THE166LIFESTYLE

BOOKS BY MARC LAWSON

It's the End of the Church as We Know It

AVAILABLE FROM DESTINY IMAGE PUBLISHERS

THE 166 LIFESTYLE

THE NEW NORMAL CHRISTIAN LIFE

MARC LAWSON

DESTINY IMAGE® PUBLISHERS, INC.

P.O. Box 310, Shippensburg, PA 17257-0310

"Speaking to the Purposes of God for This Generation and for the Generations to Come."

This book and all other Destiny Image, Revival Press, MercyPlace, Fresh Bread, Destiny Image Fiction, and Treasure House books are available at Christian bookstores and distributors worldwide.

For a U.S. bookstore nearest you, call 1-800-722-6774.

For more information on foreign distributors, call 717-532-3040.

Reach us on the Internet: www.destinyimage.com.

ISBN 10:   0-7684-3158-1

ISBN 13:   978-0-7684-3158-2

For Worldwide Distribution, Printed in the U.S.A.

1 2 3 4 5 6 7 8 9 10 11 / 13 12 11 10

TABLE OF CONTENTS

FOREWORD

As we see the moral and ethical meltdowns in our society today, it is blatantly obvious that the Christian Church is not having the significant positive and righteous effect on our increasingly secular culture that is needed. And the latest "brands" of churches are increasingly more of the seeker-friendly stripe, which seem to compromise more and more standards to remain "relevant" to this culture. Evidence clearly suggests the Christian Church is losing ground—not only to secularism, humanism, and the spirit of the world, but even to Islam. This book doesn't expose the problems within the Church itself because my first book, *It's the End of the Church as We Know It*, does.

While there is nothing necessarily "new" about churches that don't accurately preach the Gospel of the Kingdom or speak the truth (apostasy has been around since the beginning…), still the reactionary bent of many of these churches is troubling. It is possible one can swing the pendulum too far. By reacting to religion and replacing it with a type of lawlessness, many churches have lost the holiness, power, and fruitfulness that they could have had. While I won't question the motives of those leading these works, the strong overreaction to the religious spirit in many institutional churches has helped create this new strain.

One of the clearest actions that can be taken to right this floundering ship, which is the state of the Church, is to focus on what the Church and the people of God *can* do rather than what they *can't*. For too long, Church leaders have told God's people, *"Don't do this,"* or *"Don't do that."* Psalm 110:3 says, *"Your people will volunteer freely in the day of Your power…"* We have seen this to be true in our local setting. People will respond and want to be part of the solution! Why don't we tell leaders and the Church the words of Jesus that tell us what we *can* do? Yes, *what we can do* is what this book is about.

7

We are human *be*-ings, not human *do*-ings, so, of course, we must learn to become, to *be* who we are in Christ. But a huge part of learning that is to learn how to listen and respond to those passionate stirrings and impulses to do the Father's will coming from "Jesus in us" that rise up when injustice, sickness, or bondage is seen and not responded to. How we live is more important than simply telling others what we believe, which has been the preoccupation of the Church for too long. Less talk and more action is what is needed. Let's not simply win arguments; let's win souls, lives, and cities!

This book, *The 166 Lifestyle*, helps answer this question: *How should Christian believers act the rest of the week when they are not in church?* It is about the other 166 hours of the week when we are not in the two-hour Sunday service. Instead of "the Christian life" springing from the effect of a two-hour Sunday morning church service, why don't we recapture the essence of the Christian life—*a change in lifestyle?* This will encompass our habits, choices, use of time, talents, and finances. It also is reflected in the priorities of our life. Are we living each day for Jesus and His Kingdom, or do we give Him lip service? Are we true disciples, or do we cautiously follow Him from the sidelines? Remember hearing of people whose conversion transformed their daily lives? That is what happened to my wife, Linda, and me. Few leaders still preach transformation but instead have settled into talking about "coming to the service" or "coming to the meeting." The true meaning of Christian "service" as a lifestyle is hesitatingly or rarely addressed in most church services. By defining "church" as a meeting to attend rather than a lifestyle to be lived, we end up with a lopsided faith based on our definition of God and how He operates.

But there is a New Reformation coming when the leaders and saints wake up to and recognize the glory of Christ that is in us. And as we realize what we have and who we really are, we will go, preach, and heal, and God's power and glory will come out of us, transforming everyone and everything we encounter!

So they departed and went through the towns, preaching the gospel and healing everywhere (Luke 9:6 NKJV).

CHAPTER 1

THE 166 FACTOR— "THE REST OF THE STORY"

I pray also that the eyes of your heart may be enlightened in order that you may know the hope to which He has called you, the riches of His glorious inheritance in the saints, and His incomparably great power for us who believe.

—EPHESIANS 1:18-19 (NIV)

In our church and ministry, we have a ministry philosophy the Lord gave us we call "The 166 Factor." While I mentioned it briefly in my first book, I want to clearly explain it here. Do you know how many hours there are in a week? There are 168: 24 hours a day times 7 days equals 168 hours in a week. So what is the 166 Factor? The 166 Factor is the number of hours we have in a week *less* the two hours we go to church each week, assuming we go once for two hours. The 166 Factor is the answer to this question: As a Christian believer, what do you do with your life during the time you are not in church? How do you act during that time? Are you consistent with your fire for God outside the building the rest of the week? This is in sharp contrast to the meeting-centric, market-driven church culture that has been "running the table" for years in its quest to direct and define the course of American and Western Christianity.

Therefore He says: "Awake, you who sleep, arise from the dead, and Christ will give you light." See then that you walk circumspectly, not as fools but as wise, redeeming the time, because the days are evil (Ephesians 5:14-16 NKJV).

The Bible says to redeem the time, to rescue and ransom our allotted time on earth so it is wisely used. That word *redeem* means "to rescue from loss or improve the opportunity."[1] There are other passages that refer to this as well.

*Be wise in the way you act toward outsiders; **make the most of every opportunity**. Let your conversation be always full of grace, seasoned with salt, so that you may know how to answer everyone* (Colossians 4:5-6 NIV).

We have been conditioned to believe that those with the most influence in the Church today will have the final say on what God is doing in this generation. That is wrong. Some of the most high-profile leaders now won't even be remembered a generation from now. God is beginning to take the ministry out of the hands of those who would keep the ministry, resources, and gifting within the control of an elite few and in a confined space—behind a pulpit, on a colossal stage, or behind a camera. There is a revolution that has already begun among the Body of Christ that could define the Church for a generation. Leaders who presently have the most influence will end up having only a marginal voice in the days ahead because they built their ministries on many of the things that the Spirit is now removing from the Church. While they may continue acting as if things are the same, the Lord will not be with them, and, like Saul in the latter days of his life, they will be paranoid of the Mighty Warriors the Lord raises up who are the "real deal." They will *not* have it.

The fruit of the righteous is a tree of life, and he who wins souls is wise (Proverbs 11:30 NIV).

...But wisdom is proved right by her actions (Matthew 11:19 NIV).

In Proverbs 11 Solomon implies that wisdom is revealed in our use of time and equates it with winning souls! These passages suggest that to redeem the time we must use wisdom and that it is wise to win souls. Most of us would agree with this, but we don't see ourselves as polished soul-winners. However, we are all able to bring the Kingdom and lay the evidence of it at people's doors, and they can decide what to do with it.

Time is the only thing that we have an allotted amount of here on earth. While worship, adoration, praise, and prayer are all activities we can participate in when we enter Heaven, there are many things we cannot accomplish anywhere but on earth. Winning souls and bringing the Kingdom to the lost is absolutely the number one priority. And while many of us get "off the hook" on this by saying, "I'm not an evangelist," Jesus never looked at or referred to it that way. Jesus told His Church to do only two main things: win the lost and make disciples. Winning is a challenge, but discipleship takes a lot longer.

WE EXERCISE OUR FAITH HERE ON EARTH

I tell you that He will avenge them speedily. Nevertheless, when the Son of Man comes, will He really find faith on the earth? (Luke 18:8 NKJV).

When we get to Heaven, do you think we will exercise faith as we do here? Based on most passages about Heaven in Scripture, I think that there must be an instant manifestation by just thinking of what is needed. And I know there is no sickness, grief, depression, rape, violence, bondage, abuse, etc., in Heaven. Scripture is clear that Heaven is not the place we get saved or "come to Jesus." That must happen on earth. The sick must be healed *on earth*. Possibly some kind of faith is exercised there in Heaven, but I am certain that most kinds are exercised here on earth!

All of us who consider ourselves born-again Christians should live our lives on this earth not for ourselves, but for the Lord and His purposes. I can't emphasize enough how important it is we make good use of our time while on the earth, but the more crucial questions we must ask are: Are we serving God's purpose for our life while we are here? Are we doing the task that only we can do? Are we ministering to the people the Lord has sent our way? And are we effective and fruitful and not just busy? An overriding concern we should have is that the time we spend here on the earth with family, friends, career, hobbies, or ministry be fruitful, effective, and lasting. Otherwise, we take up space here simply to ingest oxygen and be great consumers! We must realize that we exist at this time in history to bring God's Kingdom to people. We don't just want to do busy work for Jesus; we want to fulfill God's purpose for our life and help change someone's destiny. Life is a gift, and we must not squander it.

> *Then Jesus answered and said: "A certain man went down from Jerusalem to Jericho, and fell among thieves, who stripped him of his clothing, wounded him, and departed, leaving him half dead. Now by chance a certain priest came down that road. And when he saw him, he passed by on the other side. Likewise a Levite, when he arrived at the place, came and looked, and passed by on the other side. But a certain Samaritan, as he journeyed, came where he was. And when he saw him, he had compassion. So he went to him and bandaged his wounds, pouring out oil and wine; and he set him on his own animal, brought him to an inn, and took care of him. On the next day, when he departed, he took out two denarii, gave them to the innkeeper, and said to him, 'Take care of him; and*

whatever more you spend, when I come again, I will repay you.' So which of these three do you think was neighbor to him who fell among the thieves?" (Luke 10:30-36 NKJV).

The story of the Samaritan is a good example of persons coming upon an opportunity to minister and help someone outside of a religious setting in a way that could make a difference. While a number of people mention this as justification for mercy ministry to the homeless, there is no indication that the man mugged in this passage was homeless—or jobless, for that matter. He obviously had some things on him thieves wanted to steal. In addition, it is a clear example there is a time we need to step into our neighbors' lives and help them out. While giving the homeless food and a bed is merciful, it is a fact that these acts of kindness fail to move them to change their lifestyles in the long term. They rarely do. Jesus said, "The poor will always be with you." That is why those who work in inner-city or "street" ministries have realized the need to invest only in those who are disciples and are able to turn their lives around. This story of the "Good Samaritan" is a great example of somebody moving out of his comfort zone in order to help the helpless. While we don't have any idea of the long-term effect of the Samaritan's kindness toward that "certain man" who was mugged, we do know it was the right thing to do. It also is a clear example of those who, by cultural religious standards, were viewed as the godly people of their day. Yet the Levite and the temple priest were blind to the opportunity for ministry right under their noses. Neither would leave their *religious comfort zone* to help someone on the opposite side of the road, even a victim of a robbery and mugging! This is also one of the lessons the Church is now facing. Are we willing to break out of our comfort zones to bring God's glory to the deepest areas of darkness? This challenge shines light on the disparity between what is really going on in our society and those adhering to their forms of religious piety.

There are many things we can *only do on earth* and *not* in Heaven. Here is a short list:

- Win souls

- Marry

- Raise godly children and pass godly heritage on to them

- Cast out devils

- Heal the sick

- Raise the dead

- Preach the Gospel to the poor

- Bind up the broken-hearted

- Cleanse those who have leprosy/AIDS/blood diseases

- Prophesy destiny and purpose to folks

My generation's time on this earth has a specific assignment from God that He wants accomplished for the Kingdom. Acts 13:36 says, *"For David, after he had served the purpose of God in his own generation, fell asleep, and was laid among his fathers and underwent decay."*

The Bible declares that David, described as "a man after [God's] own heart," served His specific purpose in the time allotted him on earth (see 1 Sam. 13:14 NKJV). It's essential that we understand the gravity of this whole concept of stewardship. It simply means that our time, financial resources and assets, and gifts are not our own, but exist to progress and accelerate God's purposes while we are here on the earth. We are not to just take up space but to make an impact for *Him*. I want to do that, you want to do that, and all those who

are committed lovers of Jesus want to do that. But something fundamental and rudimentary must change in the way we view church and
ministry—fundamental, because it must be foundational to our belief
system; and rudimentary, because it needs to be a part of our daily
practice, our lifestyle.

A NEW VIEW

First, our view of *Church* must change. We must see that *we are the
Church*. We don't *"go to church,"* because we *are the Church!* We must
see that the Church is not simply a meeting; as we live out our lives in a
way that fulfills the purpose God has for us, we manifest His presence
on the earth.

God wants us to be delivered of a meeting mentality. Otherwise
we will assume that what occurs in a two-hour meeting once a week is
what God is doing on the earth. What happens in our meetings may be
wonderful and glorious, but we can't simply contain God in the box we
know as church. We can't limit Him to having access to our lives two
hours a week. God is everywhere all the time and is capable of anything,
anywhere, anytime, and anyplace. We need to have a long-term mentality concerning our Christian faith, where we are living our life for
God all week. Ananias and Sapphira had this "meeting mentality," which
allowed them to live a hypocritical lifestyle.

> But a certain man named Ananias, with Sapphira his
> wife, sold a possession. And he kept back part of the
> proceeds, his wife also being aware of it, and brought a
> certain part and laid it at the apostles' feet. But Peter
> said, "Ananias, why has Satan filled your heart to lie to
> the Holy Spirit and keep back part of the price of the land
> for yourself? While it remained, was it not your own? And
> after it was sold, was it not in your own control? Why

17

have you conceived this thing in your heart? You have not lied to men but to God."

Then Ananias, hearing these words, fell down and breathed his last. So great fear came upon all those who heard these things. And the young men arose and wrapped him up, carried him out, and buried him. Now it was about three hours later when his wife came in, not knowing what had happened. And Peter answered her, "Tell me whether you sold the land for so much?"

She said, "Yes, for so much." Then Peter said to her, "How is it that you have agreed together to test the Spirit of the Lord? Look, the feet of those who have buried your husband are at the door, and they will carry you out." Then immediately she fell down at his feet and breathed her last. And the young men came in and found her dead, and carrying her out, buried her by her husband. So great fear came upon all the church and upon all who heard these things (Acts 5:1-11 NKJV).

FREEDOM FROM THE CONTROL
OF MONEY OR TIME

Ananias and Sapphira were "known" to the people in that church as extravagant givers. They had some kind of reputation for that, it seems. They were giving way beyond the 10 percent of tithing. Some scholars believe that when Barnabas, who was a new convert, came into the church, his giving and generosity exceeded theirs. Some believe that Ananias and Sapphira were jealous that he might steal their position as the big givers.

The main thing is that all the giving here was publicized. We've made such a deal about bringing things out in the open. What if every week we published the amounts people gave? I don't believe people could handle that yet, but it sure would get rid of the financial pretense. Remember, we are only giving out of what we have. As long as the financial arena is off limits to the Holy Spirit, most people will be stuck in a meeting mentality, rather than a Christian lifestyle of sacrifice.

I believe there may be few poor people in hell, but *many* rich and wealthy, those with means. Why? Because many people believe success and favor from God is only measured by financial blessing or business success. Now the Bible is clear that blessing comes from the Lord, and anyone with common sense knows that to have abundance feels better than experiencing lack. However, many who appear successful have little faith. This is because they trust in their own ability to plan or sell or make money, all the while not really giving God credit for His blessing and somehow believing their success is due to their self-effort. Yet in James it says the poor are rich in faith (see James 2:5). Why? Because they have learned how to exercise faith for the basic needs of life rather than assuming it was always there.

The story of the rich man in hell trying to get help from poor Lazarus is an example of a man who trusted in himself rather than God.

> *Now the poor man died and was carried away by the angels to Abraham's bosom; and the rich man also died and was buried. In Hades he lifted up his eyes, being in torment, and saw Abraham far away and Lazarus in his bosom. And he cried out and said, "Father Abraham, have mercy on me, and send Lazarus so that he may dip the tip of his finger in water and cool off my tongue, for I am in agony in this flame." But Abraham said, "Child, remember that during your life you received your good things, and likewise Lazarus bad things; but now he is being comforted here, and you are in agony. And besides all this, between us and you there is a great chasm fixed,*

so that those who wish to come over from here to you will not be able, and that none may cross over from there to us." And he said, "Then I beg you, father, that you send him to my father's house—for I have five brothers—in order that he may warn them, so that they will not also come to this place of torment." But Abraham said, "They have Moses and the Prophets; let them hear them." But he said, "No, father Abraham, but if someone goes to them from the dead, they will repent!" But he said to him, "If they do not listen to Moses and the Prophets, they will not be persuaded even if someone rises from the dead" (Luke 16:22-31).

While this story is disturbing, it clearly reveals how important it is *how we live* while here on earth. Somehow Christians think that God cares more about them having all their finances in perfect order before He can use them. Some even think we have to be out of debt, own our house, and pay off all our bills before God will require us to give Him our money. The truth is that it was never *our* money to begin with. This is a lie perpetuated by hell to keep us in slavery to our possessions. Our debt, bills, taxes, etc., were not initiated by God but us. Why is it we give God "credit" for our debt and our bills, but when people begin to prosper they think, *It's my money; I earned it; I worked hard for it?* Let's give God credit for what He does do and take responsibility for our own bills and problems. Most times when we have provision problems it is not because of God, but us. I address the whole issue of provision and serving mammon in Chapter 5.

A second important fact about stewardship is God requires us to be accountable to Him for the handling of our money and resources both when we are alive here on earth and when we bow the knee before Him after we are dead. When we're dead is not a good time to negotiate with God why we couldn't let go of things while on earth. Those who have more in this life will be held accountable to a higher standard. In addition, whatever holds us captive here will pull on us there.

> *And He told them a parable, saying, "The land of a rich man was very productive. And he began reasoning to himself, saying, 'What shall I do, since I have no place to store my crops?' Then he said, 'This is what I will do: I will tear down my barns and build larger ones, and there I will store all my grain and my goods. And I will say to my soul, "Soul, you have many goods laid up for many years to come; take your ease, eat, drink and be merry."' But God said to him, 'You fool! This very night your soul is required of you; and now who will own what you have prepared?' So is the man who lays up treasure for himself, and is not rich toward God"* (Luke 12:16-21).

Freedom can be defined as *no longer being controlled by our possessions or our passions so we can live and serve God unimpeded.* Money and financial resources are a wonderful tool and even a weapon we can use to further the work of Kingdom expansion. But we must be free of a love of money to be readily able to use it for that purpose. We must be delivered of being owned or controlled by anything but God. Our time and money really is not our own, and we will be required to account for it at the Great White Throne Judgment (see Rev. 20:11-12).

WHAT *IS* MINISTRY?

Ministry literally means helping, waiting, and serving. But today many feel ministry is for the special ones selected by the Lord, an extremely elite company of perfected saints. This superstar mentality of ministry is wrong. Ministry does not simply mean:

- Preaching on television

- Singing

- Teaching

- Holding a microphone

- Praying over people

Paul defined ministry, and we should look at his criteria.

> *Therefore, if anyone is in Christ, he is a new creation; the old has gone, the new has come! All this is from God, who reconciled us to Himself through Christ and gave us the ministry of reconciliation: that God was reconciling the world to Himself in Christ, not counting men's sins against them. And He has committed to us the message of reconciliation* (2 Corinthians 5:17-19 NIV).

Ministry is being a representative of Christ to those who do not know the Kingdom. We are God's Kingdom ambassadors. We represent the King and His Kingdom wherever we go, not theoretically, but in reality. Ministry is serving and sharing God's power, love, and heart to anyone, anywhere, anytime, and anyplace. It is not successful only when done with colorful eloquence or passionate presentation, but it is successful when we get to introduce people to Jesus and they make Him King!

> *Jesus said to them, "Did you never read in the Scriptures, 'The stone which the builders rejected, this became the chief corner stone; this came about from the Lord, and it is marvelous in our eyes'?* ***Therefore I say to you, the kingdom of God will be taken away from***

you and given to a people, producing the fruit of it.
And he who falls on this stone will be broken to pieces;
but on whomever it falls, it will scatter him like dust
(Matthew 21:42-44).

We are filled with the Spirit of God for a purpose. From the beginning, God's purpose was to have fellowship with man and to cause him to be like God on the earth. God's command to Adam and Eve was: *"Be fruitful and increase in number; fill the earth and subdue it. Rule over the fish of the sea and the birds of the air and over every living creature that moves on the ground"* (Gen. 1:28-29 NIV). That command is still active today. The Bible says that *"The highest heavens belong to the Lord, but the earth He has given to man"* (Ps. 115:16 NIV). Our ultimate purpose as Christians is to be like God on the earth. We are called to exercise dominion over the earth and subdue it for God.

We must embrace our destiny, *which is one of warfare and conquest,* not sitting around drinking tea and singing our favorite worship songs, as good as they are. We can't have peace and love without taking dominion and subduing our enemies. My generation didn't want to war; they just wanted to have peace and love. But we must take the fight to the enemy. The greatest defense is offense.

> *...The Son of God appeared for this purpose, to destroy the works of the devil* (1 John 3:8).

SEEING GOD AS HE REALLY IS

He is King of kings. Our definition of God must truly reflect God as He really is, not as so many have made Him out to be. Jesus has courage and is not a whiny failure. We must get used to seeing God back us up big time! We must step out and believe God is going to back us up; when He does, our courage will rise! We will also begin to be those "dread champions" who will arise in the last days doing the exploits of God with power! (see Jer. 20:11).

It really is the end of church as we know it. But it is the beginning of a new manifestation of the Church on the earth that will send fear into the camp of the evil one as Jesus will be seen as He really is, the Savior of the world, and the King of kings and Lord of lords. The Church as we know it must come to an end, but in its place will arise the Church as *He knows it to be*—without spot or wrinkle, and regal in Her authority—*"as awesome as an army with banners"* (Song of Sol. 6:4,10).

OUR VIEW OF CHURCH MUST CHANGE

The Church is to primarily be an expression of the Kingdom of God. While the Kingdom of God is the rule and reign of God, the Church is the visible manifest expression of that Kingdom in the earth. The Church holds several key purposes in the earth.

First, the Church should hold up the truth as a foundation for society. Right now the Church is wavering on standing up for the truth of God's Word in many areas. The most notable currently is the support of the institution of marriage and the rejection of homosexuality as an alternative lifestyle. If this is not done, this society as we know it will collapse. Every great society before us that tolerated perversion and licentiousness has come to an abrupt end.

> *If I am delayed, you will know how people ought to conduct themselves in God's household, which is the church of the living God, the pillar and foundation of the truth* (1 Timothy 3:15 NIV).

If the Church won't stand up for the truth, who will? The Church is to be salt and light to this world (see Matt. 5:13-14). This aspect of light is intriguing, if we realize that by saying and doing nothing we participate in keeping the status quo of darkness and ignorance. Jesus said, *"I am the light of the world"* (see John 8:12; 9:5). So we are to reflect His light that shines in us in every place we go. The prophetic ministry must be taken out of the church box and brought out into the open in the marketplace. We can't keep this light of God's truth hidden in conferences and ministry times during church services.

Second, the Church must visibly demonstrate the Kingdom of God through confronting darkness with the light of the Gospel of the Kingdom. While social work such as feeding the hungry, clothing the needy, and helping the unfortunate in practical ways is essential, there is a much greater need right now for the Church to reveal God's glory through miraculous demonstrations of God's power and love. Signs and wonders, miracles, and demonstrations of God's power are desperately needed to defeat the onslaught of darkness our culture is accepting and endorsing more and more each day.

There is no surer way to express God's love for man as when an individual has had their space invaded by God's delivering and healing power. God is truly a "space invader" who cannot sit by and do nothing as a person succumbs to the bondage of sickness or torment. What kind of love does it show the world for the Church to sit on our hands while every day we walk by many people who just need one touch from Jesus? Just look at one example:

> *Now there is in Jerusalem by the Sheep Gate a pool, which is called in Hebrew, Bethesda, having five porches. In these lay a great multitude of sick people, blind, lame, paralyzed, waiting for the moving of the water. For an angel went down at a certain time into the pool and stirred up the water; then whoever stepped in first, after the stirring of the water, was made well of whatever disease he had. Now a certain man was there who had an infirmity thirty-eight years. When Jesus saw him lying there, and*

*knew that he already had been in that condition a long
time, He said to him, "Do you want to be made well?"
The sick man answered Him, "Sir, I have no man to put
me into the pool when the water is stirred up; but while
I am coming, another steps down before me." Jesus said to
him, "Rise, take up your bed and walk." And immediately
the man was made well, took up his bed, and walked...*
(John 5:2-9 NKJV).

Can you imagine the pandemonium if believers were to start doing
the works of Jesus like this in the mall, the video store, or the grocery
store? *Wow!* What would happen if someone in a wheelchair was pulled
out of it and started to walk in a mall? Would that be something? We
have seen it happen many times. Have you?

Finally, the Church must express God's wisdom. We must reveal to
the earth a way of doing things with the mind of God. Presently when
unbelieving folks think of the Church, they think, *A sweet, but outmoded
institution.* So what did we do to combat that? We made sure we stayed
a stiff institution, but we changed our methods so they weren't so outmoded. This is what a lot of the seeker-friendly thing is about: show the
lost we can be "wired," hip, and contemporary. While all this effort to
be contemporary is needed, without a message that changes people's lives
with the power of God, all we have is yet another institution doing dead
works. Even with good motives, we seem to keep doing things that don't
quite work.

We have to realize that the Gospel of the Kingdom is about God's
supernatural power invading our lives and destroying the works of the
evil one. The wisdom of God is how to go about the delivering of its
message with effect.

*To the intent that now the manifold wisdom of God might
be made known by the church to the principalities and*

powers in the heavenly places, according to the eternal
purpose which He accomplished in Christ Jesus our Lord,
in whom we have boldness and access with confidence
through faith in Him (Ephesians 3:10-12 NKJV).

OUR NEW COVENANT INHERITANCE

"This is the covenant that I will make with them after
those days," says the Lord: "I will put My laws upon their
heart, and on their mind I will write them." He then says,
"And their sins and their lawless deeds I will remember
no more." Now where there is forgiveness of these things,
there is no longer any offering for sin. Therefore, breth-
ren, since we have confidence to enter the holy place by
*the blood of Jesus, by a new and **living way** which He*
inaugurated for us through the veil, that is, His flesh, and
since we have a great priest over the house of God, let us
draw near with a sincere heart in full assurance of faith,
having our hearts sprinkled clean from an evil conscience
and our bodies washed with pure water. Let us hold fast
the confession of our hope without wavering, for He who
promised is faithful; and let us consider how to stimulate
one another to love and good deeds, not forsaking our own
assembling together, as is the habit of some, but encour-
aging one another; and all the more, as you see the day
drawing near" (Hebrews 10:16-25).

To say that an understanding of the New Covenant is essential to
live a victorious, overcoming Christian life would be a great understate-
ment! We not only need to grasp the significance of what it implies but
begin to believe in it and walk in it. It is all about believing that what
the Word says about us is really true!

It is not enough just to have an intellectual understanding of our New Covenant inheritance. To actually possess our inheritance, we have to exercise faith that it is true. If we are going to believe, we must let go of all former understandings that are inadequate and unfruitful. Unfortunately, many of us have been taught that the New Covenant is the Law "Lite." We have grace for this and grace for that, but on the big issues, the Law rules. That is simply not so, and that is the reason so many live empty-handed, always asking God to give them something He has already taken care of in Christ.

We have a saying in our church: "Let Jesus get His money's worth, and let Him get what He paid for" (on the Cross). In other words, Jesus went to great and considerable effort that we might be *"sons (and daughters) of glory"!* He went all the way and gave us His best. Why can't we give Him our best? Let us believe and receive all that He paid for on the Cross—deliverance from sin, healing, prosperity, a sound mind, and victory over the enemy!

Contrary to popular belief, salvation doesn't just mean freedom from the penalty of sin but total and complete emancipation from all its past, present, and future effects on us! Now that's Good News!

> For it was fitting for Him, for whom are all things, and through whom are all things, **in bringing many sons to glory**, to perfect the Author of their salvation through sufferings. For both He who sanctifies and those who are sanctified are all from one Father; for which reason He is not ashamed to call them brethren, saying, "I will proclaim Your name to My brethren, in the midst of the congregation I will sing Your praise." And again, "I will put My trust in Him." And again, "Behold, I and the children whom God has given Me." Therefore, since the children share in flesh and blood, He Himself likewise also partook of the same, that through death He might render powerless

him who had the power of death, that is, the devil, and might free those who through fear of death were subject to slavery all their lives. For assuredly He does not give help to angels, but He gives help to the descendant of Abraham (Hebrews 2:10-16).

*How will we escape if we neglect so great a **salvation?** After it was at the first spoken through the Lord, it was confirmed to us by those who heard, God also testifying with them, both by signs and wonders and by various miracles and by gifts of the Holy Spirit according to His own will* (Hebrews 2:3-4).

This passage says we must not neglect *such a great salvation.* Salvation in the New Testament is primarily translated from the root Greek word *sozo.*[2] This verb implies deliverance, emancipation, healing, rescue, recovery, and restoration. There is nothing implied in this translation of the word that suggests salvation is merely a rescue reluctantly approved by God or even a "get-out-of-hell-free" card. The concept of this word is far broader than simply an escape from eternal damnation. It implies not just a rescue but a translation and transfer from the kingdom of darkness into the Kingdom of light.

While most evangelicals teach that the Gospel is only about salvation or entrance into the Kingdom, the Gospel is much more than that. Jesus taught more about the Kingdom than simply how to get in. Jesus taught about Kingdom values, stewardship, callings, and priorities. While they all can be considered controversial, the primary reason the Church has historically avoided these teachings is because of the tremendous controversies they foster. By not telling the whole story, we are left with the sense that what we have heard *is* the whole story.

THE REST OF THE STORY...

The great American radio personality, Paul Harvey, who passed away recently, used the phrase, "And that's...the rest of the story" each time he did his radio show to communicate to people that there is far more going on there than we hear or see on the surface. His commentaries and true stories illustrate that there is a much larger world out there with more interesting people and situations than the typical version of events we commonly hear through the media.

Just because bookstores or highly popular and influential Christian leaders espouse something doesn't mean it is the only truth. Truth is true until something *more true comes on the scene* to reveal its true priority. Just because "everybody knows" something doesn't make it any more the truth than "facts" announced on the cover of Internet blogs or supermarket tabloids. The criteria for apostolic leadership in the New Testament weren't popularity or influence but adherence to preaching the Gospel's truth and demonstrating it with signs and wonders. The Church has been teaching a watered-down definition of salvation that implies, "If God had His way, you'd be burning in hell. But thanks to Jesus, you can barely escape! Of course, the rest of your life here on earth is one trial and failure after another sent by God to perfect you since you don't deserve this salvation anyway. And these sicknesses and calamities you experience? They too are sent by God to give Him glory as you suffer. If you are lucky, maybe you will only experience a little bit."

The problem with this line of reasoning is that by and large the Western Church is equating suffering with simply putting up with and accommodating unbelief. It is as if we are catering to unbelief, thinking that it is somehow God's mysterious will! As Bill Johnson of Redding, California, has said, "God is *not* mysteriously bad, but mysteriously *good.*"[3] Instead of authentic suffering and persecution that could come from sharing the authentic Gospel, we are taught by nearly everyone, including many mainstream Charismatic and Pentecostal leaders, that experiencing and enduring sicknesses like cancer or asthma gracefully is tantamount to suffering for the Gospel. These well-intentioned definitions of events, however, are still wrong.

This next example I give might cause people to get upset with me, but please try and follow the illogical nature of what is occurring. It is appalling that many large and small ministries today, even Charismatic ones, accommodate unbelief and resignation to defeat through things like ministries to the deaf, cancer support groups, and the like. God, of course, wants to minister to everyone, but like Reinhard Bonkke said in a recent blog, "Any doctrine or philosophy that doesn't lend itself as conductor of the power of God is a waste of time."[4] Jesus' first priority when He came upon the deaf in the Gospels wasn't to encourage them to teach other believers how to sign, but to get them healed. Making accommodation for diseases is as good as waving a white flag over the good folks who battle them daily and saying, "God is just not big enough to heal and deliver you." When we do this, we make an accommodation for the weakness of our message and the greatness of our unbelief. Allowing the culture to define our message is an error and a trap; we must hold up and adhere to a high standard even if it appears to be unreachable. It isn't! With God ALL things are possible. Is God the problem here? NO! It is the smallness of our faith and largeness of the excuses for our unbelief.

> *After these things there was a feast of the Jews, and Jesus went up to Jerusalem. Now there is in Jerusalem by the sheep gate a pool, which is called in Hebrew Bethesda, having five porticoes. In these lay a multitude of those who were sick, blind, lame, and withered, [waiting for the moving of the waters; for an angel of the Lord went down at certain seasons into the pool and stirred up the water; whoever then first, after the stirring up of the water, stepped in was made well from whatever disease*

with which he was afflicted.] A man was there who had been ill for thirty-eight years. When Jesus saw him lying there, and knew that he had already been a long time in that condition, He said to him, "Do you wish to get well?" The sick man answered Him, "Sir, I have no man to put me into the pool when the water is stirred up, but while I am coming, another steps down before me." Jesus said to him, "Get up, pick up your pallet and walk." Immediately the man became well, and picked up his pallet and began to walk. Now it was the Sabbath on that day. So the Jews were saying to the man who was cured, "It is the Sabbath, and it is not permissible for you to carry your pallet." But he answered them, "He who made me well was the one who said to me, 'Pick up your pallet and walk.'" They asked him, "Who is the man who said to you, 'Pick up your pallet and walk'?" But the man who was healed did not know who it was, for Jesus had slipped away while there was a crowd in that place. Afterward Jesus found him in the temple and said to him, "Behold, you have become well; do not sin anymore, so that nothing worse happens to you." The man went away, and told the Jews that it was Jesus who had made him well. For this reason the Jews were persecuting Jesus, because He was doing these things on the Sabbath. But He answered them, "My Father is working until now, and I Myself am working." For this reason therefore the Jews were seeking all the more to kill Him, because He not only was breaking the Sabbath, but also was calling God His own Father, making Himself equal with God. Therefore Jesus answered and was saying to them, "Truly, truly, I say to you, the Son can do nothing of Himself, unless it is something He sees the Father doing; for whatever the Father does, these things the Son also does in like manner. For the Father loves the Son, and shows Him all things that He Himself is doing; and the Father will show Him greater works than these, so that you will marvel" (John 5:1-20).

ENDNOTES

1. *Merriam-Webster's Collegiate Dictionary*, 11th ed., s.v. "Redeem."

2. StudyLight.org, *The New Testament Greek Lexicon Online,* s.v. "Sozo," http://www.studylight.org/lex/grk/view.cgi?number=4982.

3. Bill Johnson, *The King and His Kingdom,* CD of message given at NorthGate Church of Atlanta, September 10, 2006.

4. Reinhard Bonnke, Facebook blog of September 29, 2009, http://www.facebook.com/evangelistreinhardbonnke.

CHAPTER 2

A MEETING-CENTRIC CHURCH CULTURE

Blessed are those who have been persecuted for the sake of righteousness, for theirs is the kingdom of heaven.

—MATTHEW 5:10

What do I mean by *meeting-centric?*

Here is the definition of *centric*: "located in or at a center; concentrated about or directed to a center."[1]

So when I say meeting-centric faith (or Christianity or church culture), I mean the cultivation of an entire lifestyle around an event. In this case, I am referring to the typical Sunday church service that takes approximately 2 hours out of that person's 168 hour week. When a person becomes born-again into a meeting-centered mentality of Christianity, it is as if that person needs to wait till he or she goes to the weekly meeting to hear God's voice. If an encounter with God is only centered on the Sunday meeting, then there is little to no discipleship. The hard work of mentoring and character development and modeling is left to the Holy Spirit whom new Christians are often never introduced to—or are even taught to ignore. We must teach folks to see that we *are* the Church. We don't just "go to church," because we *are* the Church! Yes, we go to those meetings and activities at the buildings the church is using. But we must look beyond meetings to see that being the Church means that we don't act one way two hours a week and then another way the other 166. We must see that we are to live out our life in a way that fulfills the purpose God has for us as we manifest His presence on the earth.

> *From that time Jesus began to show His disciples that He must go to Jerusalem, and suffer many things from the elders and chief priests and scribes, and be killed, and be raised up on the third day. Peter took Him aside and began to rebuke Him, saying, "God forbid it, Lord! This shall never happen to You." But He turned and said to Peter, "Get behind Me, Satan! You are a stumbling block to Me; for you are not setting your mind on God's interests, but man's." Then Jesus said to His disciples, "If anyone wishes to come after Me, he must deny himself, and take up his cross and follow Me. For whoever wishes to save his life will lose it; but whoever loses his life for My sake will find it"* (Matthew 16:21-25).

As we read in this passage, even those who love the Lord deeply, like Peter, can assume they need to "help the Lord out," and, even worse, feel like they know how. Many of the problems the Church has are tied to well-meaning people with good motives who are led by their carnal thinking and reasoning. Double-mindedness is such a regular part of the way of thinking in most churches and ministries that it is considered "normal." In Matthew 4:17, Jesus says, *"Repent, for the kingdom of heaven is at hand."*

Repent! The Kingdom of God is at hand. This is what Jesus first had to say. *He exclusively had one message to preach.* Over 160 times, in nearly every story and parable, this Kingdom is mentioned. Jesus was always talking about and referencing the Kingdom. The Kingdom is *not* the Church, but the Church is supposed to be an expression of the Kingdom on the earth. Is it? Most places I look, I don't see it. Jesus said, "God is like this...The Kingdom of God is like..." His statements absolutely confronted the religious system of the day.

He said *repent* (which simply means change the way you think and look at things); He didn't say cry, sob, or run to the altar. When we equate an emotional response with repentance, we will always get an outcome that doesn't result in lifestyle change. Repentance moves people to effect a complete turning around and a change of mind, ways, habits, and intentions! Here are some honest questions: If the church leaders of today have the right message, then why does the response to their message appear to bring little to no change of habits, lifestyles, values, ethics, and morality? And why do all the polls indicate that righteousness, morality, and cultural change is not only going the wrong direction in the Church but in our society as well? Why in the early years of our nation could one preacher like George Whitefield or Jonathan Edwards with the right message be so effective in changing his culture, yet today, even with all the technological tools at their disposal, our leaders have such little success making that same difference?

I believe our present compromised system has helped fashion a compromised message. Most pastors whom I have known over the years, of churches small, big, and huge, are, by and large, like anyone else attempting to do God's will. Most feel like their job is akin to cleaning sand off the beach. Many are in survival mode or caution mode. If things seem great outwardly, "Don't rock the boat"; if not, then, "We need to be careful." But these are not apostolic mindsets! An authentic apostolic message will produce a real life-changing response, a change of mind, and a rending of the heart.

The Kingdom of Heaven (the regime, rule, and reign of God's authority and dominion on earth—or anywhere—without limits) *is at hand* (which means right here, right now, in the midst of you, as plain as the nose on your face). While this is plain and simple, we seemingly have a hard time having faith for something we can't see. However, Jesus said the Spirit was like the wind (see John 3:8). You can see its effects and its force, but it is not visible to the eye. He was talking of a real dimension right in front of all of us that could be accessed by faith, as He modeled for His followers.

In this world the blind are blind, but in Jesus' world the blind see! In this world the lame can't walk, but in Jesus' world the lame can walk! In this world the deaf need hearing aids, but in Jesus' world, the deaf can hear! In this world the dead are dead, but in Jesus' world the dead rise!

Up is down, in is out, rich is poor, poor is rich, last are first, and first, last; it is a parallel dimension right alongside our fallen world, but the rules are different there! There are no wheelchair ramps, no handicapped parking, no deaf section! It is wrong that we spend so much of our life accommodating the failure of our faith and our lack of bringing in the Kingdom.

Jesus' message went so against the flow of the religious establishment that they couldn't deal with Him! He tweaked all the religious elements in His culture. Maybe we need to use His same approach since our approaches don't seem to be helping us.

Today we have even the basic order and structure of the Church backwards. Imagine getting one of those "assemble yourself" kits for a swing set or BBQ grill or bike. You take out the instructions that go A, B, C, D, etc., and are to be done in the "manufacturer's order of assembly." You begin with F, then go over to Q, then make your way to D, and on and on. How do you think that would work for you? Not so great.

Paul wrote about how God designated things to be formatted in the Church:

> *And God has appointed these in the church: first apostles, second prophets, third teachers, after that miracles, then gifts of healings, helps, administrations, varieties of tongues* (1 Corinthians 12:28 NKJV).

1. *Apostles*: senders

2. *Prophets*: seers

3. *Teachers*: searchers of the Scriptures

4. *Miracles*: doers of signs and wonders

5. *Gifts of Healings*: releasers of the supernatural

6. *Helps*: supporters

7. *Administrations*: providers of solutions

8. *Varieties of tongues:* receivers and speakers of heavenly mysteries

While most pastors are well-meaning people, they are frequently concerned with only two things: salvation and protection for the sheep. Pastors and administrators may have done an admirable job in winning a huge section of the world to Christ, but I wonder what could happen if we really functioned according to God's design. Pastors, evangelists, and even administrators by and large are leading the American Church, which leads to a church focusing primarily on what happens in and around the Sunday meeting, creating an atmosphere that is imbalanced spiritually. With administrators, pastors, teachers, and evangelists at the helm, we have a meeting-centric faith based on an excellently packaged, entertaining Sunday meeting. In this church culture, the only time God does something is "at church." When does God speak, or when do we feel His presence? At church. When we define "church" as a meeting to attend rather than as the lifestyle of the believer, our faith becomes lopsided along with our view of God and how He operates. Everything is about "the meeting" and "the service." We even back off on being too bold or aggressive because we might "run off people." It is as if the whole fate of the Church is resting on having a good service, a good meeting with excellent fluff.

GOVERNMENT PRIORITIES

Here is what this meeting-centric church culture looks like:

- *Pastoral:* people's comfort and safety

- *Administrative:* things and money

- *Teaching-focused:* doctrine is what *we* teach, often in order to defend our territory

- *Evangelistic:* salvation message *only*

The perception of God in a pastoral government is primarily anxiety and fear. The great concern is *losing what we have.* There is also a fear that if and when any obstacles or opposition come our way it indicates that the Lord is behind it, so this is "how He directs us." In addition, in this type of church culture or atmosphere, the supernatural is suspect and thought to be deceptive and unreliable. With everyone protecting their turf, things, and assets, there is no forward-advancing mentality. And in this environment anything supernatural means, "You can be and probably already are deceived, so I will protect you from yourself." A pastoral government is filled with anxiety and control. Why? By keeping you in line you will continue to need me, *your pastor.* The vast majority of people living in this kind of church are taught subliminally to stay powerless and mostly helpless, dependent on leadership. In this atmosphere, many times good reasons are made up for suffering to keep the leader in his job.

In 1994, a church that I planted pulled out of a church-planting denomination that operated and had an atmosphere like this. While it felt so strange to be leaving our supposed security and "covering," within 10 days our church was caught up in a move of the Spirit that lasted over five years. God used it to send missionaries to nations like Norway, France, Romania, Jordan, and Israel. Also, other churches and ministries were birthed from it. When I pulled out of one thing, I wasn't exactly sure what we were going into, but I knew God was doing it. I knew we needed to get out of the old to go into the new. While it was a major shift and shock, we have been pursuing it ever since. We had to make a choice to move forward for the Kingdom. I look back on that decision now, and it was absolutely not the safest or most comfortable way to go. But there has to be resoluteness, a determination in us that old ways must give place to the new.

> ...*He takes away the first in order to establish the second* (Hebrews 10:9).

The absence of a Kingdom or overcoming mentality in churches helps create an attitude of, "We are only lowly sinners working out our salvation... We're not fulfilling our calling, for how can we know His will? We are just lowly servants waiting for further instructions." In 1996, Rick Joyner prophesied a spiritual civil war coming to the American Church. Like the Civil War, it too would pit brother against brother, and would be over the issue of spiritual slavery, to end the injustice on these ministry "plantations."[2]

I think that the timing of the meltdown of American business markets in the last few months was a sign of the beginning of the meltdown of the giant "ministry plantations" where most of the Body was in slavery to a few. Let's hope that what is happening in the natural we will also get to see happen in the spiritual. For many of these institutions it was over a long time ago. To relish or adhere to these ways of man versus the ways of God is a dangerous trap and will be a snare to us. Jesus even said, "*...Thus you nullify the word of God for the sake of your tradition*" (Matt. 15:6 NIV). The devil uses these things and the lusts of man to trap us into this world's system of operation. This causes us to compromise our entire "way of doing business." We attempt to fight the devil, but he already has us snared in his ways.

One of the reasons people get burned out from going to church is that they were told a number of stories that never came true. And I don't mean those wonderful testimonies of God's love and mercy but just an idealistic and unrealistic view of living that revolves around only "going to church" instead of being the Church. This happens as we are *reasoning in our hearts,* **not** *just our minds.*

> *And the scribes and the Pharisees began to reason, saying, "Who is this who speaks blasphemies? Who can forgive sins but God alone?" But when Jesus perceived their thoughts, He answered and said to them,* **"Why are you reasoning in your hearts?"** (Luke 5:21-22 NKJV).

The main reason for this double-mindedness is our need to resort to reasoning things out rather than hearing and obeying by faith. The problem is made worse by taking that reasoning out of our heads where it belongs and bringing it into our hearts. Because it is with our hearts we are to believe, *not* with our heads! We'll never believe using only our logic and brain power.

> *For with the heart one believes unto righteousness, and with the mouth confession is made unto salvation* (Romans 10:10 NKJV).

To resort to reasoning in our minds is simply prideful mental gymnastics to make sure we cover all our bases in case God doesn't come through. One of the weirdest things is many times we do this especially when God authentically and legitimately speaks to us, when we have been given an authentic word from God about something. But unfortunately then we attempt to bring it to pass, do it in our own strength and with our own abilities!

> *This is the only thing I want to find out from you: did you receive the Spirit by the works of the Law, or by hearing with faith? Are you so foolish? Having begun by the Spirit,*

are you now being perfected by the flesh? (Galatians 3:2-3)

The Greek word for reasoning is *dialogizomai,* where we get the English word *dialogue,* which means, "a conversation between two or more persons; an exchange of ideas or opinions on a particular issue."[3] Here's the breakdown of the Greek word:

- *Dia:* through, on account of, because of;

- *Logizomai:* to reckon, consider, regard, suppose.[4]

To give ourselves over to reasoning is to entertain an argument with God in our heart: *How am I gonna do that?* or, *Are you kidding me? Do you know what it will mean if I have to do that?* Peace begins to come as we learn to acknowledge and obey truth, but peace is only truly realized when we submit to the Person (Jesus) who is the Truth. When we learn to obey *Him* and *His Word,* we can begin to walk in that peace. And as mentioned earlier, fear rather than peace is the prevailing atmosphere in most churches that are built around the meeting-centric culture.

ENDNOTES

1. *Merriam-Webster's Collegiate Dictionary,* 11th ed., s.v. "Centric."

2. Rick Joyner, "Civil War in the Church," *MorningStar Prophetic Bulletin* (Summer 1996).

3. *Merriam-Webster's Collegiate Dictionary,* 11th ed., s.v. "Dialogue."

4. StudyLight.org, *The New Testament Greek Lexicon Online,* s.v. "Dialogizomai," http://www.studylight.org/lex/grk/view.cgi ?number=1223.

CHAPTER 3

SUBPRIME

All of us are now keenly aware of the subprime mortgage meltdown and the ensuing havoc it caused to America and the world's financial and banking systems, helping send the world economies into a tailspin.

The subprime mortgage financial crisis of 2007-9 was a sharp rise in home foreclosures that started in the United States during the fall of 2006 and became a global financial crisis within a year. The crisis began with the bursting of the housing bubble in the U.S. and high default rates on "subprime," adjustable rate, "Alt-A," and other mortgage loans made to higher-risk borrowers with lower income or lesser credit history than "prime" borrowers. The share of subprime mortgages to total originations increased from 9% in 1996, to 20% in 2006. Further, loan incentives including "interest only" repayment terms and low initial teaser rates (which later reset to higher, floating rates) encouraged borrowers to assume mortgages believing they would be able to refinance at more favorable terms later. While U.S. housing prices continued to increase during the 1996-2006 period, refinancing was available. However, once housing prices started to drop moderately in 2006-2007 in many parts of the U.S., refinancing became more difficult. Defaults and foreclosure activity increased dramatically. By

October 2007, 16% of subprime loans with adjustable rate mortgages (ARM) were 90 days delinquent or in foreclosure proceedings, roughly triple the rate of 2005. By January of 2008, this number increased to 21%. As of December 22, 2007, a leading business periodical estimated subprime defaults would reach a level between U.S. $200-300 billion.

A subprime borrower is one who cannot qualify for prime financing terms but can qualify for subprime financing terms. The failure to qualify for prime financing is due primarily to low credit scores. A very low score will disqualify. A middling score might or might not, depending mainly on the down payment, the ratio of total expense (including debt payments) to income, and ability to document income and assets.[1]

The bottom line was that mortgage lenders took a lot of risks to get mortgages for those who could least afford it, offering teaser rates that in three years would rise to a level that was unaffordable. While the possibility of helping first-time buyers get a house was a good thing, it was still a huge risk. In other words, the lower-middle class got taken because they didn't realize that the higher rates would put them out of the range to pay. Then the banks packaged these exotic mortgages, bundled them with other things, and sold them as derivatives. Giant international financial, insurance, and brokerage houses bought these by the billions, gambling on their ability to make money from them. Apparently, it didn't work, did it? Now the federal government has been putting together stimulus packages to pay for this and to keep the banking system solvent and working. I believe the world's events speak to us in natural terms many times of what is occurring in the lives of God's people and even His purposes on the earth. So I felt there was a lesson in the whole subprime mortgage meltdown that we could use.

I strongly sensed the Lord showed me there was a lesson in this if we could see it. I am *not* saying the Lord caused this mortgage mess. Instead, it was the lenders who were fulfilling government mandates to lend, lend, and lend some more to the lower-middle class. They had to keep coming up with more and more exotic mortgages to creatively finance these folks who honestly had no ability to pay. The government created the mandates; then the lenders were punished by the market as defaults began.

Now—several months after the markets first crashed and the economy started tanking—I feel strongly that what happened and *continues* to happen in the financial, automotive, and other sectors of the economy is a natural sign of things to happen or already happening in the Spirit. *Many times we see natural indicators signaling what the Spirit is doing invisibly: "However, the spiritual is not first, but the natural; then the spiritual"* (1 Cor. 15:46). First and foremost, this financial crisis exposes how fragile and propped-up many of those banks were, concocting all manner of exotic mortgages to get people into these homes. Here are some things to note:

One clear root of this crisis was *compromise.* The banks compromised their standards of lending–doing just about anything to get anybody and everybody into these new homes.

Even the people moving in couldn't possibly ignore the fact that in two years their rates would go up and they would have to pay double the sum. Everyone denied reality and just looked the other way, assuming that somehow things would be different later. Isn't this what many or most of the seeker and emergent churches are doing? Aren't they just changing the rules to do whatever it takes to fill these buildings with people? Are they really all born-again and followers of Jesus now, or just a bunch of compromised people in a quasi-spiritual purgatory?

Second, autos and vehicles can represent a prophetic type for individual people's ministries. In the failure of the *big* three automakers in America, we can see an analogy of the Church's failure to give the

Body legitimate ministry training and the ability to get around (in ministry). One of the chief reasons for the auto crisis was the failure of leadership to take the industry into the future with fuel-efficient cars and/or alternative fuels like electricity and hydrogen. Another was that retired employees demanded huge pensions of up to 90 percent of pay based on today's salaries. That's in addition to Social Security. Some of the GM pensioners retired with double what they made in their lifetime based on the rate of inflation, etc. Obviously the unions had a huge part to play here as well, in robbing the future to pad their pockets.

Third, those in leadership of these failing companies have to take the primary blame for attempting to get something for nothing and for continuing to play the odds when they were operating on such shaky ground all along.

Their denial of the numbers not adding up should have been a clear sign to them all that what they were doing was just not sustainable in the short OR long term! It's like the old joke in which people ask the new car or appliance dealership that is selling items for less than they paid for them how they can have such low prices. The answer is always *volume,* because "We sell so many more!" How can you lose money on each item you sell and by selling more still make money? Answer—you can't!

Firstborn

Now, let's look at this word *prime,* which basically means "first." The first or prime always has held a significant place in society. For example, in ancient Israel, there was great significance placed on the firstborn in a family. We all know the story of how Jacob came with a meal of game, deceived his father Isaac, who was old and blind, and took Esau's birthright blessing. Remember that Esau and Jacob were twins, but Esau came out first, so he was the firstborn and entitled to all that entails.

Jacob said to his father, "I am Esau your firstborn; I have done as you told me. Get up, please, sit and eat of my game, that you may bless me" (Genesis 27:19).

The first son born to a couple was required to be specially dedicated to God. The firstborn son of newly married people was believed to represent the *prime* of human vigor (see Gen. 49:3; Ps. 78:51). In memory of the death of Egypt's firstborn and the preservation of the firstborn of Israel, all the firstborn of Israel, both of man and beast, belonged to Yahweh (see Exod. 13:2,15; compare 12:12-16). This meant that the people of Israel attached unusual value to the eldest son and assigned special privileges and responsibilities to him. He was presented to the Lord when he was a month old. Since he belonged to the Lord, it was necessary for the father to buy back the child from the priest at a redemption price not to exceed five shekels (see Num. 18:16). The husband of several wives would have to redeem the firstborn of each.

The birthright of a firstborn included a double portion of the estate and leadership of the family. As head of the house after his father's death, the eldest son customarily cared for his mother until her death, and he also provided for his sisters until their marriage. The firstborn might sell his rights as Esau did (see Gen. 25:29-34) or forfeit them for misconduct as Reuben did because of incest (see Gen. 35:22; 49:3-4).

First Day

In the same way, the Lord gave specific significance to the *first* day of a festival or a feast. Let's look at what happened on the first day:

1. Leaven was removed from houses (see Exod. 12:15).

2. A holy assembly was called (see Exod. 12:16).

3. The Tabernacle was set up (see Exod. 40:2).

4.   No work was done on the first day of the Feast of Unleav-
     ened Bread and the Feast of Booths; the Passover lamb
     was sacrificed (see Lev. 23:5-8; 23:33-36).

5.   Early morning on the first day of the week is when
     they found the stone rolled away and Jesus raised (see
     Mark 16:2-4).

6.   Paul told the Corinthian Church to set aside and save
     their offerings on the first day of every week so that no
     offerings would be received when he came (see 1 Cor.
     16:2).

This principle of the first is a big deal. For example, Jesus many times
said that something had to happen first before something else could happen
(see Matt. 5:24; 6:33; 7:5; 12:29). In other words, sometimes certain pre-
conditions must be met to see things happen, to see breakthroughs.

> *Why do you look at the speck that is in your brother's eye,*
> *but do not notice the log that is in your own eye? Or how*
> *can you say to your brother, "Let me take the speck out*
> *of your eye," and behold, the log is in your own eye? You*
> *hypocrite, first take the log out of your own eye, and then*
> *you will see clearly to take the speck out of your brother's*
> *eye* (Matthew 7:3-5).

In deliverance, we also see this principle:

> *Or how can anyone enter the strong man's house and carry*
> *off his property, unless he first binds the strong man? And*
> *then he will plunder his house* (Matthew 12:29).

Peter Lord has said, "Keep the main thing the main thing."[2] We do that by knowing what we are called to do and not getting distracted with all the other lesser things that come up. So many times all the enemy needs to do is simply get us off the path God has called us to.

"First things first" is an old saying, and it's true that if we don't prioritize our time and life we face an ever-increasing demand on our life. Unless we decide what's important and do it first, we may end up doing it last or never at all. This was the foremost key to the financial market and business collapses we have seen. These companies lost their way and got off the original path by chasing quick bucks instead of long-term profitability.

> Another of the disciples said to Him, "Lord, permit me **first** to go and bury my father." But Jesus said to him, "Follow Me, and allow the dead to bury their own dead" (Matthew 8:21-22).

A certain disciple's father had passed away, and he asked the Lord if he could go bury him. While Jesus' answer sounds incredibly insensitive, it was in order that Jesus might clarify the priority we should have concerning the Kingdom and following Jesus.

> But seek **first** His kingdom and His righteousness, and all these things will be added to you. So do not worry about tomorrow; for tomorrow will care for itself. Each day has enough trouble of its own (Matthew 6:33-34).

> And everyone who has left houses or brothers or sisters or father or mother or children or farms for My name's sake, will receive many times as much, and will inherit eternal life. But many who are first will be last; and the last, first (Matthew 19:29-30).

*...Grace to you and peace, from Him who is and who was and who is to come, and from the seven Spirits who are before His throne, and from Jesus Christ, the faithful Witness, **the Firstborn of the dead**, and the Ruler of the kings of the earth. To Him who loves us and released us from our sins by His blood—and He has made us to be a kingdom, priests to His God and Father—to Him be the glory and the dominion forever and ever. Amen* (Revelation 1:4-6).

*For He rescued us from the domain of darkness, and transferred us to the kingdom of His beloved Son, in whom we have redemption, the forgiveness of sins. He is the image of the invisible God, **the Firstborn of all creation.** For by Him all things were created, both in the heavens and on earth, visible and invisible, whether thrones or dominions or rulers or authorities—all things have been created through Him and for Him. He is before all things, and in Him all things hold together. He is also Head of the body, the church; and He is the Beginning, the Firstborn from the dead, so that He Himself will come to have first place in everything* (Colossians 1:13-18).

*But you have come to Mount Zion and to the city of the living God, the heavenly Jerusalem, and to myriads of angels, to the general assembly and **church of the firstborn** who are enrolled in heaven, and to God, the Judge of all, and to the spirits of the righteous made perfect, and to Jesus, the Mediator of a new covenant, and to the sprinkled blood, which speaks better than the blood of Abel* (Hebrews 12:22-24).

Jesus was the Firstborn, the Forerunner, and the Pacesetter. That is why he is called the Alpha, the First of firsts! First things first: we must keep Jesus and His Kingdom the main thing.

ENDNOTES

1.   Wikipedia, s.v. "Subprime Mortgage Crisis," http://en .wikipedia.org/wiki/Subprime_mortgage_crisis#Mortgage_market.

2.   Peter Lord, *Prayer,* audiotape from Jesus '77 Festival.

CHAPTER 4

EXTREME CHURCH MAKEOVER

In answer to your inquiry, I consider that the chief dangers which confront the coming century will be religion without the Holy Ghost, Christianity without Christ, forgiveness without repentance, salvation without regeneration, politics without God, and heaven without hell.

—WILLIAM BOOTH

I t's *time for an extreme Church makeover!* The Church in America needs an extreme church makeover. It needs to be turned inside out and upside down. We don't need to just tweak a couple of items; we need a whole new operating system as well as a whole new way of doing business that works and bears fruit. Without a radical priority change, we will continue to be ineffective, irrelevant, and fruitless, unable to change our increasingly wicked culture. So we need a new **church** culture if we hope to reform our world and culture. And it has become clear to me recently that one of our primary callings as a ministry is to help awaken the American church culture out of its present fruitless, faddish, and market-driven state.

The Church in America is now much more market-driven than Spirit-led because it is led primarily by highly-gifted administrators and pastors whose main concerns are the people's salvation, then protection. While this may sound noble, virtuous, and even self-sacrificing, it is neither biblical nor is it in line with what apostolic Christianity looks like in the Book of Acts or the rest of the New Testament. As a result, and due to the significant lack of spiritual discernment in most pastor-led church leadership, the fads and trends that the Church wants, she gets. Whatever she wants to eat, she is allowed to feed on. Very few are getting exercise of their spiritual gifts, and fear and anxiety are the primary forces that move day-to-day operations. It is as if mom and dad are gone and the indulgent aunts and uncles are running things. Due to this, spiritual fruit is virtually nonexistent, and people are somehow content to sit and listen to messages designed for spiritual babies.

Leaders have traded influence and apostolic anointing for a sappy, ineffective, watered-down message with no teeth. Instead of boldness, we hear words like *caution* as an excuse to avoid becoming a militant, spiritually aggressive church. Instead of the radically sacrificial lifestyles we see the New Testament apostles had, too many of today's leaders are a pompous bunch of rich, spoiled, self-indulgent sissies, too scared to rebuke a cold and too self-indulgent to care.

Some ministry behemoths are so quick to compromise and prone to personal excess that large legal expenditures are now included as a significant part of the budget of most big, successful American ministries. Instead of exercising restraint or feeling a twinge of conscience, they say, "Well, so-and-so does it, so I'll do it, too." They have bodies, bucks, and big buildings, but integrity is on the decline.

It is amazing the correlation between what is happening with many giant American businesses like GM and Citigroup and these huge American ministries, which suck up huge amounts of resources but are becoming even more self-indulgent and unfruitful. Do these ministry leaders, many of whom are more salespeople than fishers of men, really think the Holy Spirit is going to allow them to run these "ministries" forever? Just as American businesses are going to have to either get rid of the excess and get back to serving customers or die, so these monstrous "ministry machines" are going to go the way of the dinosaur unless they repent and change. They are bloated and ineffective, yet amazingly addicted to millions a day to survive. Being big isn't the problem, and being "persecuted" isn't the problem. Our prayer should be, "Lord put out of business any and all of these supposed 'ministries' that have now stopped ministering and have instead become platforms for influence and riches for their leaders instead of serving your Kingdom's purposes. The King is coming and is requiring an accounting of how they have been 'doing the Lord's business.' Come, Lord, and clean house!" The Church needs to wake up because unless authentic apostolic leadership steps in to straighten things out, we are in real trouble. Our message and the representation of Jesus we have been communicating must change!

When a well-known minister died a few years ago, the Lord told me that his passing represented a changing of the guard in which "the pointing of the finger" in accusation would end. In its place would come new leaders who would be "pointing their fingers" in order to point people in the direction of their destiny!

Bill Johnson says, "To represent Jesus authentically, we must *re-present* Him and His Kingdom in a more authentic way."[1] This must be done with great integrity that authentically communicates His values and love yet moves people to focus on their purposes and destinies. God intentionally leaves no mold, pattern, or formula for how the Church is to be established; the main point is to follow the Word and listen to His voice.

Apostolic and prophetic churches will be more and more the order of the day while churches that practice the seeker-friendly model will be more and more absent of God's presence as the Lord says, "Enough is enough." While the Lord blesses things He won't inhabit, the difference between a little blessing and His manifest glory will be so stark and clear that only agnostics and the hard-hearted will stick with these religious facades.

> *Consequently, you are no longer foreigners and aliens, but*
> *fellow citizens with God's people and members of God's*

*household, built on the **foundation of the apostles and prophets,** with Christ Jesus Himself as the chief Cornerstone* (Ephesians 2:19-20 NIV).

NEW GOVERNMENT, NEW PRIORITIES

Obviously the churches that begin to be led by apostolic messages and mandates will look radically different, and they will have real and lasting fruit. Of course, a new wineskin brings a different set of priorities and governing core principles. Based on the gifts God has set in *His* order in the Church, as enumerated in First Corinthians 12:28, we have a new "way of doing business."

- Apostles advancing the Kingdom

- Prophets seeing this supernatural realm

- Teachers understanding the Kingdom

- Workers of miracles (including evangelists and pastors) engaging in supernatural activity

- Saints doing ministry (see Matt. 10:7-9)

No longer dependent on their district or their denomination's latest mandates, these new churches will follow God's pattern. In addition to having these new priorities, they will then also have new core values. Here is our latest list of core values we teach our newcomers as they come into the church.

CORE VALUES OF NORTHGATE CHURCH

Grace is the "operating system" in which we do all we are called to do. The key component of the outpouring of the Spirit in the Book of

Acts was *grace!* *"And with great power the apostles gave witness to the resurrection of the Lord Jesus. And great grace was upon them all"* (Acts 4:33 NKJV).

Liberty in the Spirit is encouraged in the personal lives of believers, in the operations of ministries, in using spiritual gifts, as well as in all meetings (see 1 Cor. 8:9; 2 Cor. 3:17; Gal. 2:4; James 1:25).

Reality is accentuated rather than theory; implementation is emphasized over exhortation, and action over passivity. We are unafraid to acknowledge failure even as we pursue success. In the words of G.K. Chesterton, "If a thing is worth doing, it is worth doing badly." Christianity is modeled as our *lifestyle* over a Sunday- or meeting-based Christianity. The Church is defined as any two gathered in His name (see Matt. 18:20). The Church is not the Kingdom but the vehicle to extend the Kingdom on the earth.

Integrity requires a love for the Spirit of Truth. *"Then you will know the **truth**, and the **truth** will set you free" (John 8:32 NIV). "Yet because I tell the **truth**, you do not believe Me!"* (John 8:45 NIV).

Giving: God is a giver, so we encourage tithing, caring for the poor, and liberal, hilarious giving (see 2 Cor. 9:7-9).

Servanthood is elevated and honored, especially in those courageous enough to take responsibility (see Matt. 23:8-10). Titles and positions are downplayed, and authority is not trusted to the irresponsible, regardless of how gifted they may be. The willing, eager, and early are rewarded.

Wisdom is sought after. To be wise, we win souls, encourage listening, choose to have a teachable spirit, seek out correction, and avoid fruitless associations (see most of Proverbs, especially 11:30).

Boldness: Since boldness was the prime request of prayer meetings in the Book of Acts, we ask for and exercise it. Also, since cowards and unbelievers are the first groups thrown into Hell, we stress the benefit of walking in boldness and confidence (see Acts 4:31; Rev. 21:8).

Victory: We attempt to remove excuses and unbelief so we might live a theology of victory, learning how to be winners rather than teaching things that legitimize failure and a lack of power (see James 1:22-24; 1 Cor. 15:57).

Presence Over the "Package": We become what we behold, so we practice passionate worship and pursue regular times of soaking and being filled with God's presence (see Gen. 30:37-43; 2 Cor. 3:18). I like to say, "We will always come down on the side of having His Presence over the package we project."

God Friendly: Though we attempt to be relevant, meetings are designed first to attract God rather than people. The companion of fools suffers harm, so we won't compromise to accommodate the carnal and uncommitted (see 2 Cor. 3:18; Prov. 13:20). Real love isn't mushy tolerance but a sincere offer of the truth and a commitment to a relationship with believers as they become disciples and fulfill their destiny.

Prophetic ministry is highly valued, and we encourage all believers to receive and operate in this gift (see Acts 2:17-18; 1 Cor. 14:1). Since God does nothing without informing His prophets, we want to listen to what God's prophets are hearing so we will have success (see Amos 3:7; 2 Chron. 20:20).

Ministry: Our goal is to attempt to release believers into ministry without qualification. This rapidly exposes heart issues (see Luke 9, 10, and 11). We don't attempt to perfect the saints before they can function, as that is the Holy Spirit's job. We give opportunity, and people can accept or reject it.

Power: The Gospel of the Kingdom requires a demonstration of God's power rather than a declaration of man's wisdom through powerless talk (see 1 Cor. 2:4). Signs, wonders, and miracles are a regular thing rather than a random occurrence.

Apostolic Ethic: The apostles were "sent ones," commissioned to train and send believers into their fields of ministry. We feel called as an apostolic center to train and send into the local, regional, and international harvest.[2]

> *But you will receive power when the Holy Spirit comes on you; and you will be My witnesses in Jerusalem, and in all Judea and Samaria, and to the ends of the earth* (Acts 1:8 NIV).

When we discard human methods and get in line with God's way of doing church, we begin to see the fruit and the manifest Presence we have all longed to see. Look at some Bible passages that others have told us just won't work for us today:

> *"And these signs will accompany **those who believe**: In My name they will drive out demons; they will speak in new tongues; they will pick up snakes with their hands; and when they drink deadly poison, it will not hurt them at all; they will place their hands on sick people, and they will get well." After the Lord Jesus had spoken to them, He was taken up into heaven and He sat at the right hand of God. Then the disciples went out and preached everywhere, and the Lord worked with them and confirmed His word by the signs that accompanied it* (Mark 16:17-20 NIV).

> *The next day the crowd that had stayed on the opposite shore of the lake realized that only one boat had been there, and that Jesus had not entered it with His disciples, but that they had gone away alone. Then some boats from Tiberias landed near the place where the people had eaten the bread after the Lord had given thanks. Once the crowd realized that neither Jesus nor*

His disciples were there, they got into the boats and went to Capernaum in search of Jesus. When they found Him on the other side of the lake, they asked Him, "Rabbi, when did You get here?" Jesus answered, "I tell you the truth, you are looking for Me, not because you saw miraculous signs but because you ate the loaves and had your fill. Do not work for food that spoils, but for food that endures to eternal life, which the Son of Man will give you. On Him God the Father has placed His seal of approval." Then they asked him, "What must we do to do the works God requires?" Jesus answered, "The work of God is this: to believe in the one He has sent." So they asked Him, "What miraculous sign then will You give that we may see it and believe You? What will you do? Our forefathers ate the manna in the desert; as it is written: 'He gave them bread from heaven to eat.'" Jesus said to them, "I tell you the truth, it is not Moses who has given you the bread from heaven, but it is My Father who gives you the true bread from heaven. For the bread of God is He who comes down from heaven and gives life to the world." "Sir," they said, "from now on give us this bread." Then Jesus declared, "I am the bread of life. He who comes to Me will never go hungry, and he who believes in Me will never be thirsty. But as I told you, you have seen Me and still you do not believe. All that the Father gives Me will come to Me, and whoever comes to Me I will never drive away. For I have come down from heaven not to do My will but to do the will of Him who sent Me (John 6:22-38 NIV).

One of the most vivid contrasts between this new breed of lifestyle-changing churches and meeting-centric churches will be the magnitude, as well as the multitude, of miracles, signs, and wonders. Miracles are a regular part of the lifestyle of these churches that the Lord is already raising up.

APOSTOLIC SIGNS AND WONDERS

In my former book, Theophilus, I wrote about all that Jesus began to do and to teach (Acts 1:1 NIV).

This Scripture is crucial because it runs counter to the wrong teaching we have been programmed with—the idea that we must teach something first before we can then do it. This passage reveals another priority: *doing*, then *teaching*, not teaching, then somehow doing.

*Men of Israel, listen to this: Jesus of Nazareth was a Man **accredited by God to you by miracles, wonders and signs**, which God did among you through Him, as you yourselves know* (Acts 2:22 NIV).

1. *Tongues:* They spoke in tongues (see Acts 2:2-4; 8:17; 10:44-46)

2. *A sense of awe:*

*Everyone was filled with awe, and **many** wonders and miraculous signs were done by the apostles* (Acts 2:43 NIV).

*Now, Lord, consider their threats and enable Your servants to speak Your word with great boldness. Stretch out Your hand to heal **and perform miraculous signs and wonders through the name of Your holy servant Jesus*** (Acts 4:29-30 NIV).

3. *Unselfish giving:*

All the believers were together and had everything in common. Selling their possessions and goods, they gave to anyone as he had need (Acts 2:44-45 NIV).

There were no needy persons among them. For from time to time those who owned lands or houses sold them, brought the money from the sales and put it at the apostles' feet, and it was distributed to anyone as he had need (Acts 4:34-35 NIV).

4. *Miraculous healing of lifelong conditions:*

Then Peter said, "Silver or gold I do not have, but what I have I give you. In the name of Jesus Christ of Nazareth, walk." Taking him by the right hand, he helped him up, and instantly the man's feet and ankles became strong (Acts 3:6-7 NIV).

"What are we going to do with these men?" they asked. "Everybody living in Jerusalem knows they have done an outstanding miracle, and we cannot deny it" (Acts 4:16 NIV).

5. *Boldness:*

When they saw the courage of Peter and John and realized that they were unschooled, ordinary men, they were astonished and they took note that these men had been with Jesus (Acts 4:13 NIV).

After they prayed, the place where they were meeting was shaken. And they were all filled with the Holy Spirit and spoke the word of God boldly (Acts 4:31 NIV).

6. *Premature death by prophecy* (see Acts 5:1-11).

7. *Peter's shadow healed the sick and delivered the demonized* (see Acts 5:15-16).

8. *Philip's healings, deliverances, and translation—at least 15 miles away!* (See Acts 8:6-8;38-40.)

9. *Peter healed a paralytic and raised Dorcas from the dead* (see Acts 9:33-34;36-41).

10. *Paul's handkerchiefs healed and delivered by contact* (see Acts 19:11-12)

You should get the picture by just glancing at these and other passages that there was a vivid and thick supernatural atmosphere of signs, wonders, and supernatural phenomena. The impossible was normal; the supernatural was normal; the miraculous was normal. For them, normal was what we would call revival today. The believers were more interested in being in God's presence than in just going to meetings. This is a deep contrast to the entertainment-laden, seeker-sensitive gatherings that represent a large segment of American Christianity today.

ENDNOTE

1. Bill Johnson, *The King and His Kingdom*, CD of message given at NorthGate Church, Atlanta, September 10, 2006.

2. Material from NorthGate Church, © Mighty Warrior Ministries.

CHAPTER 5

THE MAMMON-DRIVEN CHURCH

(With Apologies to Rick Warren)

No one can serve two masters; for either he will hate the one and love the other, or he will be devoted to one and despise the other. You cannot serve God and wealth. For this reason I say to you, do not be worried about your life, as to what you will eat or what you will drink; nor for your body, as to what you will put on. Is not life more than food, and the body more than clothing? Look at the birds of the air, that they do not sow, nor reap nor gather into barns, and yet your heavenly Father feeds them. Are you not worth much more than they? And who of you by being worried can add a single hour to his life? And why are you worried about clothing? Observe how the lilies of the field grow; they do not toil nor do they spin, yet I say to you that not even Solomon in all his glory clothed himself like one of these. But if God so clothes the grass of the field, which is alive today and tomorrow is thrown into the furnace, will He not much more clothe you? You of little faith! Do not worry then, saying, "What will we eat?" or "What will we drink?" or "What will we wear for clothing?" For the Gentiles eagerly seek all these things; for your heavenly Father knows that you need all these things. But seek first His kingdom and His righteousness, and all these things will be added to you (Matthew 6:24-33).

He who is faithful in a very little thing is faithful also in much; and he who is unrighteous in a very little thing is unrighteous also in much. Therefore if you have not been faithful in the use of unrighteous wealth, who will entrust the true riches to you? And if you have not been faithful in the use of that which is another's, who will give you that which is your own? No servant can serve two masters; for either he will hate the one and love the other, or else he will be devoted to one and despise the other. You cannot serve God and wealth (Luke 16:10-13).

BREAKING THE BACK OF MAMMON

Jesus made it exceedingly clear what the number one impediment to serving God is. It is not a lack of faith; it is not a lack of knowledge or wisdom or the need for a clear "word." All these things are excuses and evasions from addressing the real barrier, which is serving another—mammon. In Jesus' day *mammon* was the Greek form of a Syrian or Aramaic word for "money," "riches," "property," "worldly goods," or "profit."[1] You can't serve two purposes and accomplish one fully. It has to be one or the other. And anyone watching the financial and stock market collapse and severe economic contraction globally can see the "downside" of what is supposed to be the "good life." I am certain that a major part of the reason for this financial chaos was the reckless derivatives trading based on subprime loans. The greed to make a fortune was the driving force behind most of the reckless trading, using Wall Street like it was a casino.

Do you not know that to **whom you present yourselves slaves to obey, you are that one's slaves whom you obey,** *whether of sin leading to death, or of obedience leading to righteousness?* (Romans 6:16 NKJV).

If anyone teaches otherwise and does not consent to wholesome words, even the words of our Lord Jesus Christ, and to the doctrine which accords with godliness, he is proud, knowing nothing, but is obsessed with disputes and arguments over words, from which come envy, strife, reviling, evil suspicions, useless wranglings of men of corrupt minds and destitute of the truth, who suppose that godliness is a means of gain. From such withdraw yourself. Now godliness with contentment is great gain. For we brought nothing into this world, and it is certain we can carry nothing out. And having food and clothing, with these we shall be content. But those who desire to be rich fall into temptation and a snare, and into many foolish and harmful lusts which drown men in destruction and perdition. **For the love of money is a root of all kinds of evil,** *for which some have strayed from the faith in their greediness, and pierced themselves through with many sorrows. But you, O man of God, flee these things and pursue righteousness, godliness, faith, love, patience, gentleness* (1 Timothy 6:3-11 NKJV).

Do not lay up for yourselves treasures on earth, where moth and rust destroy and where thieves break in and steal; but lay up for yourselves treasures in heaven, where neither moth nor rust destroys and where thieves do not break in and steal. For **where your treasure is, there your heart will be also** (Matthew 6:19-21 NKJV).

69

Worrying about our supply is like bringing an offering to this demon god mammon. Self-preservation is what mammon works on and what mammon uses to manipulate us. Bitterness comes when we feel that this god (mammon) hasn't taken care of us, hasn't provided for us. This split commitment is the reason greed is likened to idolatry by the apostle Paul.

> *Put to death, therefore, whatever belongs to your earthly nature: sexual immorality, impurity, lust, evil desires and* **greed, which is idolatry** (Colossians 3:5 NIV).

> *Give us this day our daily bread. And forgive us our debts, as we also have forgiven our debtors. And do not lead us into temptation, but deliver us from evil. [For Yours is the kingdom and the power and the glory forever. Amen.] For if you forgive others for their transgressions, your heavenly Father will also forgive you. But if you do not forgive others, then your Father will not forgive your transgressions* (Matthew 6:11-15).

> *Then Jesus said to His disciples, "If anyone desires to come after Me, let him deny himself, and take up his cross, and follow Me. For whoever desires to save his life will lose it, but whoever loses his life for My sake will find it. For what profit is it to a man if he gains the whole world, and loses his own soul? Or what will a man give in exchange for his soul? For the Son of Man will come in the glory of His Father with His angels, and then He will reward each according to his works. Assuredly, I say to you, there are some standing here who shall not taste death till they see the Son of Man coming in His kingdom* (Matthew 16:24-28 NKJV).

Unless the Lord builds the house, its builders labor in vain. Unless the Lord watches over the city, the watchmen stand guard in vain. In vain you rise early and stay up late, toiling for food to eat—for He grants sleep to those He loves (Psalm 127:1-2 NIV).

PROVISION FROM THE UNSEEN REALM

It is amazing to me that Elijah, who called a three-and-a-half year drought, called fire from heaven, and destroyed over 400 of baal's prophets, needed the Lord to provide for him during the drought that he called! Elijah was engaged in a confrontation between true and false religion (*"How long will you waver between two opinions?"* see 1 Kings 18:21 NIV). The ministries of both Elijah and his successor, Elisha, were intended to demonstrate the supremacy of Yahweh of the Hebrews over baal of the Canaanites. The worship of baal-melqart (the Tyrian counterpart of the Canaanite baal) was imported to Israel as part of the dowry of Jezebel, the Phoenician princess King Ahab married (see 1 Kings 16:31-33). Ahab later institutionalized the worship of baal as the state religion of Israel. The story of Elijah must be read against the backdrop of this spiritual conflict, notably the supremacy of Yahweh over the domains traditionally ascribed to baal by the Canaanites:

- Baal controls the rain/rides upon the clouds vs. Yahweh controls the rain/rides upon the clouds in the whirlwind

- Baal is the god of fertility vs. Yahweh provides food and vegetation that sustain life

- Baal controls fire vs. Yahweh commands fire and lightning

- Baal controls life vs. Yahweh alone has power over barrenness, sickness, life, and death

Elijah is the prophet of the wilderness and wandering—rugged and austere. Elijah's miracles, with few exceptions, are works of wrath and destruction. He is the "prophet of fire," an abnormal agent working for exceptional ends, and he is the messenger of vengeance—sudden, fierce, and overwhelming. Yet Elijah still had to trust in his God for daily bread.

> *And Elijah the Tishbite, of the inhabitants of Gilead, said to Ahab, "As the Lord God of Israel lives, before whom I stand, there shall not be dew nor rain these years, except at **my** word"* (1 Kings 17:1 NKJV).

Obedience positions us for provision and blessing, and Elijah was, in his calling, wisely doing that which God had called him to do. While he could do extraordinary things in that calling, he was still reliant on the Lord for his daily meal, and His provision came in the form of a brook and ravens delivering his food.

> *Then the word of the Lord came to him, saying, "Get away from here and turn eastward, and hide by the Brook Cherith, which flows into the Jordan. And it will be that **you shall drink from the brook, and I have commanded the ravens to feed you there."** So he went and did according to the word of the Lord, for he went and stayed by the Brook Cherith, which flows into the Jordan. The ravens brought him bread and meat in the morning, and bread and meat in the evening; and he drank from the brook* (1 Kings 17:2-6 NKJV).

If we operate under a works paradigm, then we think our acts of obedience qualify us for something, but that isn't what happened here. Elijah's obedience to his calling is what positioned him for God's unique miraculous provision. He was doing what God called him to, and God was paying his bills, putting food on the table. By aligning himself to God's purpose for his life, provision was available for him to partake of. Obedience to our destiny positions us for provision.

God provided for Elijah even though eventually the brook dried up and the ravens stopped the pizza deliveries...

> And it happened after a while that the brook dried up, because there had been no rain in the land. Then the word of the Lord came to him, saying, "Arise, go to Zarephath, which belongs to Sidon, and dwell there. See, **I have commanded a widow there to provide for you**" (1 Kings 17:7-9 NKJV).

OK, you have got to see the bizarreness of this command. Could God pick a more unlikely candidate to take care of Elijah? Elijah called a drought, which the Lord didn't even command him to call (using his own creativity there), and, due to that, he experienced a little difficulty finding food and water. Then the Lord sent him to mooch off a poor widow—who was probably having a horrible time finding food herself. Just the idea that Elijah would *even do this* is humorous to me. He goes to a poor old lady and tells her to give him a big gulp full of water and some bread—what obedience he had to the Lord!

> So he arose and went to Zarephath. And when he came to the gate of the city, indeed a widow was there gathering sticks. And he called to her and said, "Please bring me a little water in a cup, that I may drink." And as she was going to get it, he called to her and said, "Please bring me a morsel of bread

in your hand." So she said, "As the Lord your God lives, I do not have bread, only a handful of flour in a bin, and a little oil in a jar; and see, I am gathering a couple of sticks that I may go in and prepare it for myself and my son, that we may eat it, and die" (1 Kings 17:10-12 NKJV).

So it looks like she was worse off than Elijah—on the verge of death herself when Elijah showed up.

*And Elijah said to her, "**Do not fear**; go and do as you have said, but make me a small cake from it first, and bring it to me; and afterward make some for yourself and your son. For thus says the Lord God of Israel: 'The bin of flour shall not be used up, nor shall the jar of oil run dry, until the day the Lord sends rain on the earth.'" So she went away and did according to the word of Elijah; and she and he and her household ate for many days. The bin of flour was not used up, nor did the jar of oil run dry, according to the word of the Lord which He spoke by Elijah* (1 Kings 17:13-16 NKJV).

So let's just recap…It stopped raining in the land, and there was a famine because Elijah said so. God did not tell Elijah to cause the drought, but he did that on his own! Elijah caused it to stop raining, but he couldn't even provide for himself. The Lord had to send the ravens to feed him. He was just in the right place to receive it. Then, God had to command the widow to feed Elijah through her. Get it? Following our calling positions us for God-sent provision.

Therefore I tell you, do not worry about your life, what you will eat or drink; or about your body, what you will wear. Is not life more important than food, and the body more important than clothes? Look at the birds of the air; they do not sow or reap or store away in barns, and yet your heavenly Father feeds them. Are you not much more valuable than they? Who of you by worrying can add a single hour to his life? And why do you worry about clothes? See how the lilies of the field grow. They do not labor or spin. Yet I tell you that not even Solomon in all his splendor was dressed like one of these. If that is how God clothes the grass of the field, which is here today and tomorrow is thrown into the fire, will He not much more clothe you, O you of little faith? So do not worry, saying, "What shall we eat?" or "What shall we drink?" or "What shall we wear?" For the pagans run after all these things, and your heavenly Father knows that you need them. But seek first His kingdom and His righteousness, and all these things will be given to you as well. Therefore do not worry about tomorrow, for tomorrow will worry about itself. Each day has enough trouble of its own (Matthew 6:25-34 NIV).

When we are brought into the world, we become God's responsibility for provision. Our obedience to our call aligns us to receive it. The position to receive provision is in God's house! If we get in the right position, which is fulfilling our calling, then we are in the right place to get provision. If your priority is to take care of your own provision, you may provide for yourself, but you won't receive God's best way because you are pursuing your own ends and seeking the Kingdom last. Obedience only places us in position to be blessed and to be supplied for. We need not ask God to do what is *our* job to do. We need to ask God to show us His will but trust that in doing it, *He will provide*!

You will keep him in perfect peace, whose mind is stayed on You, because he trusts in You....Lord, You will establish

75

peace for us, for You have also done all our works in us (Isaiah 26:3,12 NKJV).

God has spelled out His will for us in Matthew 10:6-9. He even tells us the seven words to say as we preach His Gospel, *"The kingdom of heaven is at hand"* (Matt. 10:7). We only need ask God to show us how to specifically perform His will within the framework of our lives. The Church has taken up so much of its time attempting to provide for itself and figure out ways to get "the wealth of the wicked" (see Prov. 13:22). If we will realign our lifestyles and priorities to *do* His will, the provision will come. Preaching the Gospel is a Heaven-approved mandate, and Heaven has no unfunded mandates.

ENDNOTE

1. StudyLight.org, *The New Testament Greek Lexicon Online,* s.v. "Mammonas," http://www.studylight.org/lex/grk/view.cgi?number=3126.

CHAPTER 6

PROVISION FROM UNSEEN REALMS

Blessed be the God and Father of our Lord Jesus Christ, who according to His abundant mercy has begotten us again to a living hope through the resurrection of Jesus Christ from the dead, to an inheritance incorruptible and undefiled and that does not fade away, reserved in heaven for you, who are kept by the power of God through faith for salvation ready to be revealed in the last time.

—1 PETER 1:3-5 (NKJV)

If something is hidden to us, it could be right in front of us, even in the natural world. What you *can't* see can be more real than what you can! What you see with the eyes of your spirit is not necessarily here now, but you can get access to it. There is another dimension we can tap into, and that is God's infinite supply. Even here on earth God knows where all the riches and treasures are!

> *I walk in the way of righteousness, in the midst of the paths of justice, to endow those who love me with wealth, that I may fill their treasuries* (Proverbs 8:20-21).

God wants to bless and prosper us. This verse seems to say God truly likes to bless His kids, especially those who love Him the most! This is a real and legitimate message in the Scriptures that we cannot deny. Even though ministers have succumbed to greed and avarice and taken this message to extremes, it is still a valid truth. Many times things are only proven when we hang on to them after they have been misused and abused. The answer to abuse and misuse is not *no* use but *proper* use. Fire is great in a fireplace but obviously can cause a lot of harm if it isn't contained. Many truths God reveals have to go through a crucible of testing that refines the rightness and accuracy of the message. Throwing everything out is an overreaction.

There are hidden treasures...

> *He tunnels through the rock; His eyes see all its treasures. He searches the sources of the rivers and brings hidden things to light* (Job 28:10-11 NIV).

And also out-in-the-open treasures...

> *For every animal of the forest is mine, and the cattle on a thousand hills. I know every bird in the mountains, and the creatures of the field are Mine* (Psalm 50:10-11 NIV).

INSTANT TRANSFER OF WEALTH

A day is coming—and I believe, for many, is already here—when those God has been able to trust with a few things will be given many things. God rewards the faithful. There is a vast and sudden transfer of wealth coming, and I believe that the recent financial collapse was the first step in this process. It has happened before and will happen again. When we see things like this happen nationally or globally, it is a clear sign that God is dealing with finances.

Example #1   The Wealth of Egypt

*He brought out Israel, **laden with silver and gold,** and from among their tribes **no one faltered**. Egypt was glad when they left, because **dread of Israel** had fallen on them. He spread out a cloud as a covering, and a fire to give light at night. They asked, and He brought them **quail** and satisfied them with the **bread of heaven.** He opened the rock, and water gushed out; like a river it flowed in the desert. For He remembered His holy promise given to His servant Abraham. He brought out His people with rejoicing, His chosen ones with shouts of joy; He gave them the lands of the nations, and they fell heir to what others had toiled for—that they might keep His precepts and observe His laws* (Psalm 105:37-45 NIV).

Example #2   Aramean Army Supply

And it happened after this that Ben-Hadad king of Syria gathered all his army, and went up and besieged Samaria. And there was a great famine in Samaria; and indeed they besieged it until a donkey's head was sold for eighty shekels of silver, and one-fourth of a kab of dove droppings for five shekels of silver. Then, as the king of Israel was passing by on the wall, a woman cried out to him, saying, "Help, my lord, O king!" And he said, "If the Lord does not help you, where can I find help for you? From the threshing floor or from the winepress?" Then the king said to her, "What is troubling you?" And she answered, "This woman said to me, 'Give your son, that we may eat him today, and we will eat my son tomorrow.' So we boiled my son, and ate him. And I said to her on the next day, 'Give your son, that we may eat him'; but she has hidden her son." Now it happened, when the king heard the words of the woman, that he tore his clothes; and as he passed by on the wall, the people looked, and there underneath he had sackcloth on his body. Then he said, "God do so to me and more also, if the head of Elisha the son of Shaphat remains on him today." But Elisha was sitting in his house, and the elders were sitting with him. And the king sent a man ahead of him, but before the messenger came to him, he said to the elders, "Do you see how this son of a murderer has sent someone to take away my head? Look, when the messenger comes, shut the door, and hold him fast at the door. Is not the sound of his master's feet behind him?" And while he was still talking with them, there was the messenger, coming down to him; and then the king said, "Surely this calamity is from the Lord; why should I wait for the Lord any longer?" (2 Kings 6:24-33 NKJV).

Then Elisha said, "Hear the word of the Lord. Thus says the Lord: 'Tomorrow about this time a seah of fine flour shall be sold for a shekel, and two seahs of barley for a shekel, at the gate of Samaria.'" So an officer on whose hand the king leaned answered the man of God and said, "Look, if the Lord would make windows in heaven, could this thing be?" And he said, "In fact, you shall see it with your eyes, but you shall not eat of it" (2 Kings 7:1-2 NKJV).

One key thing about this sudden transfer is that there are two different kinds of people involved in this and their responses will determine whether they will receive or not. There are those who believe God for great things, who have been faithful in little, working with what they have and believing for more, and these people will be good receivers.

Then there are those like the four lepers (see Second Kings below) who said to themselves, "We'll die if we sit, and we'll die if we go. Let's go!" When you have nothing left to lose, your courage jumps to new levels. I think a lot of people are sitting outside the walls of the churches right now like those lepers who maybe didn't fit in or were cast out of their churches for this or that reason—none scriptural—who will run back into their destinies when they are desperate enough.

> Now there were **four leprous men** at the entrance of the gate; and they said to one another, "Why are we sitting here until we die? If we say, 'We will enter the city,' the famine is in the city, and we shall die there. And if we sit here, we die also. Now therefore, come, let us surrender to the army of the Syrians. If they keep us alive, we shall live; and if they kill us, we shall only die." And they rose at twilight to go to the camp of the Syrians; and when they had come to the outskirts of the Syrian camp, to their surprise no one was there. For the Lord had caused the army of the Syrians to hear the noise of chariots and the noise of horses—the noise of a great army; so they said to one another, "Look, the king of Israel has hired against us the kings of the Hittites and the kings of the Egyptians to attack us!" Therefore they arose and fled at twilight, and left the camp intact—their tents, their horses, and their donkeys—and they fled for their lives. And when these lepers came to the outskirts of the camp, they went into one tent and ate and drank, and carried from it silver and gold and clothing, and went and hid them; then they came back and entered another tent, and carried some from there also, and went and hid it.
>
> Then they said to one another, "We are not doing right. This day is a day of good news, and we remain

silent. If we wait until morning light, some punishment will come upon us. Now therefore, come, let us go and tell the king's household." So they went and called to the gatekeepers of the city, and told them, saying, "We went to the Syrian camp, and surprisingly no one was there, not a human sound—only horses and donkeys tied, and the tents intact." And the gatekeepers called out, and they told it to the king's household inside.

So the king arose in the night and said to his servants, "Let me now tell you what the Syrians have done to us. They know that we are hungry; therefore they have gone out of the camp to hide themselves in the field, saying, 'When they come out of the city, we shall catch them alive, and get into the city.'"

*And one of his servants answered and said, "Please, let several men take five of the remaining horses which are left in the city. Look, they may either become like all the multitude of Israel that are left in it; or indeed, I say, they may become like all the multitude of Israel left from those who are consumed; so let us send them and see." Therefore they took two chariots with horses; and the king sent them in the direction of the Syrian army, saying, "Go and see." And they went after them to the Jordan; and indeed all the road was full of garments and weapons which the Syrians had thrown away in their haste. So the messengers returned and told the king. Then the people went out and plundered the tents of the Syrians. **So a seah of fine flour was sold for a shekel, and two seahs of barley for a shekel, according to the word of the Lord** (2 Kings 7:3-16).*

There is also the group like the officer the king leaned on, the gate-keeper, whose own unbelief killed him. While it was Elisha who declared his end, it was his own unbelief that took him. Sometimes when things seem to get worse and worse, it seems like there is nothing left to believe for, and when hope is gone, then people start pronouncing judgment on themselves. That is what the king's officer did.

> *Now the king had appointed the officer on whose hand he leaned to have charge of the gate. But the people trampled him in the gate, and he died, just as the man of God had said, who spoke when the king came down to him. So it happened just as the man of God had spoken to the king, saying, "Two seahs of barley for a shekel, and a seah of fine flour for a shekel, shall be sold tomorrow about this time in the gate of Samaria." Then that officer had answered the man of God, and said, "Now look, if the Lord would make windows in heaven, could such a thing be?" And he had said, "In fact, you shall see it with your eyes, but you shall not eat of it." And so it happened to him, for the people trampled him in the gate, and he died* (2 Kings 7:17-20 NKJV).

It is interesting that Scripture says that *the people trampled him* at the gate trying to get through to the abundance! Here is a lesson for all those whose ambition it is to be a gatekeeper or a leader in the Church. The leaders should be the ones who serve rather than those who bottle up the provision. If you don't get out of the way when people are hungry, you might end up dead.

We can live out of the other realm that is *not* of this world. This involves not only things on this earth but even supernatural transfers and the release of angel's food and Heaven's bread. It has happened before and will happen again. This realm of provision is where we pull from the Kingdom to supply us in this earthly realm. We are not finding hidden things in this world, but literally pulling our source of supply into this dimension from the Kingdom through supernatural means.

SUPERNATURAL MULTIPLICATION
OF NATURAL THINGS

1. Loaves and fish

> *Do you still not understand? Don't you remember the five
> loaves for the five thousand, and how many basketfuls you
> gathered? Or the seven loaves for the four thousand, and
> how many basketfuls you gathered?* (Matthew 16:9-10
> NIV).

2. Oil in jars

> *The wife of a man from the company of the prophets cried
> out to Elisha, "Your servant my husband is dead, and you
> know that he revered the Lord. But now his creditor is
> coming to take my two boys as his slaves." Elisha replied to
> her, "How can I help you?* **Tell me, what do you have in
> your house?"** *"Your servant has nothing there at all," she
> said, "except a little oil." Elisha said, "Go around and ask
> all your neighbors for empty jars. Don't ask for just a few.
> Then go inside and shut the door behind you and your
> sons. Pour oil into all the jars, and as each is filled, put
> it to one side." She left him and afterward shut the door
> behind her and her sons. They brought the jars to her and
> she kept pouring. When all the jars were full, she said to
> her son, "Bring me another one." But he replied, "There
> is not a jar left." Then the oil stopped flowing. She went
> and told the man of God, and he said, "Go, sell the oil
> and pay your debts. You and your sons can live on what is
> left"* (2 Kings 4:1-7 NIV).

3. Bread and oil

> *For thus says the Lord God of Israel: "The bin of flour shall not be used up, nor shall the jar of oil run dry, until the day the Lord sends rain on the face of the earth." So she went away and did according to the word of Elijah; and she and he and her household ate for many days. The bin of flour was not used up, nor did the jar of oil run dry, according to the word of the Lord which He spoke by Elijah* (1 Kings 17:14-16 NKJV).

4. Angelic food

> *He lay down and slept under a juniper tree; and behold, there was an angel touching him, and he said to him, "Arise, eat." Then he looked and behold, there was at his head a bread cake baked on hot stones, and a jar of water. So he ate and drank and lay down again* (1 Kings 19:5-6).

5. Bread of Heaven (manna)

> *So it came about at evening that the quails came up and covered the camp, and in the morning there was a layer of dew around the camp. When the layer of dew evaporated, behold, on the surface of the wilderness there was a fine flake-like thing, fine as the frost on the ground. When the sons of Israel saw it, they said to one another, "What is it?" For they did not know what it was. And Moses said to them, "It is the bread which the Lord has given you to eat. This is what the Lord has commanded, 'Gather of it every man as much as he should eat; you shall take an omer*

apiece according to the number of persons each of you has in his tent.'" The sons of Israel did so, and some gathered much and some little. When they measured it with an omer, he who had gathered much had no excess, and he who had gathered little had no lack; every man gathered as much as he should eat. Moses said to them, "Let no man leave any of it until morning" (Exodus 16:13-19).

6. Fed by birds

"It shall be that you shall drink of the brook, and I have commanded the ravens to provide for you there." So he went and did according to the word of the Lord, for he went and lived by the brook Cherith, which is east of the Jordan. The ravens brought him bread and meat in the morning and bread and meat in the evening, and he would drink from the brook (1 Kings 17:4-6).

7. Cash from fish

"Nevertheless, lest we offend them, go to the sea, cast in a hook, and take the fish that comes up first. And when you have opened its mouth, you will find a piece of money; take that and give it to them for Me and you" (Matthew 17:27 NKJV).

8. Great catch of fish

When He had finished speaking, He said to Simon, "Put out into the deep water and let down your nets for a catch." Simon answered and said, "Master, we worked hard all night and caught nothing, but I will do as You say and let down the nets." When they had done this, they enclosed a great quantity of fish, and their nets began to break; so they signaled to their partners in the other boat for them to come and help them. And they came and filled both of the boats, so that they began to sink. But when Simon Peter saw that, he fell down at Jesus' feet, saying, "Go away from me Lord, for I am a sinful man!" For amazement had seized him and all his companions because of the catch of fish which they had taken (Luke 5:4-9).

CHAPTER 7

OVERCOMING THE POVERTY SPIRIT

Poverty with its horrible effects is one of the greatest hindrances to the people of God entering into their inheritance and being a blessing to the nations (see Gen. 12:2-3). Seeing the terrible effect poverty has on people makes unbelievers question why a loving God could allow the kind of suffering it brings. Poverty is defined as "the state of one who lacks a usual or socially acceptable amount of money or material possessions; scarcity, dearth."[1] God's creation was never meant to experience this horrible condition—it was a result of the Fall.

While much attention has been given to the effects poverty creates concerning material and monetary things, there is a clear correlation between material and spiritual blessing or lack of it. While it is *not* true that only good things happen to good people and bad things happen to bad people, ample biblical evidence reveals God's desire to bless, heal, and prosper His children. *"Beloved, I pray that in all respects you may prosper and be in good health, just as your soul prospers"* (3 John 1:2). Why would God intentionally want His children to suffer in such a way that not only hurts them but makes Him look like a terrible dad? In the Book of Proverbs, poverty is blamed more on man's selfishness, neglect, and laziness than anything God—or even the devil—might have done.

Lack of self control

- Neglecting discipline (see Prov. 13:18)

- Being hasty (see Prov. 21:5)

- Being a heavy drinker (see Prov. 23:21)

- Being a glutton (see Prov. 23:21)

Laziness

- Following empty pursuits (see Prov. 28:19)

- Talking instead of working (see Prov. 14:23)

Forgetting the poor

- Not giving to the poor (see Prov. 28:27)

- Oppressing the poor (see Prov. 22:16)

- Giving to the rich (see Prov.22:16)

Not only is God *not* responsible for the effects or the causes of nearly all poverty, but He even grants us redemption from it in Jesus Christ!

> *For you know the grace of our Lord Jesus Christ, that though He was rich, yet for your sake He became poor, so that you through His poverty might become rich* (2 Corinthians 8:9).

> *Christ redeemed us from the curse of the Law, having become a curse for us—for it is written, "Cursed is everyone who hangs on a tree"—in order that in Christ Jesus the blessing of Abraham might come to the Gentiles, so that we would receive the promise of the Spirit through faith* (Galatians 3:13-14).

Through the cross of Christ we receive the promise of the Spirit through faith, delivering us from a life of poverty and lack. To consistently do without is not God's intentional will for us. While some may suffer lack from time to time, God takes care of His children. It's a historic fact that when pagan cultures are converted to Christianity they begin to experience blessing economically and materially. This is because God never intended His children to suffer lack this way.

> *Oh, fear the Lord, you His saints! There is no want to those who fear Him. The young lions lack and suffer hunger; but those who seek the Lord shall not lack any good thing* (Psalm 34:9-10 NKJV).

POVERTY MENTALITY

While we can be guaranteed deliverance from poverty in Christ, we must deal with the wrong attitudes, thoughts, and mentalities that are contrary to defeating poverty in our lives. Here are a few:

1. Myth of limited resources

This mentality supposes that God has some kind of supply problem or limits on His ability to provide. It says, *"If they get something, I won't."* Some folks raised in a large family with limited resources can struggle with this concept. One woman we were counseling told me that she grew up in a family of eight children, and every Friday night they would have pizza and cola. She was only allowed one slice of pizza and a half glass of cola. Consequently, the poverty mentality of her parents was passed to her. God has access to every resource on this planet, and because we have a relationship with Him, we also have that same access in Jesus' name! This poverty spirit does attempt to get folks to look around at what others have or don't have; it stirs up envy and provokes people to jealousy. In God's economy, it is foolish to think that something is being taken away from us simply because others have it. The whole premise the Green Party is using to curtail worldwide growth and development is that there simply are not enough resources to go around. But the Kingdom has an unlimited supply, and when God wants to, He materializes things or multiples natural things like oil and bread and fowl.

> *For every beast of the forest is Mine, and the cattle on a thousand hills* (Psalm 50:10 NKJV).

> *"The silver is Mine, and the gold is Mine," declares the Lord of hosts* (Haggai 2:8).

2. Myth of limited opportunity to receive

The poverty spirit attempts to convince folks that *"Others can be blessed, but I can't."* It attempts to keep that person in a works mentality regarding their provision so they keep going around the cul-de-sac but never seem to make progress. This spirit works to get you where you have no choices left. Many people in poverty are enslaved to mammon and spend all of their lives focused on money rather than God. It works to create a greed for things, which is a form of idolatry. Greed is idolatry.

> *Therefore consider the members of your earthly body as dead to immorality, impurity, passion, evil desire, and greed, which amounts to idolatry* (Colossians 3:5).

This spirit also attempts to get people trusting in the natural realm, keeping them in severe unbelief and convinced that natural rather than spiritual principles will help them succeed and get blessed. People with a spirit of poverty may have little or they may have a lot, but whatever they have, it is never quite enough. One way this spirit can rob us is to turn us to look toward having stuff rather than the anointing and the Holy Spirit. Do we want the cash to feed the 5,000 or the power to train 5,000 to feed themselves? The spirit of poverty moves people to stay carnally minded, to hold back even from tithing. I have been a Christian for 33 years and have never seen someone who tithes faithfully stay in the bondage of this spirit. All of the Christians I know who prosper, are debt free, and have wealth, tithe faithfully. They also give and sow to projects and missions. I have never seen Christians prosper who won't tithe. They always seem to stay in a never-never land of missed opportunities.

3. Financial distraction

The spirit of poverty is a demon assigned to keep people from walking in their potential. It can go at this one of two ways, but both ways can certainly work. *First*, this spirit may even allow us to receive things and to possess and acquire finances in order to keep us from fulfilling our destinies in God. Did you know that one study discovered that within two or three years about 80 percent of lottery winners end up in worse shape financially than before they won? Have you ever wondered at the wealth rock stars and entertainers have and how quickly it goes through their fingers? This spirit causes people with money to say, "I'm going to serve the Lord and people with my money someday, but just let me make some more." Obviously, they never do and never will.

The *second* way this spirit limits people's potential is by pushing them to become underachievers and reducing them to being dreamers only instead of doers. If people only theorize about things and never really accomplish something, they can become accustomed to it and live their lives thinking a good week is when one of their theories was proved, though it was never acted on. These people are chasing fantasies, and Scripture is clear this kind of poverty keeps them under a strong delusion. These are the folks who are always looking for the big score, always trying to get people who have earned real money to part with it so they can follow their schemes and dreams.

He who works his land will have abundant food, but he who chases fantasies lacks judgment (Proverbs 12:11 NIV).

There is real Kingdom treasure available to us that is more valuable then authentic veins of gold underground that have to be dug up and mined. There are hidden nuggets of truth and insights in God that can save us years if we would only invest time in them. Instead of chasing phantom investment schemes and multi-level marketing nonsense, why don't we spend time seeking the Kingdom by plumbing the depths of the Word of God? It is a much better investment of time and energy. *Money is our least valuable resource.* Yet we won't be trusted with true riches (anointing and power) if we don't learn how important money is and how to handle it. To have the true riches we also must be able to handle money. Luke 16 is all about the correlation between the two.

Now He was also saying to the disciples, "There was a rich man who had a manager, and this manager was reported to him as squandering his possessions. And he called him and said to him, 'What is this I hear about you? Give an accounting of your management, for you can no longer be manager.' The manager said to himself, 'What shall I do, since my master is taking the management away from me? I am not strong enough to dig; I am ashamed to beg. I know what I shall do, so that when I am removed from the management people will welcome me into their homes.' And he summoned each one of his master's debtors, and he began saying to the first, 'How much do you owe my master?' And he said, 'A hundred measures of oil.' And he said to him, 'Take your bill, and sit down quickly and write fifty.' Then he said to another, 'And how much do you owe?' And he said, 'A hundred measures of wheat.'

> *He said to him, 'Take your bill, and write eighty.' And his master praised the unrighteous manager because he had acted shrewdly;* **for the sons of this age are more shrewd in relation to their own kind than the sons of light.** *And I say to you, make friends for yourselves by means of the wealth of unrighteousness, so that when it fails, they will receive you into the eternal dwellings. He who is faithful in a very little thing is faithful also in much; and he who is unrighteous in a very little thing is unrighteous also in much.* **Therefore if you have not been faithful in the use of unrighteous wealth, who will entrust the true riches to you?** *And if you have not been faithful in the use of that which is another's, who will give you that which is your own? No servant can serve two masters; for either he will hate the one and love the other, or else he will be devoted to one and despise the other.* **You cannot serve God and wealth**" (Luke 16:1-13).

We think that somehow the more we have, then the more God can do something with, the more God can use. But Jesus could always take a little and make a lot of something with it. When the disciples told Him that people needed food and had come a long way, He only asked them what they had. After blessing a couple fish and five loaves of bread, they fed 5,000 families and had 12 giant baskets brimming over. Now that is the way God operates. How about the widow and the oil that just kept on flowing? God loves to multiply a little and make it a lot!

> *One day Jesus was praying in a certain place. When He finished, one of His disciples said to Him, "Lord, teach us to pray, just as John taught his disciples." He said to them, "When you pray, say: 'Father, hallowed be Your name, Your kingdom come.* **Give us each day our daily bread.**

*Forgive us our sins, for we also forgive everyone who sins against us. And lead us not into temptation.'" Then He said to them, "Suppose one of you has a friend, and he goes to him at midnight and says, 'Friend, lend me three loaves of bread, because a friend of mine on a journey has come to me, and I have nothing to set before him.' Then the one inside answers, 'Don't bother me. The door is already locked, and my children are with me in bed. I can't get up and give you anything.' I tell you, though he will not get up and give him the bread because he is his friend, yet because of the man's **boldness** he will get up and give him as much as he needs"* (Luke 11:1-8 NIV).

As we see here, God honors boldness, and I wrote a whole chapter in my first book about this. But boldness is not only the way we get His Gospel mandate accomplished, it is what keeps the bread coming! When something great is produced, many times it comes out of something small or weak. It is interesting that the *wise* men who discovered where Jesus was needed to have revelation from above to even find Him in that small, unlikely place. Solomon said, *"...He who wins souls is wise"* (Prov. 11:30 NIV). So we have to think differently, think wisely. Wisdom is *what* to *do!*

The Lord cares about numbers and wants all men to be saved. No question—the mark of the beast is an economic mark. The love of money is the root of *all* evil, and so one of the ultimate tests at the end is an economic test (see 1 Tim. 6:10; Rev. 13:17). *Now* is the time to grow in trusting the ultimate Source. He will provide through unlikely sources. Remember Elijah was even told, "A widow will provide for you." The stock market in Heaven never crashes, so God's supply never runs out. Every Christian can write checks to expend His heavenly account, and we are called to live with those windows of Heaven opened to us. I personally have never met anyone who is tithing who has chronic financial problems. Also, all the people I know who have significant wealth, always tithe. It is true that things may happen and they may suffer loss, but the person who tithes closes many doors to the enemy and actually, according to this passage, opens up the window of Heaven!

> *"I the Lord do not change. So you, O descendants of Jacob, are not destroyed. Ever since the time of your forefathers you have turned away from My decrees and have not kept them. Return to Me, and I will return to you," says the Lord Almighty. "But you ask, 'How are we to return?' Will a man rob God? Yet you rob Me. But you ask, 'How do we rob You?' In tithes and offerings. You are under a curse— the whole nation of you—because you are robbing Me. Bring the whole tithe into the storehouse, that there may be food in My house. Test Me in this," says the Lord Almighty, "and **see if I will not throw open the floodgates of heaven and pour out so much blessing that you will not have room enough for it.** I will prevent pests from devouring your crops, and the vines in your fields will not cast their fruit," says the Lord Almighty. "Then all the nations will call you blessed, for yours will be a delightful land," says the Lord Almighty* (Malachi 3:6-12 NIV).

That's what God wants to do; He wants to open the floodgates of Heaven and pour out so much blessing there is no more need *if* we will tithe to the place of the storehouse. It's one of the only places God says, "Test Me." He promises the blessing if we meet His conditions.

But there is another place where a door of poverty can be opened up in our lives.

> *Now this is what the Lord Almighty says: "Give careful thought to your ways. You have planted much, but have*

*harvested little. You eat, but never have enough. You drink, but never have your fill. You put on clothes, but are not warm. You earn wages, only to put them in a purse with holes in it." This is what the Lord Almighty says: "Give careful thought to your ways. Go up into the mountains and bring down timber and build the house, so that I may take pleasure in it and be honored," says the Lord. "You expected much, but see, it turned out to be little. What you brought home, I blew away. Why?" declares the Lord Almighty. "Because of My house, which remains a ruin, **while each of you is busy with his own house.** Therefore, because of you the heavens have withheld their dew and the earth its crops. I called for a drought on the fields and the mountains, on the grain, the new wine, the oil and whatever the ground produces, on men and cattle, and on the labor of your hands." Then Zerubbabel son of Shealtiel, Joshua son of Jehozadak, the high priest, and the whole remnant of the people obeyed the voice of the Lord their God and the message of the prophet Haggai, because the Lord their God had sent him. And the people feared the Lord* (Haggai 1:5-12 NIV).

The problem here was that the people put their own houses, careers, and problems first rather than the Kingdom of God. Message: "Seek first the Kingdom." Put Him first every day! He says if we put Him first, we will be taken care of. He doesn't want to be *in* our lives; He wants to *be our life!*

Like I say, if you want His life, then adopt His lifestyle! Things that used to hold us back have no more sway in our lives when we commit our time to Him. When Jesus is really King of our lives, He is King of our schedules! For too long believers have gone to church on Sunday, paid their tithes, and then lived for themselves, serving their own pleasure and interests the rest of the week. Then they wonder why their lives are so messed up! You have heard, "Whatever we bind in Heaven gets bound on earth too." But we bind the enemy when we follow the Lord. The blessings of God cause far more people to come to Him than calamities and difficulties. We want His blessings. As we are blessed, we bless. But let's take it a step further. If we are called to be a blessing to the nations, we should bless out of our need as well. We should ask for seed to sow and then sow that. The goal is to be a conduit for His supply to others; as we bless others, we will get it back on our own head as well!

While everyone would say they are waiting for something to sow, remember what Jesus did with just a little? How are we going to see financial miracles if we just want to see the blessing first? We should be the blessing, and then we'll see the blessing!

> *Remember this: Whoever sows sparingly will also reap sparingly, and whoever sows generously will also reap generously. Each man should give what he has decided in his heart to give, not reluctantly or under compulsion, for God loves a cheerful giver. And God is able to make all grace abound to you, so that in all things at all times, having all that you need, you will abound in every good work. As it is written: "He has scattered abroad His gifts to the poor; His righteousness endures forever." Now He who supplies seed to the sower and bread for food will also supply and increase your store of seed and will enlarge the harvest of your righteousness. You will be made rich in every way so that you can be generous on every occasion, and through us your generosity will result in thanksgiving to God. This service that you perform is not only supplying the needs of God's people but is also overflowing in many expressions of thanks to God* (2 Corinthians 9:6-12 NIV).

Rick Joyner feels that another one of the biggest doors to letting the spirit of poverty in our life is *criticism!*[2] The pointing of the finger, the judging, analyzing, and calling everything into question... We must realize we all have two main ways to respond to just about anything: we either accuse, criticize, and complain or we intercede, pray, minister, and intervene. We can either be part of the problem or help *fix it!*

*"Is this the kind of fast I have chosen, only a day for a man to humble himself? Is it only for bowing one's head like a reed and for lying on sackcloth and ashes? Is that what you call a fast, a day acceptable to the Lord? Is not this the kind of fasting I have chosen: to loose the chains of injustice and untie the cords of the yoke, to set the oppressed free and break every yoke? Is it not to share your food with the hungry and to provide the poor wanderer with shelter—when you see the naked, to clothe him, and not to turn away from your own flesh and blood? Then your light will break forth like the dawn, and your healing will quickly appear; then your righteousness will go before you, and the glory of the Lord will be your rear guard. Then you will call, and the Lord will answer; you will cry for help, and He will say: Here am I. **If you do away with the yoke of oppression, with the pointing finger and malicious talk, and if you spend yourselves in behalf of the hungry and satisfy the needs of the oppressed, then your light will rise in the darkness, and your night will become like the noonday.** The Lord will guide you always; He will satisfy your needs in a sun-scorched land and will strengthen your frame. You will be like a well-watered garden, like a spring whose waters never fail. Your people will rebuild the ancient ruins and will raise up the age-old foundations; you will be called*

Repairer of Broken Walls, Restorer of Streets with Dwell-ings. If you keep your feet from breaking the Sabbath and from doing as you please on My holy day, if you call the Sabbath a delight and the Lord's holy day honorable, and if you honor it by not going your own way and not doing as you please or speaking idle words, then you will find your joy in the Lord, and I will cause you to ride on the heights of the land and to feast on the inheritance of your father Jacob." The mouth of the Lord has spoken (Isaiah 58:5-14 NIV).

We can experience these living waters! If we put away criticism and judgment and instead become those who intercede, we will receive bless-ing and be blessed. Intercession means we lay ourselves down to create a way for change to come. While there is always a legitimate place for criticism *that brings change*, we have to be willing to ***fix the problems*** in our own house first. Jesus could be accused of criticizing the Jews, the Pharisees, the Sadducees, the Jewish leaders, and everyone else. But ***He was there to fix the problem!*** We can't fix anything if we deny there is a problem. To criticize without being willing to lift a finger to change something is simply counter-productive. The pointing of the finger has no place. We must be able to preach to the hardest cases in love and still win. We have to be willing to bring light into the darkness, not simply curse it. Sitting on the sidelines saying nothing while it is obvious the ship is going down is neither righteous nor noble. Get in the game and let's fix this mess!

ENDNOTE

Merriam-Webster's Collegiate Dictionary, 11th ed., s.v., "Poverty."

Rick Joyner, *Overcoming Evil in the Last Days* (Shippensburg, PA: Destiny Image, 2009).

CHAPTER 8

WAKE THE LIVING DEAD!

I was praying a few years ago and had a vision of one of those zombie films (think Michael Jackson's "Thriller" music video) where all the zombies were walking during the night. When they came upon a normal, healthy person they would bite and devour him and make him into a zombie like them. Then the healthy person walked around and became one of them, wandering as one of the living dead...alive but dead. I said, "What was that, Lord?" The Scripture in Galatians came to me about "biting and devouring one another," and then He said, "That is a significant part of My Church. Wake them up!"

> *For you were called to freedom, brethren; only do not turn your freedom into an opportunity for the flesh, but **through love serve one another.** For the whole Law is fulfilled in one word, in the statement, "You shall love your neighbor as yourself." But **if you bite and devour one another, take care that you are not consumed by one another*** (Galatians 5:13-15).

There are several important things about this passage that merit attention. In these days when the Body of Christ is waking up to freedom from legalism and the freedom to be who they are called to be in Christ, there will be a tendency to go into the "Wild Wild West" of lawlessness. New territories require pioneers to go in there, and these pioneers may be folks with a thick-skinned nature. Nevertheless, the freedom to go where we have never gone before doesn't allow us to neglect the reason for our freedom. We are to serve one another

166 LIFESTYLE

through love. The reason the zombies were biting each other was they had no love and no reason for their freedom. So they wandered and bit and devoured and wandered and bit and devoured. God wants to heal the wounded and get them back on track! And I feel like the Lord has made it clear *we can wake these living dead* and get them to arise like the awesome army we see in Ezekiel:

> *The hand of the Lord was upon me, and He brought me out by the Spirit of the Lord and set me in the middle of a valley; it was full of bones. He led me back and forth among them, and I saw a great many bones on the floor of the valley, bones that* **were very dry.** *He asked me, "Son of man, can these bones live?" I said, "O Sovereign Lord, You alone know." Then He said to me, "Prophesy to these bones and say to them, 'Dry bones, hear the word of the Lord! This is what the Sovereign Lord says to these bones: I will make breath enter you, and you will come to life. I will attach tendons to you and make flesh come upon you and cover you with skin; I will put breath in you, and you will come to life. Then you will know that I am the Lord.'" So I prophesied as I was commanded. And as I was prophesying, there was a noise, a rattling sound, and the bones came together, bone to bone. I looked, and tendons and flesh appeared on them and skin covered them, but there was no breath in them. Then He said to me, "Prophesy to the breath; prophesy, son of man, and say to it, 'This is what the Sovereign Lord says: Come from the four winds, O breath, and breathe into these slain, that they may live.'" So I prophesied as He commanded me, and breath entered them; they came to life and stood up on their feet—a* **vast army** *(Ezekiel 37:1-10 NIV).*

> *Arise, shine, for your light has come, and the glory of the Lord rises upon you. See, darkness covers the earth and thick darkness is over the peoples, but the Lord rises upon you and His glory appears over you* (Isaiah 60:1-2 NIV).

It's obvious that even with all our technology, marketing, and sales hype, the American Church needs a huge dose of integrity, authenticity, passion, and real power. Way too many people aspire to minister to be revered by the crowds and as a "stepping-stone" to *"my own ministry."* Way too many now view prophecy as an endorsement of "what God is doing in my life." Few real apostles are emerging to speak into the many awful scenarios where sin, false doctrine, and heresies are being allowed to continue. Authentic prophets are few and far between, and the Church has few platforms to allow their words of warning or reproof to be heard. Bottom line: the Church is not looking her best right now. We cannot expect to have Christ's power in the Church if we refuse to live as He said to live, act as He said to act, and *not* act as He said *not* to act.

We have slogans, gimmicks, marketing, graphics, cool Websites, and everything else, but *we need the real deal.*

Instead of just being a catchy slogan to put on wristbands, the question, "What Would Jesus Do?" ought to be the primary question we ask to determine how to live our lives, do our ministries, and have a church life. One of the strongest passages that we see about this comes not from Jesus but from one of His disciples:

> *We know that we have come to know Him if we obey His commands. The man who says, "I know Him," but does not do what He commands is a liar, and the truth is not in him. But if anyone obeys His word, God's love is truly made complete in him. This is how we know we are in Him: whoever claims to live in Him must walk as Jesus did* (1 John 2:3-6 NIV).

According to this passage, we are called not just to obey His words but also to live out His life and lifestyle, led by the Holy Spirit. The definition of a disciple is one who is becoming like his master. To "walk as Jesus did" isn't referring to the primary mode of transportation at the time, which was walking or riding an animal, but is about imitating the way Jesus dealt with people and situations as He "walked through His daily life." And perhaps the greatest encouragement we have about this is that Jesus said we could do this!

Look at this passage in the New American Standard:

> *…He who has seen Me has seen the Father; how can you say, "Show us the Father"? Do you not believe that I am in the Father, and the Father is in Me? The words that I say to you I do not speak on My own initiative, but the Father abiding in Me does His works. Believe Me that I am in the Father and the Father is in Me; otherwise believe because of the works themselves. Truly, truly, I say to you, he who believes in Me, the works that I do, he will do also; and greater works than these he will do; because I go to the Father. Whatever you ask in My name, that will I do, so that the Father may be glorified in the Son. If you ask Me anything in My name, I will do it. If you love Me, you will keep My commandments* (John 14:9-15).

The Message:

> *…To see Me is to see the Father. So how can you ask, "Where is the Father?" Don't you believe that I am in the Father and the Father is in Me? The words that I speak to you aren't mere words. I don't just make them up on My own. The Father who resides in Me crafts each word into a divine act. Believe Me: I am in My Father and My*

Father is in Me. If you can't believe that, believe what you see—these works. The person who trusts Me will not only do what I'm doing but even greater things, because I, on My way to the Father, am giving you the same work to do that I've been doing. You can count on it. From now on, whatever you request along the lines of who I am and what I am doing, I'll do it. That's how the Father will be seen for who He is in the Son. I mean it. Whatever you request in this way, I'll do. If you love Me, show it by doing what I've told you (John 14:9-15).

Amplified:

...Anyone who has seen Me has seen the Father. How can you say then, Show us the Father? Do you not believe that I am in the Father, and that the Father is in Me? What I am telling you I do not say on My own authority and of My own accord; but the Father Who lives continually in Me does the (His) works (His own miracles, deeds of power). Believe Me that I am in the Father and the Father in Me; or else believe Me for the sake of the [very] works themselves. [If you cannot trust Me, at least let these works that I do in My Father's name convince you.] I assure you, most solemnly I tell you, if anyone steadfastly believes in Me, he will himself be able to do the things that I do; and he will do even greater things than these, because I go to the Father. And I will do [I Myself will grant] whatever you ask in My Name [as presenting all that I AM], so that the Father may be glorified and extolled in (through) the Son. [Yes] I will grant [I Myself will do for you] whatever you shall ask in My Name [as presenting all that I AM]. If you [really] love Me, you will keep (obey) My commands (John 14:9-15).

What does this lifestyle—the 166 lifestyle—look like and what are we supposed to do and be? He gives us several promises here, so we'll take them one by one.

1. Representation

First, Jesus says in verses 9 and 10, *"You want to see God? You want to see the Father? Then look at Me!"* For us to see how God thinks, works, and acts, all we have to do is look at Jesus. It is not complicated or mysterious. Jesus says that He did *nothing* excepting that which He saw the Father doing. This would best be described by the word *representation*. Jesus represents (or re-presents) His *Dad* to the world and to His people.

> *The Son is the radiance of God's glory and the exact representation of His being, sustaining all things by His powerful word...* (Hebrews 1:3 NIV).

2. Authentication

Second, in John 14:11 Jesus says, *"Believe in Me because I am in the Father and He in Me, but if that doesn't suffice, how about believing because of the works themselves?* **They** *will testify to the Father working in Me!"* So Jesus is saying, *"If you can understand that I am the exact representation of the Father, then you can also see How He works through and in Me."* The best word to describe this would be *authentication*. In other words, this is the real deal, the authentic, not a cheap imitation. We are seeing God's perfect form through His Son and His works.

3. Demonstration

Third, in John 14:12, Jesus tells us if we just believe in Him we also can do the same kind of works and even greater ones, because in a short while Jesus will be going back to Heaven to be with His Dad. Basically there is no limit to what *we* can do if we just believe in Him. So the operative word here is *demonstration*.

My message and my preaching were not with wise and persuasive words, but with a demonstration of the Spirit's power, so that your faith might not rest on men's wisdom, but on God's power (1 Corinthians 2:4-5 NIV).

4. Validation

Fourth, in John 14:13-14, Jesus says that based on the preceding line of reasoning, He will then give us whatever we ask for in His name and back up all our requests personally. The criteria here is found in verses 9-12: Jesus is the exact representation of the Father, and so He manifests what the Father desires (which authenticates Him), then demonstrates it to show His Father's will and reveal His glory! It is in that succession that we come to this passage. It is all about giving glory to God and honoring His name, not about us looking good or being cool. It isn't about our needs or wants, our likes or dislikes, but about God's name and His fame! The word here is *validation*. These greater works validate believers as evidence of God's presence within and among them. The dictionary defines *validate* as "to make legally valid; to grant official sanction to by marking; to support or corroborate on a sound or authoritative basis."[1]

When they saw the courage of Peter and John and realized that they were unschooled, ordinary men, they were astonished and they took note that these men had been with Jesus. But since they could see the man who had been healed standing there with them, there was nothing they could say (Acts 4:13-14 NIV).

Now as we look at Jesus doing ministry we see at least three things that His specific ministry was: it was *strategic, intentional, and targeted.* I regularly define terms because I have discovered that, for many people, clear definitions can help in the comprehension of important concepts. Here are the definitions to these three terms:

Strategic: "of, relating to, or marked by strategy; Necessary to or important in the initiation, conduct, or completion of a strategic plan; of great importance within an integrated whole or to a planned effect."[2]

As we see by the above definition, *strategic* implies that the Father had a specific purpose in sending Jesus to the lost sheep of Israel first. God had always said that Israel was His chosen people and the apple of His eye. So He sent His Son to His people first to offer God's plan of salvation and the truth about the Kingdom to them.

Intentional: "done by intention or design."[3]

> *For we are His workmanship, created in Christ Jesus for good works, which God prepared beforehand that we should walk in them* (Ephesians 2:10 NKJV).

The word *intentional* means what it says: to minister in a way intended to accomplish a certain thing. We don't live our lives by accident but on purpose. To minister with the intent of bringing all people to repentance, salvation, and deliverance for their sins and iniquities so they can serve the living God!

> *All Your works shall give thanks to You, O Lord, and Your godly ones shall bless You. They shall speak of the glory of Your kingdom and talk of Your power; To make known to the sons of men Your mighty acts and the glory of the majesty of Your kingdom* (Psalm 145:10-12).

Many of us live our work lives with intent to excel and glorify God in our jobs. In our families, we do certain things with the intent that we will have Heaven in our home. Others regularly donate to their retirement fund so they will have a nest egg someday. These are all done with specific intent. Things don't happen by accident *most* of the time. And as a believer in God, angels, and demons, I honestly don't believe in the idea of experiencing a "coincidence." When I tell God something we need and someone hands us that within 24 hours without even knowing us, that is *not* a coincidence, but it is an answer to prayer.

Targeted: "to make a target of; to set as a goal; to direct or use toward a target."[4]

To be a good sniper, for example, requires polished marksman skills in addition to the ability to stay in a position for hours and days. It takes intense training and discipline. In the Vietnam War it took hundreds of bullets for each enemy kill. Snipers would have to take three days to crawl 100 yards. Hidden because of their camouflaged clothing, they nevertheless had to learn to be still within their surroundings and blend in. They had to deal with bodily functions, wildlife, and other inconveniences or dangers without losing their focus. But these snipers got the kill with determination and specific targeting. You can see how crucial it is to focus on a target. When you refine your focus, it's amazing how things become clear to you.

> *Leaving that place, Jesus withdrew to the region of Tyre and Sidon. A Canaanite woman from that vicinity came to Him, crying out, "Lord, Son of David, have mercy on me! My daughter is suffering terribly from demon-possession." Jesus did not answer a word. So His disciples came to Him and urged him, "Send her away, for she keeps crying out after us." He answered, "I was sent only to the lost sheep of Israel"* (Matthew 15:21-24 NIV).

- *Strategic:* not coincidental; purposeful.

- *Intentional:* not accidental; deliberate.

- *Targeted:* not haphazard; focused.

5. *Partnership*

Jesus equates our love for Him with doing what He tells us to do. Our obedience to Jesus is a way to express our love for Him, yet His love and acceptance of us is not dependent on our obedience.

Doing things with Him is what He wants. He doesn't need us to do stuff *for* Him but instead *with* Him (see 2 Cor. 6:1). When He describes His yoke as easy, it conveys a picture of us yoked with Him, like two oxen pulling a wagon. Of course, we don't literally do that, but it is a partnership event; it's a team sport.

If you go into business to fulfill a lifelong dream or a call of God, that is wonderful, but don't go into business only to provide a ministry with money. Why? Because you are then going into it out of need, not a call, and God can use other ways to fund ministry. While the motive and reason is good, God doesn't expect us to go around the mountain to get over the mountain.

> *The God who made the world and all things in it, since He is Lord of heaven and earth, does not dwell in temples made with hands; nor is He served by human hands, as though He needed anything, since He Himself gives to all people life and breath and all things* (Acts 17:24-25).

People who try to do things *for* God usually make wrong decisions. Sincerity doesn't keep you safe—you can still die.[5]

When David brought the ark into Jerusalem, he had it set on a new oxcart, which was never God's directive for moving the ark, and brought it to the city. David was a man with God's heart about things, but he missed the obvious and it cost Uzzah his life (see 2 Sam. 6:1-8). So what the Philistines got away with (if you can call plagues of rats and tumors getting away with something) will kill God's people because they are supposed to know better. We can't respond just to a need, or even out of our own compassion; we must respond to the word of the Lord.

Therefore, we are ambassadors for Christ, as though God were making an appeal through us; we beg you on behalf of Christ, be reconciled to God. He made Him who knew no sin to be sin on our behalf, so that we might become the righteousness of God in Him (2 Corinthians 5:20-21).

And what about all the wonderful folks who "start a ministry" only because the need is there? While this sounds admirable, and while it is true that every Christian believer has a call and ministry, good motives are no guarantee of success or safety. We must first and foremost be directed by the Lord Himself. He "will make us fishers of men" (see Matt. 4:19). We can't just run ahead and "do something." The safest place to be is in the center of God's will and purpose for your life.

I have a unique testimony about how the safest place is in the Lord's will. A sweet young lady came to us recently after finishing her schooling on the West Coast. Her dad lived in Woodstock, near our ministry, and through a friend of ours she had heard of us and felt the call of God to be with us. She was a phenomenal musician and writer, and we had her booked to do some music that morning at church. She had relocated here, moved in with her dad, and was working a job at the Georgia Aquarium downtown. Sometimes she would pull a 12-hour Saturday shift and wouldn't get home till after 1:00 in the morning. That Sunday she was so exhausted from the day before that she wanted to sleep in, but she was scheduled to be at church at 9:30 A.M. to run over her songs. When her alarm went off, she had a splitting headache and was going to call to say she was "too tired to play" and go back to sleep. But right before she did, she smelled the scent of gas. She called her dad, who was out of town, and he told her to get out of the house immediately while he called the furnace repairman. When she showed up at church she still had a splitting headache, but she pressed through and did her music. After the service, she told us her dad called and said that the repairman discovered a gas leak and the headache she had was due to her breathing the natural gas.

He said it was incredible she woke up and got out of the house because in a few minutes she would have gone to sleep and never gotten up, dying of asphyxiation. So coming to church to play and fulfill her calling literally saved her life! She was saved by being in her place of safety in the middle of God's will. If she would have listened to her flesh she would have gone back to sleep and never gotten up—a scary thought! Thank You, Jesus!

> *Therefore Jesus answered and was saying to them, "Truly, truly, I say to you, the Son can do nothing of Himself, unless it is something He sees the Father doing; for whatever the Father does, these things the Son also does in like manner. For the Father loves the Son, and shows Him all things that He Himself is doing; and the Father will show Him greater works than these, so that you will marvel. For just as the Father raises the dead and gives them life, even so the Son also gives life to whom He wishes. For not even the Father judges anyone, but He has given all judgment to the Son, so that all will honor the Son even as they honor the Father. He who does not honor the Son does not honor the Father who sent Him"* (John 5:19-23).

> *But He answered them, "My Father is working until now, and I Myself am working"* (John 5:17).

> *For in Christ Jesus neither circumcision nor uncircumcision means anything, but **faith working through love*** (Galatians 5:6).

Our faith-in-action should be motivated by love and not a need for affirmation or recognition. Too many people want to launch out into something for the wrong reasons. Moving into ministry causes rejection and "daddy issues" to surface or be exposed in our lives. While the person needs to step out, when these things surface (which they will), he or she should be willing to deal with them. Deal with these issues and keep going; ministry should be to serve God's purposes first, not simply as a way of getting esteem from God.

Being led by the Spirit doesn't mean being goofy or without direction and purpose. Spirit-led believers may be unpredictable, but they are not flaky or unfaithful. Being a Spirit-filled believer shouldn't mean we are lazy, weird, and unreliable. Hearing from Heaven should shake us and break us, but it should also make us. We should begin to grow in grace and stability as we humble ourselves and jettison everything that holds us back. We need to let go of everything that slows us or makes us stop!

> *But He said, "I must preach the good news of the kingdom of God to the other towns also, because that is why I was sent"* (Luke 4:43 NIV).

So we must redefine—or rather *rightly define*—some terms because we are currently living out of unbiblical definitions.

All these terms must be redefined:

- Preaching

- Gospel

- Ministry

- Church

- Leadership

- Love

- Relationship

- Fellowship

So, for example, we must clarify that love is more than a feeling and an act of giving. We must also redefine what fellowship means and how this affects our friendships and relationships. Scripture doesn't describe fellowship as a potluck dinner or hanging out in someone's home group. First John 1:7 says, *"But if we walk in the Light as He Himself is in the Light, we have fellowship with one another, and the blood of Jesus His Son cleanses us from all sin."* This verse implies that fellowship among believers necessitates a lifestyle of true discipleship and honesty where people are growing in truth and expressing what God is doing in them one to the other. This term *fellowship* has been so dumbed down that it is applied to nearly any scenario where believers get together (it is important and necessary for believers to get together, but true fellowship is more than this). And more and more people today refer to themselves as "Christian"—even if they have not been to a church in years or are not born again. There is a large and growing group of people who see themselves as Christians culturally, seeing no need to involve themselves in a local church.

We should be pursuing connections because there are some wonderful Spirit-led relationships that will take us far and open doors for us in realms we never thought imaginable. In the same way, we also can be used to help other people enter into their destinies.

> ***As you go***, *preach this message: "The kingdom of heaven is near." Heal the sick, raise the dead, cleanse those who have leprosy, drive out demons. Freely you have received, freely give. Do not take along any gold or silver or copper in your belts; take no bag for the journey, or extra tunic, or sandals or a staff; for the worker is worth his keep* (Matthew 10:7-10 NIV).

The temptation has always been to water down the Gospel message so we are then not quite so offensive. Where there is greater boldness, there will be greater power. Real love is bold. Real love does what Jesus said. When you operate in power, others are obligated to either surrender or fight against you (persecution).

The biggest enemy of real ministry is counterfeit ministry without fruit—or just busy activities with no substance. When we operate in these realms then our conscience is excused, and we do just enough talking about power to get us off the hook. There is a place in the Spirit where the enemy can't go. But it is also a place where only you and God can go. Flesh cannot thrive in this atmosphere. First Corinthians 1:29 says, *"That no flesh should glory in His presence"* (NKJV). On Pike's Peak, a line called the "snake line" is drawn across a section of the mountain, demarcating the area above which snakes cannot exist. Once a hiker crosses this line, he or she is comforted by the fact that a snake cannot survive past this point. The higher we go in God and the more God manifests Himself, the more exacting He is. I am not talking about legalism. I am talking about personal expectations. God knows what we know, whether we act like we know it or not. A good example of God's exacting nature is when Peter gave no warning to Sapphira that her husband was dead. She had no "second chance." We can't be spiritual adults and expect to be treated like new believers.

DOING STUFF WITHOUT GOD
JUST DOESN'T WORK

The number one reason there is not a move of God somewhere is always the same: lawlessness. People doing what is right in *their own eyes*.

When we make up stuff instead of following the Lord's pattern and His design then we have a problem.

- Jesus told us how to pray: we won't do it; we think there is a better way.

- Jesus told us how to fast: we won't do it; we think there is a better way.

- Jesus told us how to preach: we won't do it; we think there is a better way.

- Jesus showed us apostolic strategies: we won't do it; we think there is a better way.

- Jesus showed us about taking cities: we won't do it; we think there is a better way.

- Jesus told us unity with God leads to unity with each other: we won't do it.

- Jesus showed us how to walk in righteousness, peace, and joy: we won't do it.

We would rather walk in self-righteousness, strife, and anger than in joy.

In Romans 9:1-33, 10:1-3;12-21, Paul speaks ablout Israel, but in the middle of that discussion, he contrasts the Gospel of Jesus Christ with the Law and Israel's response to it. We need to decide now which covenant we want to walk and live in. Is it the Law or Grace? In some ways, grace is more exacting as to our faith.

> ***Christ is the end of the law so that there may be righteousness for everyone who believes.*** *Moses describes in this way the righteousness that is by the law: "The man who does these things will live by them." But the righteousness that is by faith says: "Do not say in your heart, 'Who will ascend into heaven?'" (that is, to bring Christ down) "or 'Who will descend into the deep?'" (that is, to bring Christ up from the dead). But what does it say? "The word*

*is near you; it is in your mouth and in your heart," that is, the word of faith we are proclaiming: That if you confess with your mouth, "Jesus is Lord," and believe in your heart that God raised Him from the dead, you will be saved. **For it is with your heart that you believe and are justified, and it is with your mouth that you confess and are saved**. As the Scripture says, "Anyone who trusts in Him will never be put to shame." For there is no difference between Jew and Gentile—the same Lord is Lord of all and richly blesses all who call on Him, for "Everyone who calls on the name of the Lord will be saved." How, then, can they call on the One they have not believed in? And how can they believe in the One of whom they have not heard? And how can they hear without someone preaching to them? And how can they preach unless they are sent? As it is written, "How beautiful are the feet of those who bring good news!"* (Romans 10:4-15 NIV)

And from the days of John the Baptist until now the kingdom of heaven suffers violence, and the violent take it by force (Matthew 11:12 NKJV).

To say the Kingdom suffers violence means it forces its way into a space in the same way water displaces things. Have you ever seen video of the immense power of a hurricane? When it comes on shore, the tide mixed with the wind from the storm and the water makes for a giant storm surge. Anything in its way—houses, boats, cars, and buildings—is just washed away. When I was 4 years old, our family lived in Lake Charles, Louisiana, a southwestern Louisiana town about 35 miles away from the Gulf Coast. I vividly remember riding out a Category 4 hurricane in the summer of 1957. I will never forget Hurricane Audrey coming ashore and the winds and rain and the eye passing over. The storm surge came up all the way to McNeese State College right there in Lake Charles. We drove and saw it the next day. Power was out for four to five days, and the phones were not working for a month. I also remember overhearing how a little town called Cameron was completely obliterated as the 40-foot storm surge came in and washed away the town. We drove to see what was left of Cameron three weeks later, and we saw washing machines and clothing and refrigerators in the tops of 30-foot trees over a mile away from the beach. The town no longer existed. This immense power that displaces everything in its path is what the Kingdom is like. The Amplified version says it this way:

> *And from the days of John the Baptist until the present time, the kingdom of heaven has endured violent assault, and violent men seize it by force [as a precious prize—a share in the heavenly kingdom is sought with most ardent zeal and intense exertion]* (Matthew 11:12 AMP).

Isaiah says God's government will only grow and increase!

> *Of the increase of His government and peace there will be no end, upon the throne of David and over His kingdom, to order it and establish it with judgment and justice from that time forward, even forever. The zeal of the Lord of hosts will perform this* (Isaiah 9:7 NKJV).

> *...And on that day a great persecution began against the church in Jerusalem, and they were all scattered throughout the regions of Judea and Samaria, except the apostles* (Acts 8:1).

After the martyrdom of Stephen, the saints were scattered throughout the region while the apostles stayed behind in Jerusalem. Because of the scattering of the disciples after Stephen's death, the Gospel spread beyond Jerusalem into outlying areas like Samaria.

THE PHILIP/SAMARIAN CONNECTION

Philip the deacon is one of my heroes in the New Testament. He was a man who waited tables yet also experienced a translation in the Spirit of over 15 miles. He was *not* a superstar, but he was used to go to Samaria and brought revival to that whole region with miracles, signs, and wonders. The Philip/Samaria/Samaritan connection is a unique one. At the beginning of this book we saw that the story of the Good Samaritan is a powerful message for ordinary people: breaking out of our religious comfort zones will cause us to wake up to the call and destinies that are on God's people. The leaders in that story were *horrible* examples of reaching out, and we can't wait for them to come around. I thought this little study of Philip would prove enlightening to you.

Philip went down to the city of Samaria and began pro- claiming Christ to them. The crowds with one accord were giving attention to what was said by Philip, as they heard and saw the signs which he was performing. For in the case of many who had unclean spirits, they were coming out of them shouting with a loud voice; and many who had been paralyzed and lame were healed. So there was much rejoicing in that city. Now there was a man named Simon, who formerly was practicing magic in the city and astonishing the people of Samaria, claiming to be someone great; and they all, from smallest to greatest, were giving attention to him, saying, "This man is what is called the Great Power of God." And they were giving him attention because he had for a long time astonished them with his magic arts. But when they believed Philip preaching the good news about the kingdom of God and the name of Jesus Christ, they were being baptized, men and women alike. Even Simon himself believed; and after being baptized, he continued on with Philip, and as he observed signs and great miracles taking place, he was constantly amazed. Now when the apostles in Jerusalem heard that Samaria had received the word of God, they sent them Peter and John, who came down and prayed for them that they might receive the Holy Spirit. For He had not yet fallen upon any of them; they had simply been baptized in the name of the Lord Jesus. Then they began laying their hands on them, and they were receiving the Holy Spirit. Now when Simon saw that the Spirit was bestowed through the laying on of the apostles' hands, he offered them money, saying, "Give this authority to me as well, so that everyone on whom I lay my hands may receive the Holy Spirit." But Peter said to him, "May your silver perish with you, because you thought you could obtain the gift of God with money! You have no part or portion in this matter, for your heart is not right before God. Therefore repent of this wickedness of yours, and pray the Lord that, if possible, the intention of your heart may be forgiven you. For I see that you are in the gall of bitterness and in the bondage of iniquity." But Simon answered and said, "Pray to the Lord for me yourselves, so that nothing of what you have said may come upon me"

So, when they had solemnly testified and spoken the word of the Lord, they started back to Jerusalem, and were preaching the gospel to many villages of the Samaritans (Acts 8:5-25).

While the term *Samaria* was first identified with the city founded by Omri, it soon became associated with the entire region surrounding the city, the tribal territory of Manasseh and Ephraim. Finally, the name *Samaria* became synonymous with the entire Northern Kingdom (see 1 Kings 13:32; Jer. 31:5). After the Assyrian conquest, Samaria began to shrink in size. By New Testament times, it became identified with the central region of Palestine, with Galilee to the north and Judea to the south. The name *Samaritans* originally was identified with the Israelites of the Northern Kingdom (see 2 Kings 17:29). When the Assyrians conquered Israel and exiled 27,290 Israelites, a "remnant of Israel" remained in the land. Assyrian captives from distant places also settled there (see 2 Kings 17:24). This led to the intermarriage of some, though not all, Jews with Gentiles and to widespread worship of foreign gods. By the time the Jews returned to Jerusalem to rebuild the Temple and the walls of Jerusalem, Ezra and Nehemiah refused to let the Samaritans share in the experience (see Ezra 4:1-3; Neh. 4:7). The old antagonism between Israel to the north and Judah to the south intensified the quarrel.

The Jewish inhabitants of Samaria identified Mount Gerizim as the chosen place of God and the only center of worship, calling it the "navel of the earth" because of a tradition that Adam sacrificed there. Their Scriptures were limited to the Pentateuch, the first five books of the Bible. Moses was regarded as the only prophet and intercessor in the final judgment. They also believed that 6,000 years after creation, a Restorer would arise and would live on earth for 110 years. On the Judgment Day, the righteous would be resurrected in paradise and the wicked roasted in eternal fire.

In the days of Christ, the relationship between the Jews and the Samaritans was greatly strained (see Luke 9:52-54; 10:25-37; 17:11-19; John 8:48). The animosity was so great that the Jews bypassed Samaria as they traveled between Galilee and Judea. They went an extra distance through the barren land of Perea on the eastern side of the Jordan to

123

avoid going through Samaria. Yet Jesus rebuked His disciples for their hostility to the Samaritans (see Luke 9:55-56), healed a Samaritan leper (see Luke 17:16), honored a Samaritan for his neighborliness (see Luke 10:30-37), praised a Samaritan for his gratitude (see Luke 17:11-18), asked a drink of a Samaritan woman (see John 4:7), and preached to the Samaritans (see John 4:40-42). Then in Acts 1:8, Jesus challenged His disciples to witness in Samaria. Philip, a deacon, opened a mission in Samaria (see Acts 8:5).

> *But an angel of the Lord spoke to Philip saying, "Get up and go south to the road that descends from Jerusalem to Gaza." (This is a desert road.) So he got up and went; and there was an Ethiopian eunuch, a court official of Candace, queen of the Ethiopians, who was in charge of all her treasure; and he had come to Jerusalem to worship, and he was returning and sitting in his chariot, and was reading the prophet Isaiah. Then the Spirit said to Philip, "Go up and join this chariot." Philip ran up and heard him reading Isaiah the prophet, and said, "Do you understand what you are reading?" And he said, "Well, how could I, unless someone guides me?" And he invited Philip to come up and sit with him. Now the passage of Scripture which he was reading was this: "He was led as a sheep to slaughter; and as a lamb before its shearer is silent, so He does not open His mouth. In humiliation His judgment was taken away; who will relate His generation? For His life is removed from the earth." The eunuch answered Philip and said, "Please tell me, of whom does the prophet say this? Of himself or of someone else?" Then Philip opened his mouth, and beginning from this Scripture he preached Jesus to him. As they went along the road they came to some water;*

and the eunuch said, "Look! Water! What prevents me from being baptized?" [And Philip said, "If you believe with all your heart, you may." And he answered and said, "I believe that Jesus Christ is the Son of God."] And he ordered the chariot to stop; and they both went down into the water, Philip as well as the eunuch, and he baptized him. When they came up out of the water, the Spirit of the Lord snatched Philip away; and the eunuch no longer saw him, but went on his way rejoicing. But Philip found himself at Azotus, and as he passed through he kept preaching the gospel to all the cities until he came to Caesarea (Acts 8:26-40).

Philip was a respected member of the church at Jerusalem who was chosen as one of the seven first deacons (see Acts 6:5). Following Stephen's martyrdom, Philip took the Gospel to Samaria, where his ministry was blessed (see Acts 8:5-13). Subsequently, he was led south to the Jerusalem-Gaza road where he introduced the Ethiopian eunuch to Christ and baptized him (see Acts 8:26-38). He was then transported by the Spirit to Azotus (Ashdod) and from there conducted an itinerant ministry until he took up residence in Caesarea (see Acts 8:39-40). Then, for nearly 20 years, we lose sight of him. He is last seen in Scripture when Paul lodged in his home on his last journey to Jerusalem (see Acts 21:8). He had four unmarried daughters who were prophetesses (see Acts 21:9).

I so love Philip because he was a *normal* Christian who lived and did extraordinary things! He and Stephen were both deacons, but they were also "nameless, faceless" servants who changed history. The vast majority of the saints will be normal people with normal problems who serve an awesome God and will do extraordinary exploits as God is working with them. In redefining the "normal Christian life," the "166 lifestyle" will be one of amazing highs and lows. Most of the time, many saints will never even see the results of their preaching or prayers. When you heal many diseases, you are unable to see the manifestation of healing with the majority of people at the time of prayer. Many times ears and eyes being opened are visible immediately, but sometimes they aren't. Jesus told the blind man to go wash in the pool of Siloam (see John 9:7). While we love to see tumors shrink and rashes disappear, many healings will not be seen openly. We have to be used to doing God's work and glorifying Him out of the spotlight and *behind the scenes*. This is not the Hollywood, show-biz Christianity many of us are used to seeing on Christian television. Cancers inside the body and many other conditions like diabetes can't be determined to be gone on the spot.

We knocked on the door of one lady who had such severe diabetes she took over a dozen prescriptions and was in a wheelchair. We prayed and though she said she felt "warm," we saw nothing. But a month later we went back, and she was walking around without a wheelchair, and the table that used to hold 13 prescriptions had one bottle on it. She explained that within a week of our visit, she started feeling weird. She went to the doctor who determined that her diabetes was cured, her blood sugar was normal, and she felt so poorly because she was overdosing on the insulin and other drugs! She got off the drugs and was walking with no pain! We have to be willing to be nameless and faceless.

ENDNOTES

1. *Merriam-Webster's Collegiate Dictionary*, 11th ed., s.v. "Validate."

2. *Merriam-Webster's Collegiate Dictionary*, 11th ed., s.v. "Strategic."

3. *Merriam-Webster's Collegiate Dictionary*, 11th ed., s.v. "Intentional."

4.   *Merriam-Webster's Collegiate Dictionary*, 11th ed., s.v. "Targeted."

5.   Bill Johnson, *The King and His Kingdom,* CD of message given at NorthGate Church, Atlanta, September 10, 2006.

CHAPTER 9

HEALING THE WOUNDED SPIRIT

"The Spirit of the Lord is upon Me, because He has anointed Me to preach the gospel to the poor; He has sent Me to heal the brokenhearted, to proclaim liberty to the captives and recovery of sight to the blind, to set at liberty those who are oppressed; to proclaim the acceptable year of the Lord." Then He closed the book, and gave it back to the attendant and sat down. And the eyes of all who were in the synagogue were fixed on Him. And He began to say to them, "Today this Scripture is fulfilled in your hearing."

—LUKE 4:18-21 (NKJV)

The spirit of a man will sustain his infirmity; but a wounded spirit who can bear?

—PROVERBS 18:14 (KJV)

I truly believe that it is time for the Church of Jesus Christ in America and the world to wake up to her magnificent calling and rise up as an exceedingly great army. A great release of healing and deliverance needs to occur.

A couple of years ago, I was preaching a weekend in a Gulf Coast city. We took a Friday night to stir up and encourage people in their gifts so that the next morning we could take them out with us preaching. During that Friday night meeting when it was time for prayer, two ladies came forward for healing of fibromyalgia. The first one was about 25, and I got a word of knowledge she had been raped, which I whispered to her privately. She began weeping and fell on the floor. As she forgave the person who did it, the Lord told me she had a "wounded spirit," which was hindering her healing. Once she got free of the wounded spirit from the rape, she was instantly healed from five years of fibromyalgia. The next woman was clearly carrying some horrible burden. I got the same word about a wounded spirit, and the Holy Spirit uncovered that she had experienced the murders of her husband and son on the same night 14 years earlier. When she forgave the person and was healed of the wounded spirit, she was also instantly healed of 14 years of fibromyalgia.

Besides those two wonderful healing testimonies, the next morning the older lady was one of the first people to arrive—she was almost unrecognizable as she looked 15 years younger! She said she slept the whole night through with no pain for the first time in 14 years. When we announced the projects we were going to, I asked her to come with my group. As we went she said to me, "This is a miracle! I must be delivered because the place we are going today is the exact same project where my son and husband were both shot 14 years earlier!" She put her feet on that ground and by the time we knocked on the second door, she was ministering without my help. She was a spiritual dynamo there! I understand she still goes to those projects regularly, taking back the ground on which she had experienced such tragedy 14 years earlier!

After that weekend, it became clear to me that a wounded spirit is probably keeping many Christians all over the nation in a state of being like "the living dead" we talked about in Chapter 8. These folks have been bitten and even devoured by a horrible wound but are continuing on, not quitting on God, but moving ahead. They need to be healed and awakened to their purpose, callings, and destinies.

THE WAR WE ARE IN

Jesus was attacked in the wilderness on the level of His identity. The enemy's main goal is to keep us from believing and knowing who we really are, because he knows the Word. *"As a man thinks in his heart, so is he"* (see Prov. 23:7). When we begin to believe who we are in Christ, we become very dangerous to the enemy, and he knows that. His only way to maintain dominion over the earth is through man. When a human being becomes born again and walks in all that is available to him or her through Christ, satan has lost a part of his dominion. The Gospel is a declaration of war. When Jesus came to earth, it was an invasion, a spiritual D-Day if you will. Keep in mind that it took only one angel to kill all the firstborn of Egypt. It took just two to level Sodom and Gomorrah. When the angel announced to the shepherds the birth of Jesus, Scripture says, *"And suddenly there appeared with the angel a multitude of the heavenly host praising God..."* (Luke 2:13). Think of it this way, up until that point in history God sent His angelic special forces—one or two, at the most, several—to accomplish whatever specific mission He had. At this point He sent in the "ground forces." We are in a war—a war more real than any we've seen on the earth, a war with real attacks and real consequences—and if you are blinded or oblivious to it, then that's an indicator the enemy has already affected or infiltrated your thinking. One of his main goals is to make you think everything is fine and that there is no war, no spiritual warfare.

WHY WE HAVE WOUNDS

We all have wounds, and no matter how or from whom we received them, the source is still the same. When you are in a conflict or battle, you will get fired upon and could possibly take a hit. That is the enemy's job—to attempt to stop or kill you. The wounds we receive are not random hit-or-miss things but specific strategic attacks to take us out at the point of our strength. They are designed to cause us not to believe or even see our true identity, who we are in Christ.

As we will discover, each of our wounds is there by design, and we can even begin to see a pattern. We will begin to see areas that the enemy finds dangerous to him, so those are the areas we get hit in, sometimes over and over. Remember that I mentioned the word *strategic* in the last chapter? One of its key definitions is "essential to the conducting of war." *You* are a weapon in the Lord's hands! You are an instrument of judgment to the kingdom of darkness. You are a soldier in God's army who is called to bring back the captives and heal and free them! Ever see the *Rambo* movies? In the second one, he goes somewhere in Southeast Asia to get back American POWs who were still being held 10 years after the war ended. There were some great scenes in that film (as well as some great explosions), but my favorite scene is where Rambo is pulling the POWs out of their cells! That is a picture of what we are called to do! *Holy Ghost Rambos!!*

I remember a few years ago we kept having attacks in three areas in our church over and over. It was the worship team, the intercessory prayer folks, and the youth. I was discouraged till one day I realized, *Hey, wait a minute. These are the three areas of our greatest fruit. So, of course, the enemy knows how devastating each of these can be to him.* While I know we can uncover and discover our giftings, callings, and destinies through prophetic ministry and supernatural revelation, it also is important to find out how we are hurting the enemy. In that, we will begin to see our true strength. When you were growing up, what were the things in your life that you got the most hassle for? I'm not talking about misbehavior here. Was there something you liked to do that people teased you for? Was there something you wanted to be but were told you were not cut out for? That was probably very close to your calling and strength. The enemy knew if you pursued that it would be a threat to him. That is the strategy behind most of these wounds.

HOW THE WOUND WORKS

John Eldredge of *Wild at Heart* fame says,

> Much of our life ends up being shaped by our wound, in one way or another. We take a wound, and with it comes a message, a lie about us and about the world and often about God, too. The wound and lie then leads to a vow, a resolution to never, ever do again whatever it was that might have brought the wound. From the vow we develop a false self.[1]

Wound/Lie → Vow → False Self

So, for example, if your father left due to divorce, you might make a vow like, "I'll never trust anyone again," which eventually produces a false self. You might easily end up being a very independent, driven person whose mindset is, *I'm on my own now.*

VOWS WE MAKE

The vow is very powerful. We vow things to keep us from ever being hurt again to avoid pain, but these vows transform us into something other than who we are supposed to be in Christ. We then begin to believe in the lie and speak the lie, and it begins to transform us into our false self. We come into agreement with the enemy, and, in essence, call God a liar. We are created in God's image, and we, like God, speak things into existence. The enemy knows and perverts that so we will speak his plans for us into existence instead of God's. That's the only way he ever got dominion on this earth and the only way he maintains dominion today. That is why he violently attacks the human race and is a key way in which he keeps the human race enslaved.

When you make a vow to the Lord your God, you shall not delay to pay it, for it would be sin in you, and the Lord your God will surely require it of you. However, if you refrain from vowing, it would not be sin in you. You shall be careful to perform what goes out from your lips, just as you have voluntarily vowed to the Lord your God, what you have promised (Deuteronomy 23:21-23).

Even under the Law, the vows people made to each other were their contract, their word, even their bond. Because we have been given dominion and have authority to declare and rule, what we vow affects—and can even infect—us. The enemy cleverly uses our dominion mandate and ability against us.

You will also declare a thing, and it will be established for you; so light will shine on your ways (Job 22:28 NKJV).

HEALING THE WOUND

John Eldredge teaches the following about how we look at these wounds, especially as men, but the same applies to women.

When it comes to our wound, we tend to either minimize or embrace it.

We minimize it by:

1. Denying it outright. ("Naw, nothing like that ever really happened to me." Or, "I had a pretty good life.")

2. Leaving it in the past. ("That was a long time ago, and I've gotten over it." Or, "I can't remember much from my youth.")

3. Minimizing the impact of the wound. ("It just didn't really matter that much to me." Or, "Lots of tough things happen to people...so?")

We embrace it by saying:

1. "Yes, it was awful, but I deserved it."

2. "But what he said was true about me."

3. "I'm weak...take care of me. And don't ever require anything of me." (We can take the victim mentality and let the wound define us, embracing it to the point of needing the wound.)[2]

The Church is not supposed to be a hospital *or* a nursing home, but today that is often what it looks like. A hospital takes in and treats sick people, and a nursing home tries to keep you as comfortable as possible while they watch you die. Neither are biblical metaphors. We are to be a family and an army, but even the army has medics to get the wounded back up on their feet! Our mission is to heal and deliver. If the enemy can keep us perpetually handicapped and hobbled, we won't be very effective, will we? Jesus wants to set you free and turn you loose to wreak havoc on the kingdom of darkness. It's important to find out what is revealed by how and where we are wounded; it is important to renounce the vows we have made; and it is important to fall out of agreement with this false self. By the way, this is the root in most people who adopt the homosexual lifestyle. They had sexual identity problems due to the wounding they received as children. Some of them even received this root through their parent's spiritual DNA. I personally believe the homosexual lifestyle is the result of making these kinds of vows. We can have what we declare! God gave us the power of being autonomous beings, making our own choices. As the Lord begins to show us the vows we have made with the enemy, we need to renounce them and break them over our lives. We overcome by the Blood of the Lamb *and* the word of our testimony.

> *A man's stomach shall be satisfied from the fruit of his mouth, from the produce of his lips he shall be filled. Death and life are in the power of the tongue, and those who love it will eat its fruit* (Proverbs 18:20-21 NKJV).

You may have several different areas of wounding, but you will probably find that lumped together, they moved you to make a specific vow. When we fall out of agreement with our carnal man, our flesh, which is trying to protect itself from pain, and break the vows we made to ourselves, we can be free. People can pray for you, but only when you choose to let this go will you be free. Here is a prayer you can pray to get free of these wounds and the vows that keep them:

> *Lord Jesus, while I have been wounded by the enemy, I now see his plan, and more than that, I see Your call and destiny for me that has been hindered and delayed.*
>
> *I repent for attempting to take control of my life by these vows I made when I was wounded. Please forgive me for my pride and these arrogant vows that have caused me to abort my purpose and have altered my life direction. I forgive these persons* [say them by name] *who have wounded me with their curses, words, betrayals, rejection, abandonment, or whatever form of abuse. I give them to you and release them.*
>
> *I also renounce and release myself from the vows I have made to avoid pain and to escape these wounds. I fall out of agreement even with my own words and choose to run after my call and destiny in You! Free me from the prison of my own words and these vows, and let me be free and whole in* **You**, *Lord Jesus. Amen.*

ENDNOTES

1. John Eldredge, *Wild at Heart* (Nashville, TN: Thomas Nelson, Inc., 2006).

2. Eldredge, *Wild at Heart.*

CHAPTER 10

LET'S STOP DOING GOD A FAVOR

But now He has obtained a more excellent ministry, inasmuch as He is also Mediator of a better covenant, which was established on better promises. For if that first covenant had been faultless, then no place would have been sought for a second. Because finding fault with them, He says: "Behold, the days are coming, says the Lord, when I will make a new covenant with the house of Israel and with the house of Judah—not according to the covenant that I made with their fathers in the day when I took them by the hand to lead them out of the land of Egypt; because they did not continue in My covenant, and I disregarded them, says the Lord. For this is the covenant that I will make with the house of Israel after those days, says the Lord: I will put My laws in their mind and write them on their hearts; and I will be their God, and they shall be My people. None of them shall teach his neighbor, and none his brother, saying, 'Know the Lord,' for all shall know Me, from the least of them to the greatest of them. For I will be merciful to their unrighteousness, and their sins and their lawless deeds I will remember no more." In that He says, "A new covenant," He has made the first obsolete. Now what is becoming obsolete and growing old is ready to vanish away (Hebrews 8:6-13 NKJV).

The New Covenant is called a better covenant established with better promises. It isn't an optional backup plan for those times when our performance or law-based, sin-conscious plan fails us. The New Covenant is a *better* covenant with *better* promises. It was prophesied in Jeremiah:

> *"Behold, the days are coming, says the Lord, when I will make a new covenant with the house of Israel and with the house of Judah—not according to the covenant that I made with their fathers in the day that I took them by the hand to lead them out of the land of Egypt, My covenant which they broke, though I was a husband to them, says the Lord. But this is the covenant that I will make with the house of Israel after those days, says the Lord: I will put My law in their minds, and write it on their hearts; and I will be their God, and they shall be My people. No more shall every man teach his neighbor, and every man his brother, saying, 'Know the Lord,' for they all shall know Me, from the least of them to the greatest of them, says the Lord. For I will forgive their iniquity, and their sin I will remember no more"* (Jeremiah 31:31-34 NKJV).

Probably the greatest thing we see about this New Covenant is that the Lord says, *"They shall all know Me."* Instead of there being an elite, separated, priestly class of God-experts who know Him, *all* have the potential to know Him if they choose to listen and hear. Jesus stressed that the Spirit was regularly speaking, but many times, even *most* of the time, we aren't listening (see Matt. 11:15; 13:9). So hearing God's voice through the many ways He speaks is how we walk in the good of this new, better covenant. It is about hearing what God writes on our hearts and living it out.

How do we hear God? The first and primary way is the Scriptures, of course. They are the revealed will of God for our life. In His Word is life and freedom. If we will open our Bibles, we will find an unlimited resource to feed from.

A second way is hearing His voice. This may come through prayer, during worship, or when we receive prophetic ministry.

> *Therefore, as the Holy Spirit says: "****Today, if you will bear His voice****, do not harden your hearts as in the rebellion, in the day of trial in the wilderness, where your fathers tested Me, tried Me, and saw My works forty years. Therefore I was angry with that generation, and said, 'They always go astray in their heart, and they have not known My ways.' So I swore in My wrath, 'They shall not enter My rest'"* (Hebrews 3:7-11 NKJV).

A good rule of thumb to stay on track is to run every revelation, enlightenment, or "word" through the Scriptures. The Bible is clear that if we seek, we will find (see Matt. 7:7). Dig into the Scriptures because in the Word of God are treasures beyond imagining to be unearthed. Spiritual treasures of great value actually have to be dug up to be found.

We usually know when we have heard His voice. It is a very subjective thing. However, believers need to realize how heavily their spiritual foundation weighs into this. If someone has a faulty spiritual foundation, a guilt or shame-based view of God, or a perception of God as an angry father figure, the enemy can get access to our spiritual ears. One of the enemy's greatest tactics is to attempt to impersonate or confuse our hearing of the voice of God. False doctrines, spiritual strongholds, traumatic events, and rejection, where wounds remain unhealed, can allow the enemy access to our imaginations, thought processes, and dream life and can even allow us to be fooled into thinking God is saying and doing things He isn't. The answer to this is to love the truth!

Knowing about God's nature is crucial. We can all have a much greater understanding of the goodness of God because God is mysteriously *good*, not mysteriously *bad*.

> *Therefore consider the **goodness and severity** of God:*
> *on those who fell, severity; but toward you, goodness, if*
> *you continue in His goodness. Otherwise you also will be*
> *cut off. And they also, if they do not continue in unbelief,*
> *will be grafted in, for God is able to graft them in again*
> (Romans 11:22-23 NKJV).

And yet the extremes both of these attributes of God take in Scripture are very unsettling. Scripture says to consider them *both*. We do not understand how great and amazing God's grace and mercy is, but, at the same time, we also have no grasp of this thing called the severity of God. If we are discussing something that has two sides and yet omit one part, we tend to give permission to one side and communicate that the other side is unimportant. But the Word of God is a *two*-edged sword:

> *For the word of God is living and powerful, and sharper*
> *than **any two-edged sword**, piercing even to the divi-*
> *sion of soul and spirit, and of joints and marrow, and is*
> *a discerner of the thoughts and intents of the heart. And*
> *there is no creature hidden from His sight, but all things*
> *are naked and open to the eyes of Him to whom we must*
> *give account* (Hebrews 4:12-13 NKJV).

So if we are to fully comprehend and understand God's amazing good-ness, we must see it contrasted with His great severity. While our flesh is very uncomfortable with this, we can't only focus on those parts of God we like and feel comforted by. There are mysteries of God's nature that trouble and even frighten me, but a healthy fear of God can be a great asset in clearly distinguishing His voice. And the idea that we might already know all there is to know about God is simply not true. Scripture is clear that God is beyond our knowledge without the Holy Spirit revealing *Him* to us!

*He performs wonders **that cannot be fathomed,** miracles that cannot be counted* (Job 9:10 NIV).

*Oh, the depth of the riches of the wisdom and knowledge of God! How **unsearchable** His judgments, and His paths beyond tracing out!* (Romans 11:33 NIV).

*Although I am less than the least of all God's people, this grace was given me: to preach to the Gentiles the **unsearchable riches** of Christ...* (Ephesians 3:8 NIV).

So why would the Bible tell us that we *can* know Him but also say His judgments, the riches of His nature, the wonders He performs, and His ways are all unsearchable, unfathomable, and beyond finding out? Because the Bible tells us that only the Holy Spirit can search the depths of God, and abiding with the Holy Spirit is our way to acquire an understanding of God.

*But God has revealed it to us by His Spirit. **The Spirit searches all things, even the deep things of God.** For who among men knows the thoughts of a man except the man's spirit within him? In the same way no one knows the thoughts of God except the Spirit of God* (1 Corinthians 2:10-11 NIV).

If I can come to know that God is good, awesome, and kind, yet unfathomable by mere human efforts, and only searched and plumbed by His Spirit, I start to grow in humility and wisdom.

- **Goodness:** "the quality or state of being good; the nutritious, flavorful, or beneficial part of something."[1]

- **Severity:** "strict in judgment, discipline, or government; of a strict or stern bearing or manner; austere; rigorous in restraint, punishment, or requirement; maintaining a scrupulously exacting standard of behavior or self-discipline."[2]

The angel of the Lord came to me in a dream last year and informed me by pushing something in my stomach that the Lord was going to be giving me a *new revelation of the goodness of the Lord.*

Within a few weeks, we had an awesome encounter with the glory of God in our local church that went beyond any experience or outpouring I have ever seen. It lasted about seven weeks and ended right as the Lord was showing us some major lifestyle changes we would need to make to stay in the glory realm. In the last few years some voices have been somewhat flippant about these realms of God's glory and presence. Many are young men who are just now experiencing some of these things and declaring, "This is it; this is the glory." They are young, proud, and naïve, not really knowing about these things.

When the glory comes, as it did in our church for this seven-week period, His goodness comes on the scene…as well as His severity. But many can't handle goodness. They are used to their garbage and darkness and bondage, so they run from it. They freak out and make up some reason that this can't be God. When He shows up like that, it is really too good to be true. But He is good, and He is true. When we hear, *"It's the goodness of the Lord that leads men to repentance,"* it is hard for us to know exactly what that looks like (see Rom. 2:4). But we have seen that kind of repentance and change coming on people who just had to get in His presence and experience His goodness. As we experienced these 50 days of goodness, we began to understand literally what these passages of Scripture mean:

> *Goodness and mercy shall follow me…* (Psalm 23:6 NKJV).

*Oh, how great is Your **goodness**, which You have laid up for those who fear You, which You have prepared for those who trust in You in the presence of the sons of men!* (Psalm 31:19 NKJV).

*For the word of the Lord is right, and all His work is done in truth. He loves righteousness and justice; **the earth is full of the goodness** of the Lord. By the word of the Lord the heavens were made, and all the host of them by the breath of His mouth. He gathers the waters of the sea together as a heap; He lays up the deep in storehouses. Let all the earth fear the Lord; let all the inhabitants of the world stand in awe of Him. For He spoke, and it was done; He commanded, and it stood fast. The Lord brings the counsel of the nations to nothing; He makes the plans of the peoples of no effect. The counsel of the Lord stands forever, the plans of His heart to all generations. Blessed is the nation whose God is the Lord, the people He has chosen as His own inheritance. The Lord looks from heaven; He sees all the sons of men. From the place of His dwelling He looks on all the inhabitants of the earth; He fashions their hearts individually; He considers all their works. No king is saved by the multitude of an army; a mighty man is not delivered by great strength. A horse is a vain hope for safety; neither shall it deliver any by its great strength. Behold, the eye of the Lord is on those who fear Him, on those who hope in His mercy, to deliver their soul from death, and to keep them alive in famine. Our soul waits for the Lord; He is our help and our shield. For our heart shall rejoice in Him, because we have trusted in His holy name. Let Your mercy, O Lord, be upon us, just as we hope in You* (Psalm 33:4-22 NKJV).

We have told you that the Gospel is *Good News*, not bad!

The preaching of it is the declaration of a good, just King who is favorably disposed to do good on our behalf! He is good, and He wants us to show people His goodness! Every time we preach with healing, miracles, and a supernatural encounter, people have an opportunity to see His goodness in the land of the living.

One weekend I was preaching in Walla Walla, Washington, with the view to take people to preach at the liberal arts college there. As we were walking the campus, we discovered that the previous day a young man who was a Whitman College student had hanged himself in his dorm. The spirit of hopelessness hung over that place. As we talked to the students, we surmised that this student had lost all hope. One of the reasons was obvious: it is what they preach and teach on that campus—a form of nihilism through hyper-liberal and extreme environmentalism. Nihilism is a philosophy that espouses an extreme form of skepticism through the denial of all real existence or the possibility of an objective basis for truth. It believes all is nothingness or nonexistence. It can be summed up in the statement: all is nothing. Sounds really exciting and hopeful, eh? No wonder there is suicide and hopelessness!

But the Lord allowed us by His perfect timing to pray for a lot of the students reeling from this young man's suicide. One was the woman who just so happened to be hosting a group of the guy's housemates. They wanted to get out of the house where he had hanged himself. We prophesied hope to them by revealing the goodness of the Lord to everyone as we told them their destinies. The prophetic works every time in these situations! One of the three purposes of New Testament prophecy is consolation. We prayed and prophesied for a number of people needing hope that day. When I pray for people on death's door or for those mourning the death of a friend or family member, I always get this Scripture: *"I would have lost heart, unless I had believed that I would see **the goodness of the Lord in the land of the living"*** (Ps. 27:13 NKJV).

While what we are saying may sound too good to be true to a cynical, unbelieving person, the truth is that Jesus is not only our hope, He is also our Truth! Some people may say, "But Marc, you are promising people false hope. What if it doesn't work?" But hey, what if it does? (And it usually does!) *We do not have a false hope, but a living one!*

It is *not outlandish* to tell people they can experience the goodness of the Lord here on earth; it is the truth of Scripture. One of the job descriptions of angels is to minister to those who inherit salvation by bringing about God's Word on the earth to them and by bringing Heaven to earth on their behalf:

> *Are they not all ministering spirits sent forth to minister for those who will inherit salvation?* (Hebrews 1:14 NKJV).

> *Bless the Lord, you His angels, who excel in strength, who do His word, heeding the voice of His word* (Psalm 103:20 NKJV).

It is not unrealistic to promise people the Kingdom, which is righteousness, peace, and joy in the Holy Spirit. So what might this actually look like?

Imagine:

- Peace in your home;

- Joyful, obedient children;

- Healthy, loving marriages;

- Living as the head of your finances;

- Freedom from debt;

- Walking in divine health, where you are rarely sick;

- Seeing miracles happen when you pray: the blind see, the lame walk, the deaf hear;

- Living without limits: where absolutely nothing is impossible!

This is not a fantasy, but can be a reality as we progressively but comprehensively shoot for the moon in all these areas.

"SHOOT FOR THE MOON," "THE SKY'S THE LIMIT," "GO FOR IT!"

For we are God's workmanship, created in Christ Jesus to do good works, which God prepared in advance for us to do (Ephesians 2:10 NIV).

Blessed be the God and Father of our Lord Jesus Christ, who according to His great mercy has caused us to be born again to a living hope through the resurrection of Jesus Christ from the dead, to obtain an inheritance which is imperishable and undefiled and will not fade away, reserved in heaven for you, who are protected by the power of God through faith for a salvation ready to be revealed in the last time (1 Peter 1:3-5).

...We shall be satisfied [filled to overflowing] with the goodness of Your house, of Your holy temple (Psalm 65:4 NKJV).

You crown the year with Your goodness, and Your paths drip with abundance (Psalm 65:11 NKJV).

There really is another realm we can live out of that is not of this world, and it is called the Kingdom!

> *Rain down, you heavens, from above, and let the skies pour down righteousness; let the earth open, let them bring forth salvation, and let righteousness spring up together. I, the Lord, have created it* (Isaiah 45:8 NKJV).

God is changing us from the inside out, upside down... When car manufacturers build a car now on robotic assembly lines, they have different stages of accomplishment and completion. You don't put the engine in until you have a frame on, and you don't put the body panels on until the inside is completed. You don't put the seats in until the interior is finished. Bottom line—it is built from the inside out.

Whatever God does in us has to be done from the inside out. He sends His Word to us in seed form many times, and if we agree to receive it and allow it to grow, then fertilize and water it, it will grow and become a great harvest. The enemy also uses many things to cause us to run in fear from the real thing; the enemy comes sowing his tares while God sows His wheat. Every truth that comes forth in a generation is somehow abused or misused. While people will always say "heresy" about anything that is not doctrinally clear, abuse and misuse is a sure sign someone is attempting to get it right. This is one of the key ways the enemy attempts to throw people off the scent of their callings and giftings. Just as we talked about in the previous chapter on the wounded spirit, this tactic of "pushing people too far" is an old trick to get folks to "throw out the baby with the bath water."

Overreaction to anything that is the slightest bit imperfect would be considered abuse if applied to parenting, but is then somehow considered noble and honorable when it comes to the Church. There are whole ministries dedicated to finding imperfections in other ministries. These "heresy-hunters" are really just teachers or prophets who need to be delivered of the wound they received through some teaching that hurt them. While I am sorry people were hurt, maybe they should just go home and get over it. Creating whole ministries based on wounds or hurts is a colossal waste of time.

I knew of a movement that had some great insight and revelation on apostles, prophets, church planting, and many other things. It was doing really well and making an impact. Then what began right became twisted when one of the key leaders was wounded trying to bring correction to another leader who was involved in homosexuality. When confronted, this leader abused the Scriptures to avoid repenting. Eventually, he was put out of his church, but the leader who brought correction then concluded that the whole movement was lacking in right theology and a basic knowledge of Scripture. One of the brightest moves of God of the '70s and '80s ended up turning such a corner; it still is thriving and planting churches, but all the other key things it once had were lost due to the overreaction of one wounded leader. Overreaction has been a motivating force behind nearly every evil act in history. Men like Hitler, Stalin, and Mao Tse-tung all somehow became wounded and perpetrated great death on the world through their wounds and overreactions.

In the '70s, Charles Simpson, Ern Baxter, Bob Mumford, Derek Prince, and Don Basham assembled and came together as one of the first modern-era apostolic teams. The revelation they received helped bring great advancement to the Wild Wild West type of lawlessness that was part of the early days of the Charismatic Movement. In those days there was an exodus from the well-ordered institutional churches into the near anarchy of Charismatic house groups. With everyone insisting "only the Holy Spirit" could lead, you can imagine the chaos in doctrine and behavior that ensued. While these men made many mistakes—and some were whoppers—they still advanced the cause of apostolic order and government in the Church. At one time, nearly a million people worldwide looked to Charles Simpson as the key leader in this movement. Unfortunately, a lot of folks only remember the mistakes these men made, and the stigma on them all was almost too much. Nevertheless, revelations about apostles, discipleship, healing, deliverance, and spiritual liberty have all been abused and used and yet will continue to be. The lesson is this: did anyone who did something for the first time ever do it perfectly? Weren't there 10,000 experiments to perfect the lightbulb? Didn't the Wright brothers' plane only fly a few seconds? Were they all failures because they did something imperfectly? No, they were pioneers, and *they* will be remembered, *not* their critics.

> *Do not fret because of evil men or be envious of those who do wrong; for like the grass they will soon wither, like green plants they will soon die away. Trust in the Lord and do good; dwell in the land and enjoy safe pasture. Delight yourself in the Lord and He will give you the desires of your heart. Commit your way to the Lord; trust in Him and He will do this: He will make your righteousness shine like the dawn, the justice of your cause like the noonday sun. Be still before the Lord and wait patiently for Him; do not fret when men succeed in their ways, when they carry out their wicked schemes. Refrain from anger and turn from wrath; do not fret—it leads only to evil. For evil men will be cut off, but those who hope in the Lord will inherit the land. A little while, and the wicked will be no more; though you look for them, they will not be found.* **But the meek will inherit the land and enjoy great peace** (Psalm 37:1-11 NIV).

So what is our inheritance? It is the Kingdom. There are many ways of saying this in many different versions:

> *Do not be afraid, little flock, for your Father has chosen gladly to give you the kingdom* (Luke 12:32).

> *Do not be afraid, little flock, for your Father has been pleased to give you the kingdom* (Luke 12:32 NIV).

> *Do not fear, little flock, for it is your Father's good pleasure to give you the kingdom* (Luke 12:32 NKJV).

> *Do not be seized with alarm and struck with fear, little flock, for it is your Father's good pleasure to give you the kingdom!* (Luke 12:32 AMP)

Entrance is given to those who believe Him and do the will of the Father. Entrance isn't reserved for the perfect, but for the faithful. And even the person who is *least* in the Kingdom is greater than the greatest old testament prophet, John.

> *He replied, "The knowledge of the secrets of the kingdom of heaven has been given to you, but not to them. Whoever has will be given more, and he will have an abundance. Whoever does not have, even what he has will be taken from him"* (Matthew 13:11-12 NIV).

The Kingdom is about having, not knowing! It is about possessing, not suggesting! It is about keeping and giving away, but not about hoarding! It is all about possessing more and more. It is about containing it, holding on to it, and treasuring it!

RIGHTEOUSNESS...PEACE...JOY...THE KINGDOM

> *The Son of Man will send out His angels, and they will weed out of His kingdom everything that causes sin and all who do evil. They will throw them into the fiery furnace, where there will be weeping and gnashing of teeth. Then*

the righteous will shine like the sun in the kingdom of their Father. He who has ears, let him hear. The kingdom of heaven is like treasure hidden in a field. When a man found it, he hid it again, and then in his joy went and sold all he had and bought that field (Matthew 13:41-44 NIV).

People who are wounded bleed out all their lives till they get healed. But by beholding *Him* we change, and we are progressively healed so we then have a new paradigm for things. Whenever we have an overreaction, we miss the real. An overreaction to something is a lot like talking about a scene while you watch a movie: by the time you stop commenting, it is all over. We are reacting only to *what we see,* rather than to *what God sees!* God defines what is really going on. We must get God's eyes and God's ears about things so we don't miss what is really happening!

ENDNOTES

1. *Merriam-Webster's Collegiate Dictionary,* 11th ed., s.v. "Goodness."

2. *Merriam-Webster's Collegiate Dictionary,* 11th ed., s.v. "Severity."

CHAPTER 11

THE CHICKEN CONUNDRUM

*C**hicken:* "common domestic fowl; coward."[1]

Conundrum: "a riddle whose answer is or involves a pun; a question or problem having only a conjectural answer; an intricate and difficult problem."[2]

When I mention this term, the *chicken conundrum,* it refers to the huge gap between *knowing about* the actual practice of what Jesus defined as a normal Christian lifestyle versus what is really practiced. Probably the biggest reason for this huge discrepancy is fear and cowardice. We have become so "chicken" at sharing our faith or being willing to stand out in a crowd that we now have a vast gap between *what we know* (theory) and *what we do* (practice). The vast majority of long-time Christian believers, including pastors and ministry leaders, have little to no experience in the 166 lifestyle of personal ministry Jesus commands of us (winning unbelievers to the Lord, healing the sick, casting out demons, raising the dead, or preaching—by Jesus' definition, not the popular misconception.) There is a great chasm between what the great majority of Western Christians *know about ministry* versus what practice and experience they *actually have in ministry.* Few American or Western believers are actually living a "normal Christian lifestyle" by Jesus' definition.

Again, Jesus defines ministry a lot differently than the present popular church culture does. We in the Western Church have succumbed to the deception that acquiring knowledge *about* something equates with actually practicing it. For example, when I first came on the staff of a large church, some of the pastors would like to go play racquetball a couple times a week. I was invited by the "experienced" to play with them. By experienced, I mean they had played in tournaments and state championships! In other words, these guys knew what they were doing. After reading a book about racquetball, I arrived with my new equipment—racquet, balls, shoes, attire, and glasses. I felt I would do just great because my motivation was there, my knowledge of the game was there, and my equipment was right. What a shock to find out *I couldn't even score* for at least a dozen games! When theory is fleshed out in real life, it becomes practical, and when it is repeated, it becomes a lifestyle.

It is much easier to theorize, pontificate, comment, and otherwise weigh in on things we know little to nothing about than to actually attempt to do them. We live in a culture that exalts commentary and blather over accomplishment and bearing fruit. We live in a culture where Internet media like YouTube, MySpace, Facebook, and blogs make it possible for nearly everything anyone does or says to immediately be posted and then dissected by observers. The rules of commentary have changed, and now everyone with access can comment! Blather on blogs is the new rule of the day. *Blather* means "to talk foolishly at length."[3] Bottom line—we can talk and make absolutely no sense, but present our thoughts in a manner that *sounds* insightful. I believe this is what passes for a lot of the messages we hear in Sunday morning church services. They are messages, little vignettes which sound nice and cute, but the words aren't coming out of a lifestyle given to doing what Jesus did—healing the sick, raising the dead, cleansing the unclean, etc. The vast majority of pastors have very little contact with unbelievers, let alone their own church people. They stay holed up in their study, I guess… studying…and shuffling papers. Praying for the sick is done by the two faithful prayer ladies on Thursday morning. So the people get who the leader is—a theoretical expert on all things about God.

More and more issues are being decided by political correctness or mass opinion today. If it is on the Internet, some people believe it must be true. Free choice and opinions are elevated above courage, common sense, and even reason. And this mindset has made its inroads into the Church. The media culture that exalts opinion and theory over reality and experience has been bleeding over into the Church as well. This commenting on newsworthy things, giving opinions or even praying for or against things is a new form of "ministry." Instead of denying ourselves and living for Jesus, submitting our schedules and lives to fit His will and preaching and declaring the Kingdom, we have now developed whole new "acceptable" yet unbiblical forms and descriptions of ministry. We have "generals of intercession" and strategic mapping coordinators. We have mass prayer ministries that literally defy the command of Jesus that says, *"When you pray go into your closet and do it in secret"* (see Matt. 6:6). But thousands jump aboard because it is easier and less threatening to *pray* in the supposed safety of other Christians than to boldly *preach* to the lost. It is as if Christians only attempt to involve themselves in those "ministries" they perceive as safe, like the prayer meeting. Prayer meetings have great value, of course (I go to them every week) but what if we prayed **and** actually "went"? (see Matt. 9:25).

SURVEY SAYS...

A recent Barna article (February 2009) about spiritual gifts had some interesting findings that reflect and confirm much of what this book is about. The information presented in the article was taken from polling done over the last 13 years. Here are some highlights that cause me concern:

> Since 1995, the proportion of born-again adults claiming the gift of evangelism dropped from 4% to less than 1%. The stagnation of evangelism relates to many factors, but one of those is probably the fact that just 1% of Christian adults (self-described and born again) claim the gift of evangelism.

Fifteen percent of the self-identified Christian population does not know what their gift is today.

In total, over one-fifth of all the gifts cited by respondents (21%) were attributes that do not fit the biblical lists of gifts given by God. These included: a sense of humor, singing, health, life, happiness, patience, a job, a house, compromise, premonition, creativity, and clairvoyance.

Between those who do not know their gift (15%), those who say they don't have one (28%), and those who claimed gifts that are not biblical (20%), nearly two-thirds of the self-identified Christian population aren't able to apply what they know about gifts to their lives.

Thirteen percent of self-identified Christian adults claimed to have one or more of the charismatic gifts (healing, interpretation, knowledge, miracles, prophecy, tongues).

One reason the evangelical community may seem so verbal about its faith relates to the fact that more than one-quarter of them (28%) claim the gift of teaching. Possessing that gift might also raise people's expectations regarding the quality of sermons and other teaching received at their church, triggering the often-cited high turnover within evangelical congregations.[4]

My quick take on these findings is that the Body in America needs:

- Much more activation and releasing of spiritual gifts.

- Better teaching on what the gifts really are. (Did people actually say a sense of humor?)

- More emphasis on reality than theory. (When 28% of the evangelical community claims the gift of teaching, there is an overemphasis on knowledge.)

- An adjustment to the puffed-up nature of most believers in the Church. (A much higher percentage of born-again Christians claims to be a leader than cites having been given the spiritual gifts of leadership.)

Instead of people operating in the ministry of helps and doing the grunt work that must be done, ministries are created that require little to no commitment and no way to really measure results or fruit. Why do we exalt what people think versus what they have done? Shouldn't we applaud achievement rather than theory? Shouldn't we recognize fruit rather than zeal? This Barna poll reveals that pride is deep and wide in the typical American congregation. It is not about getting information, it is about getting *in formation* to find our place in God's army and do what we were born to do. Most church pastors don't have *an apostolic message* or mandate, they are only *teaching messages*.

While stadiums have been filled with city-wide prayer meetings, prayer days, and endless prayer events, little change or "fruit" (as Jesus called it) has ever come of it. While prayer is good and right and must be an integral part of the Christian life, *not one city in America or the world has ever been "won to Christ" or transformed by prayer alone.* And while there has been a proliferation of prayer "movements," many of these present a subtle danger because they give young people a supposedly biblical alternative that allows them to avoid the clear biblical mandate to preach. Instead of praying and preaching, there is an unbalanced emphasis on "prayer missionaries" given *only* to prayer and fasting and worship. We are in danger of elevating hearing from God so that we can fill prayer journals rather than doing, being, and becoming. Aren't we supposed to be lovers of God *and* deliverers of men? These movements call themselves armies and use military terms, but a cold, hard look at Scripture reveals that it only uses those terms to describe men and women like Stephen the martyr, Timothy the young apostle, Peter the preacher, or John, who was boiled in oil and wouldn't die. Soldiers who avoid their service and evade their deployment are called AWOL. Are we in danger of losing a whole generation of preachers due to the emphasis of this kind of extreme asceticism?

We are also *not* called to pay attention to special dates and events:

> *He said to them, "It is not for you to know times or epochs which the Father has fixed by His own authority; but you will receive power when the Holy Spirit has come upon you; and you shall be My witnesses both in Jerusalem, and in all Judea and Samaria, and even to the remotest part of the earth* (Acts 1:7-8).

In fact, Paul goes so far as to call these folks "puffed up" by their fleshly mind, pursuing shadows rather than Christ.

> *So let no one judge you in food or in drink, or regarding a festival or a new moon or sabbaths, which are a shadow of things to come, but the substance is of Christ. Let no one cheat you of your reward, taking delight in false humility and worship of angels, intruding into those things which he has not seen, vainly puffed up by his fleshly mind* (Colossians 2:16-18 NKJV).

Yet there are whole segments of the Church studying times, days, and seasons in God, what this year means on the Jewish calendar and other things. While Scripture clearly warns against this, and we are told *not* to do this, many believers appear to get much of their spiritual self-esteem out of following these days and dates. While studying the feasts of Israel and other things have their place, it certainly isn't to *re-place* the simple preaching of the Kingdom. God commands us *not* to study special days, but He does command us *to* preach. So what are we going to do? Which side are we going to come down on?

We are called to live for today. Jesus said, *"Each day has enough trouble of its own, so don't worry about tomorrow"* (see Matt. 6:34). Paul said we should *"redeem the time, because the days are evil"* (see Eph. 5:16). And Peter tells us that our time *"in the flesh"* should be lived for *"the will of God"* (1 Pet. 4:2). So it's clear that day by day we are to live life in faith, trusting God as we go.

> *Therefore, since Christ has suffered in the flesh, arm your-selves also with the same purpose, because he who has suffered in the flesh has ceased from sin, so as to live the rest of the time in the flesh no longer for the lusts of men, but for the will of God* (1 Peter 4:1-2).

One of the big traps that holds us back from living out a Kingdom lifestyle is a view of life where we spend an inordinate time in our life regretting mistakes from our past or worrying over our future. When we either lament the past or dread the future, we live essentially paralyzed—caught in a no-man's-land of regret and worry. There is little to be learned by spending more time on the past than the present. We just need to resolve not to make the same mistakes we made yesterday without making vows that bind us from future action in the same area if the Lord leads us there in the future. For example, if we were to go on a missions trip overseas that ended up going poorly, we might back off returning the following year. While this seems to be the route of common sense and caution, it would be wiser to study why the trip ended poorly. If it was due to a lack of good planning or the failure of leadership on the ground, those things can be addressed and fixed. If it was due to some witch doctors threatening and persecuting you because of the message, that is a good thing. It means you are on track. The point is not to make a vow like, "I'll never go back," or "God has not called me there," which then can cause you to abort that part of your destiny only because mistakes were made. Overreaction is how this stuff happens. Nothing good ever comes from overreaction. Taking action is good, but overreaction causes us to go too far.

One of the clearest commands of Jesus reveals a way of looking at life that makes sense and should give us great confidence. There is a great revelation in this for us if we are just willing to look. Jesus says in Matthew 6:33-34:

> But **seek first His kingdom** and His righteousness, and all these things will be given to you as well. Therefore do **not worry about tomorrow, for tomorrow will worry about itself.** Each day has enough trouble of its own (NIV).

This is a priority shift for most of us. He says:

1. Seek His Kingdom and righteousness;

2. Don't worry about tomorrow.

Then He even throws in a reason why we shouldn't worry. He says that "Tomorrow will worry about itself. Each day has enough trouble of its own." Another version says, "Tomorrow will care for itself. Each day has enough trouble of its own."

So our sophisticated minds may look at this and think, *Come on, He can't mean that literally. We **have to** look forward on our calendar and plan things. I mean, everybody else does.*

But Jesus is not speaking about wisely planning things, setting up things in advance, or booking classes. That is all good and necessary. He is speaking about the issue of worry and anxiety that paralyzes us and causes us to make poor choices and bad decisions. When we worry, we are putting energy into something we can't change. In another passage, Jesus also speaks about worry, *"Who of you by worrying can add a single hour to his life?"* (Matt. 6:27 NIV). So there is *nothing to be gained*—not even an hour of our lives—by worrying. It also is a colossal waste of energy, thought, and resources; if we are worrying, we are tying up precious and valuable resources that we need for that day. Worrying about what might happen tomorrow clouds the clear thinking we need to solve our problems today!

I have a good example of the negative faith worry can generate from a situation. A young Christian asked me for advice about his financial situation. This young man is a painter and work had been scarce for him during December. He was needing rent coming up in January of $700 and saw no way of getting it. He had $500 and two little jobs to do, but his work van wasn't reliable. His question is a good example of how we allow worry and anxiety about *tomorrow* to cloud our clear thinking *today.* He had gone to a car lot and found another work vehicle that would cost $500 down and then monthly car payments. His question was, "Knowing my van is working poorly, do I go get a newer van with $500 down and have a reliable work van so I can get to my jobs? Or do I use that $500 for rent?"

Here's what I told him: "You are worrying about tomorrow today." *Today* his van was unreliable but worked. He owed the $700 in two more weeks, but buying another car would be spending money for something he needed (rent) on something he *might* need. His worrying created a negative faith. It was as if he had more faith for a van breakdown than to get $200 more to pay rent or to later get a new vehicle. I told him, "Don't buy the van." He listened to me and didn't do it. Then he called me two days later and told me that within 24 hours after we talked and prayed a former customer he had done work for months before gave him $1000 as a gift, free and clear! It wasn't for any job, but because God had put him and his wife on this man's heart around Christmas time! The young man paid his rent and was able to set aside some to buy a work vehicle with cash. By not acting on his worry, he got an unexpected blessing!

Worry clouds our vision today from seeing the blessing God is sending tomorrow. Worry is negative faith for the worst to come tomorrow. God gives us enough grace to get through the things we need to handle each day. It is similar to the manna that fed God's people in the desert wilderness. While it was available fresh each day, it couldn't be stored up, or it would rot. This is how God wants us to live day-to-day, depending on Him for our supply of grace and provision. He is our daily provision! We are called to live lives that bear fruit: *"But if I am to live on in the flesh, this will mean fruitful labor for me..."* (Phil. 1:22).

This was one of the most vivid changes we had to make in our lives, ministry, and church a few years back. We decided to look at things we were doing in our schedules, relationships, and associations—even our friendships—and ask, "Is this working? *Is this actually bearing any biblical fruit?"* By doing this, we began to transition to lifestyles that were given to things that didn't just sound good theoretically but would work in the real world. A lot of Christian thought is taken up with theory and tradition. "We have *always* done this at Christmas" or "We have *always* had a youth ministry." Much of the average Christian's lifestyle is directed around survival rather than revival. We have given ourselves to living beneath a victorious overcoming life of fruitfulness in Kingdom fields of service. Instead we are content to sow in soil that produces no crop. If our Christian life isn't fruitful we may be spending our time unwisely.

> *But the seed in the good soil, these are the ones who have heard the word in an honest and good heart, and hold it fast, and bear fruit with perseverance* (Luke 8:15).

WE ARE CALLED TO ABIDE IN JESUS

> *Abide in Me, and I in you. As the branch cannot bear fruit of itself unless it abides in the vine, so neither can you unless you abide in Me. I am the vine, you are the*

branches; he who abides in Me and I in him, he bears much fruit, for apart from Me you can do nothing. If anyone does not abide in Me, he is thrown away as a branch and dries up; and they gather them, and cast them into the fire and they are burned. If you abide in Me, and My words abide in you, ask whatever you wish, and it shall be done for you. My Father is glorified by this, that you will **bear much fruit,** *and so prove to be My disciples* (John 15:4-8).

So in the real world and in real life, what does this look like? How do I need to change the way I live to accommodate it? That word *abide* suggests we are to *wait, stay, and remain.*

Wait: A waiter is always waiting on those he is serving, keeping an eye out to see if they need something from him. This implies a watchfulness and an alertness like the five virgins who were ready when the Master came (see Matt. 25:1-10).

Stay: This is the same command a lot of "masters" use to train their dogs to keep them by their side. Stay means to be in one place awaiting further instruction. Waiters in a restaurant usually have a "station" where they position themselves to wait to see if their tables need attending.

Remain: We are to remain in the correct position and place to be available for service. All three of these imperatives or commands connote a need to be available and at *His* service.

Waiting, remaining, and *staying* may make us think of lying on the ground at His feet, doing nothing. But nothing could be further from what He wants! He wants us actively engaged in doing His will *with Him,* no longer by ourselves. We are now working together with *Him*! In John 15:16 He even says:

You did not choose Me but I chose you, and **appointed you that you would go** *and* **bear fruit,** *and* **that your** *fruit would remain, so that whatever you ask of the Father in My name He may give to you* (John 15:16).

While the implications of the Barna poll sadly suggest that the American Church is so puffed up with pride through teaching it is in danger of completely forgetting her destiny and purpose, it will always help us to stay low, child-like, and humble. Neither a proud nor an insecure person can abide in Him; insecurity is a form of pride that attempts to rely on one's own works or strength. Neither can a person who is self-righteous abide in Him. A person overly concerned with doing all the right things will inevitably do the wrong one.

> *Two men went up into the temple to pray, one a Pharisee and the other a tax collector. The Pharisee stood and was praying this to himself: "God, I thank You that I am not like other people: swindlers, unjust, adulterers, or even like this tax collector. I fast twice a week; I pay tithes of all that I get." But the tax collector, standing some distance away, was even unwilling to lift up his eyes to heaven, but was beating his breast, saying, "God, be merciful to me, the sinner!" I tell you, this man went down to his house justified rather than the other; for everyone who exalts himself will be humbled, but he who humbles himself will be exalted* (Luke 18:10-14).

> *Therefore, my brethren, you also were made to die to the Law through the body of Christ, so that you might be joined to another, to Him who was raised from the dead, in order that we might bear fruit for God. For while we were in the flesh, the sinful passions, which were aroused by the Law, were at work in the members of our body to bear fruit for death. But now we have been released from*

the Law, having died to that by which we were bound, so that we serve in newness of the Spirit and not in oldness of the letter (Romans 7:4-6).

His will is fairly simple, but understanding Him is far more complex. Do we think we have to understand all there is to know about Him to please Him? We never will.

For this reason also, since the day we heard of it, we have not ceased to pray for you and to ask that you may be filled with the knowledge of His will in all spiritual wisdom and understanding, so that you will walk in a manner worthy of the Lord, to please Him in all respects, bearing fruit in every good work and increasing in the knowledge of God; strengthened with all power, according to His glorious might, for the attaining of all steadfastness and patience; joyously giving thanks to the Father, who has qualified us to share in the inheritance of the saints in Light (Colossians 1:9-12).

If we would only agree with Heaven about what our calling is, we would then get the grace to accomplish it. An account has been opened in Heaven in your name with all the grace you could possibly ever need to fulfill your calling, to operate in your gifting, and to finish *all* God has ever required you to do.

To obtain an inheritance which is imperishable and undefiled and will not fade away, reserved in heaven for you (1 Peter 1:4).

ENDNOTES

1. *Merriam-Webster's Collegiate Dictionary*, 11th ed., s.v. "Chicken."

2. *Merriam-Webster's Collegiate Dictionary*, 11th ed., s.v. "Conundrum."

3. *Merriam-Webster's Collegiate Dictionary*, 11th ed., s.v. "Blather."

4. "Survey Describes the Spiritual Gifts That Christians Say They Have," February 9, 2009, http://www.barna.org. Used by permission.

CHAPTER 12

REALLY...WHAT
WOULD JESUS DO?

POPULAR...BUT WRONG!

There is a popular trend that has so permeated the American church culture that it must be confronted straight on if we are to see an authentic move of God's power in our land. The reason I say this is because we must be clear on what "the real" is so as to experience it. This popular theology also must be held up to the light of Scripture and examined according to the criteria Jesus told us to use to determine whether something is of God or not—the question: "Does it bear fruit, and is it good fruit?" In Matthew 7:17-20, Jesus speaks of this method of inspection:

> *Even so, every good tree bears good fruit, but a bad tree bears bad fruit. A good tree cannot bear bad fruit, nor can a bad tree bear good fruit. Every tree that does not bear good fruit is cut down and thrown into the fire. Therefore by their fruits you will know them* (NKJV).

Unfortunately, an objective, unbiased, and even scientific criteria like Jesus proposed for determining whether God is truly "in" or "behind" things is rarely used by church leaders. Typically most leaders and believers weigh things by the American business definition of success: high and increasing numbers of people, greater income, and good press coverage. While these indicators may be a result of good fruit, they are not necessarily the fruit itself. And in recent days, with the economic meltdown we have all seen in the world, the illusory quality that these things had to make us feel things are really better than they appear has faded.

Things that grow quickly or become large and popular may not even be a success in God's view. One only need look at the recent American housing and financial market to see this truth: simply because something becomes huge and pervasive doesn't mean it is built on a stable foundation. The bloated nature of these banks and auto companies reflects that the prevailing line of thinking isn't always the correct one. And just because something has name recognition doesn't necessarily mean it is a sign of God's approval or His strategy. Crowds (or a lack of them) are not indicators that "God is with us." Jesus' biggest crowds left as quickly as they came. Sometimes the Lord blesses things He won't even inhabit. While He blessed Ishmael, He did that more out of His love for Ishmael's mom, Hagar, and all she endured (see Gen. 16:8-10).

ANOTHER GOSPEL

I marvel that you are turning away so soon from Him who called you in the grace of Christ, to a different gospel, which is not another; but there are some who trouble you and want to pervert the gospel of Christ (Galatians 1:6-7 NKJV).

Most of us know of the phenomenal popularity of the "What Would Jesus Do?" concept. This idea originated from the book by Charles Sheldon, *In His Steps*, written at the end of the 19th century.[1] It advocates what I will call the "social gospel," for lack of a better term. By *social gospel*, I mean feeding the poor, giving blankets to those needing warmth, finding shelter for those in need, and the like. Mr. Sheldon suggests that if Jesus were physically among us today, He would pass out food, bring blankets to the homeless, and help the poor with natural things *rather than* spiritual things. The author presents the view that doing these kinds of "good works" was what Jesus meant when He said that His followers would do "greater works" (see John 14:12). Ultimately it was this book's philosophy that caused the popularity of the WWJD wrist bands, Bibles, and other items.

While extending kindness to the "least of these" is biblically right, proper, and our heart's inclination, we must do these acts in a context where the Gospel is proclaimed, the sick are being healed, and the lame walk! When we don't, we foster a culture where there is the "social" without the "Gospel."

Charles Sheldon left this "social gospel" legacy, which has come to believe that people should do works of kindness *rather than preach*. I don't believe that he had a revelation of what true preaching really was, though he did have a revelation about self-sacrifice, which we all can appreciate in such a self-serving age. Rather he defined these kind acts as a form of preaching. He implied that Scripture's prescription to facilitate heart change could be done by walking in Christ's steps, but he didn't really know what that was. He could be credited with creating an alternative for Christians to avoid preaching or confronting the lost with the Gospel.

This unbalanced approach of equating social service with Gospel preaching has *to this day* allowed many believers a "way out" of their biblical responsibility to preach to every creature. Based on a few obscure Gospel passages pulled out of context, this way of thinking has become popular among most Christians. While his motives were charitable, Sheldon's influence has been abused by complacent believers and has led to a faddish opposite extreme to what he really wanted. This man who had a desire to see Christians live a self-denying life ended up giving ammunition to those who wanted to escape the call of the Gospel on every believer!

I am not suggesting, and neither is anyone else, that we are to ignore the poor. On the contrary, it is good, right, and kind to remember the poor, to feed and help them. The apostle Paul reminds us to remember them in Galatians 2:10, and we should not neglect or forget them. But isn't this kind of mercy outreach obvious and an example of brotherly kindness? Isn't that what the parable of the Good Samaritan was all about—don't ignore the less fortunate or cast a blind eye to the needy? While many may be incensed and offended at the thought, Jesus didn't single out the poor as His favorite and only people group to shelter, clothe, and feed. He didn't command us to *feed* the poor, He commanded us to *preach* to them. He also pointed out that the poor will be particularly receptive to the Gospel message. Jesus cast out demons from and healed and preached to many poor people.

Much of the Church has subtly allowed this shift of thinking to happen; the idea that this "social gospel is really preaching to the poor" is especially prevalent among churches that don't believe the gifts of the Spirit are necessary today. This "doing good deeds" without a Kingdom purpose or expectation of seeing God's power leaves the Church in danger of becoming a community organization without a message that brings change. One clearly recognizable Christian movement we all greatly admire illustrates this point.

The Salvation Army was birthed by the powerful desire of William Booth to get out of the pew and into the streets to "preach the Gospel to the poor." Booth was considered a heretic by many just because he wanted to preach, declare the Gospel message, and take the Scriptures *outside the church building.* Consider one of his statements:

> While women weep, as they do now, I'll fight; while little children go hungry, as they do now, I'll fight; while men go to prison, in and out, in and out, as they do now, I'll fight; while there is a poor lost girl upon the streets, while there remains one dark soul without the light of God, I'll fight, I'll fight to the very end![2]

His Gospel ministry began with fiery street preaching to the most downtrodden; consequently, aid to the poor *was a by-product.* William

Booth's goal was to preach to the poor and give aid while directing them to churches. There was no way Booth and his associates could preach to the poor without wanting to assist them with their daily struggles regarding hunger, shelter, and clothing. In time it became apparent that the "street people" they won to Christ did not feel comfortable attending the existing churches. So they opened churches and even homes to take care of the homeless and hungry.

As time passed, the Salvation Army set up centers in every city where they were preaching. Street-preaching workers reaching the lost were, in time, replaced by bell-ringing workers eager to receive offerings. Eventually this historic and revolutionary evangelistic ministry became more of a social service center for the poor where food and clothes were given away, and the Gospel was only proclaimed inside the churches they established.

The Salvation Army morphed into an exceptional social service agency, one of the largest on earth. While its kindness is legendary and its history honorable, the spiritual fruit in its outreaches is now a by-product instead of the goal. This is not an indictment, but an example *that the pure and simple effectiveness of preaching the Gospel in power can be cast aside by its sheer success and the fruit it produces.* In my opinion, this organization today bears little resemblance to what it was when it was started. To quote an old friend of mine, Larry Tomczak, "Our history does not guarantee our destiny."

BE NICE OR TELL THE TRUTH?

At a conference in Atlanta a few years ago, I heard the incredible testimony of a Bulgarian apostle who had been beaten, arrested, and deported for preaching in his homeland before Communism fell. He told amazing stories of miraculous protection from the horrific perse-cution he and the Bulgarian Church experienced under Communism. As he was preaching, he interjected this question, "What is it with you

Americans about being nice? Nice is not a fruit of the Spirit, and Jesus never said, 'Go and be nice.'" This really got me thinking!

We in America have a desire to come across as being "nice." Yet there is not one example in Scripture where Jesus taught about being nice. Jesus never said in the Sermon on the Mount, "Blessed are the nice...." Being nice is not the same as preaching the Gospel and could be one of the reasons we don't. We tend to think that God views things as we do, that love is somehow expressed in just being nice.

And we are so concerned that we might "turn someone off" when we share the Gospel that we forget the power the authentic Gospel has to set people free and set them on fire for God! Dumbing down our message to make it palatable is cowardly, compromising, ineffective, and produces bad results (fruit). The lesson should be obvious—God's ways really aren't our ways.

> "For My thoughts are not your thoughts, nor are your ways My ways," says the Lord. "For as the heavens are higher than the earth, so are My ways higher than your ways, and My thoughts than your thoughts" (Isaiah 55:8-9 NKJV).

GOOD MOTIVES

We have been erroneously taught that if we do good things and our motives are good and right, God will bless it and us. Unfortunately, that is just simply not true. The truth is Jesus only did that which the Father told Him to do. What outwardly may appear to look effective, kind, and good may not be fruitful or even that helpful! Jesus encouraged preaching the Gospel to the poor (see Matt. 11:5). He also said, *"Blessed are the poor in spirit, for theirs is the kingdom of heaven"* (Matt. 5:3). Jesus followed a clear pattern as revealed to Him by His Father, and it worked. We need to see that the method He used and the way He preached was always superior in its effects and bore much more fruit than any other way to present the Gospel that we might dream up. Simply having good motives and a charitable heart doesn't guarantee the fruit we bear will be good or lasting, nor does it equate to effective ministry based on Jesus' model.

SO *WHAT* WOULD *JESUS* DO?

If Jesus was on the streets right now in 21st-century suburban or urban America, would He hand out wristbands, give away sandwiches, and pass out cold water on street corners? Or would He bind up broken hearts, preach, cast out demons, and heal the sick? Would He go on television and plead for folks to send in money threatening to "go off the air if you don't give $100 in the next five minutes..." or would He multiply loaves and fish? Would He pass out tracts, or would He bring life and freedom through His living Word? I think in our hearts we know the answers! Jesus *would* do and *did* do what He saw His Father doing and what we read about all through the New Testament. Many of our attempts at ministry are in many ways missing the point of the example of Jesus' lifestyle. None of these "social gospel" activities are in themselves necessarily wrong, yet when they become a substitute for our primary mandate on the earth, they are out of order. Our lack of love or our cowardice to confront cannot allow us to whittle down our message!

> *Then Jesus answered and said to them, "Most assuredly, I say to you, the Son can do nothing of Himself, but what He sees the Father do; for whatever He does, the Son also does in like manner. For the Father loves the Son, and shows Him all things that He Himself does; and He will show Him greater works than these, that you may marvel. For as the Father raises the dead and gives life to them, even so the Son gives life to whom He will"* (John 5:19-21 NKJV).

JESUS' PRIORITIES

If you are still unclear, look at the priorities of Jesus, or how He spent His time in ministry. Was His ministry primarily one of "feeding the poor" or "preaching to the poor"? They are *not* the same. Did He pass out meals and water? Jesus did feed 5,000, but only after they stayed around for three days listening to Him teach and preach about the Kingdom! I think He felt it was the least He could do after they showed Him such commitment. Was He more concerned with giving them fish—or teaching them how to be "fishers of men"?

And what about the time when Jesus said to Peter three times, "Feed My sheep"? Did he mean for Peter to literally give His followers food, or was He referring to the real food He had mentioned in the Gospel—to do His Father's will?

> But He said to them, "I have food to eat that you do not
> know about." So the disciples were saying to one another,
> "No one brought Him anything to eat, did he?" Jesus said
> to them, "My food is to do the will of Him who sent Me
> and to accomplish His work" (John 4:32-34).

If you ever think, *I wonder what Jesus **really** would do,* then only look in the Scripture at how He spent His time and at His priorities. A simple analysis of the Gospels shows He spent approximately one-third of His ministry time preaching and teaching the Gospel of the Kingdom, mainly to His disciples; another third He spent casting out demons and doing miracles; and a final third He spent healing the sick.

Instead of adopting the latest politically correct Christian fad we find on the shelf of the local Christian bookstore, perhaps we should let the Word of God define our priority for us. Even if *everyone* is reading it or doing it, that doesn't make something true. There is so much information coming at Christians today it would benefit most of us to go back and *read the Bible.* Many of us have become so spiritually lazy that we have become dependent on others telling us what God is saying and what He means.

Jesus said that the things of the Kingdom would be so simple a child could understand them! Romans 3:4 says, *"Indeed, let God be true but every man a liar..."* (NKJV).

WHAT JESUS REALLY DID

Here are some Scriptures that teach what Jesus *really did,* not what we theorize Jesus *might* have done. These Scriptures are exceedingly clear— they say what they mean and mean what they say describing Jesus' activities as He preached the Gospel of the Kingdom and performed miracles. This was Jesus' lifestyle in His day-to-day life. They include, but weren't centered on, synagogue meetings or services. In fact, many of His most significant miracles and healings happened as He was "on the way" to somewhere else.

> *You know of Jesus of Nazareth, how God anointed Him with the Holy Spirit and with power, **and how He went about doing good and healing all who were oppressed by the devil**, for God was with Him* (Acts 10:38).

> *When Jesus departed from there, two blind men followed Him, crying out and saying, "Son of David, have mercy on us!" And when He had come into the house, the blind men came to Him. And Jesus said to them, "Do you believe that I am able to do this?" They said to Him, "Yes, Lord." Then He touched their eyes, saying, "According to your faith let it be to you." And their eyes were opened. And Jesus sternly warned them, saying, "See that no one knows it." But when they had departed, they spread the news*

177

about Him in all that country. As they went out, behold, they brought to Him a man, mute and demon-possessed. And when the demon was cast out, the mute spoke. And the multitudes marveled, saying, "It was never seen like this in Israel!" (Matthew 9:27-33 NKJV).

Now when He was in Jerusalem at the Passover, during the feast, many believed in His name when they saw the signs which He did (John 2:23 NKJV).

Now a certain man was there who had an infirmity thirty-eight years. When Jesus saw him lying there, and knew that he already had been in that condition a long time, He said to him, "Do you want to be made well?" The sick man answered Him, "Sir, I have no man to put me into the pool when the water is stirred up; but while I am coming, another steps down before me." Jesus said to him, "Rise, take up your bed and walk." And immediately the man was made well, took up his bed, and walked. And that day was the Sabbath (John 5:5-9 NKJV).

For this reason the Jews persecuted Jesus, and sought to kill Him, because He had done these things on the Sabbath. But Jesus answered them, "My Father has been working until now, and I have been working" (John 5:16-17 NKJV).

It certainly appears by these passages that Jesus performed a great number of signs, wonders, and miracles that He referred to as His "good works." So how then can we substitute this popular "social gospel" for Jesus' definition of good works that He clearly commanded us to do?

But realize this, that in the last days difficult times will come. For men will be lovers of self, lovers of money, boastful, arrogant, revilers, disobedient to parents, ungrateful, unholy, unloving, irreconcilable, malicious gossips, without self-control, brutal, haters of good, treacherous, reckless, conceited, lovers of pleasure rather than lovers of God, holding to a form of godliness, although they have denied its power; avoid such men as these (2 Timothy 3:1-5).

Isn't this exactly how the enemy operates? To water down the truth about these good works of power, healing, and deliverance? Isn't healing cancer patients, seeing drug addicts delivered, preaching the Good News, and binding up the broken-hearted doing "good works"? Why *wouldn't* the enemy's number one strategy be to get Christians debating whether or not to preach the Gospel and even arguing over "how it is done"? The enemy of our soul has taken entire denominations and movements captive with this delusion, some even labeling anyone truly "doing what Jesus would do" as deceived or into the occult. The enemy has sent the Church on so many bunny trails. Many ministries are pursuing anything and everything except preaching the good news of the Kingdom. There are so many diversions, detours, and excuses for not preaching that it's obvious that the enemy is propelling all this fruitless activity forward. *The enemy wants the Church caught up in obsessive activity that leads nowhere and accomplishes nothing.* He is more than happy to encourage us in those directions.

WHAT *WOULDN'T* JESUS DO?

If we look in the New Testament and simply study Jesus' lifestyle for our model of ministry, we will also see what He probably *wouldn't* do. Based on the Gospel narratives of Christ's life, we get a clear picture. Instead of buying into what is served up in Christian pop culture, the chronicle of Jesus' life in the Gospels tells us plenty. I mean, did Jesus really die on the Cross so we could do this kind of stuff? Is this the best He has for us?

If He was here now, He probably *wouldn't* express His love for humanity by only doing the following things, as kind, helpful, and politically palatable as they may appear to us:

- Bring a team of His carpenter friends to your house for a home makeover;

- Hand out cold water at interstate off-ramps;

- Wash your car;

- Mow your grass;

- Hand out turkeys on Thanksgiving and Christmas;

- Give you a bag of old clothes;

- Give you His old furniture or old shoes;

- Sell you donuts;

- Sell you cookies;

- Pat you on the back;

- Say "Try Jesus";

- Hand you a Gospel tract;

- Sew doilies and mail them to prisoners;

- Give you a car;

- Wash your hair;

- Do your nails;

- Teach English classes.

While all of these are *generous and wonderfully kind* gestures when done to others in a right spirit, I humorously and facetiously mention them only to clearly illustrate the point of how far our present Christianity has strayed from our *prime mandate!* The Church now has 1,001 diversions that take us away from the prime mission of the Church—to preach the Gospel and make disciples. Showing mercy and "doing to the least of these" should be part of every believer's lifestyle, but to equate a "silent" mercy ministry with preaching or to equate extending kindness in a Gospel vacuum is *unbalanced*—and the point of this chapter.

We have recently been spending time with several of the leaders of the Iris Ministries team led by Rolland and Heidi Baker and have been able to see this balance between bringing the Gospel message with power and helping converts with daily needs. However, it appears that when other believers see the immense success of their ministry and hear stories of how they lavishly show love to the children in their schools, some people leave their meetings thinking that all they need do is hug somebody, and then they will have conquered a nation! Of course, it is more involved than that.

Many times we Americans only want the newest formula that takes the least amount of effort. Most of these works of kindness from this "social gospel" don't require any long-term involvement or relationship. In my church's weekly outreaches many of the people who hear our preaching or who get healed or delivered need a sustained discipleship relationship. "Drive-by" good deeds won't cut it if we want long-term results. Iris Ministries has devoted their lives to minister to entire people groups, and without power they couldn't succeed. Of course, they attend to their human needs as well.

So how can each of us make this our lifestyle? Each time Jesus preached, demonstrations of power were present to illustrate and reveal the love of the Father to a lost and dying world! While "random acts of kindness" bless people and should be encouraged, there can be *no substitute* for the power of the message of the Kingdom to deliver people! As

Peter Lord said, "Keep the main thing the main thing." Jesus' lifestyle was that He healed the sick, cast out demons, and preached the message of the Kingdom. His message was crystal clear, His mission was without ambiguity, and His focus was laser accurate. He was and *is* Love in skin! He was born into our world as the Firstborn of a new race of people who would walk as sons and daughters of God. He had power and authority over His circumstances and took dominion over everything He encountered. Unless the Father sent something, Jesus didn't receive it and wasn't distracted by it.

> *For those whom He foreknew, He also predestined to become conformed to the image of His Son, so that He would be the firstborn among many brethren* (Romans 8:29).

The way we change is spelled out in these and other passages of Scripture. The first way is to repent or to change our mind. Jesus said in Matthew 4:17, *"...repent, for the kingdom of heaven is at hand."*

Change comes when we repent or change our mind. The Greek root for *repentance* means "think differently."[3] Changing the way you think will change the way you live. *"For as he thinks within himself, so he is..."* (Prov. 23:7). Many times Christians know truth only in their minds, not in their hearts—they are agnostic in their hearts.

The second way we change is through beholding and being transformed into His image, not by attempting to fix ourselves. Second Corinthians 3:17-18 says,

> *Now the Lord is the Spirit; and where the Spirit of the Lord is, there is liberty. But we all, with unveiled face, beholding as in a mirror the glory of the Lord, are being transformed into the same image from glory to glory, just as by the Spirit of the Lord* (NKJV).

While some theologians hold that, due to humanity's deep depravity, we can scarcely (or not at all) share His divine character, the Bible is quite clear that God's prescription for our deliverance involves doing the works He did as well as walking as He did. First John 2:6 says, *"The one who says he abides in Him ought himself to walk in the same manner as He walked."* To be a new creature in Christ requires us to believe and act as though our "old man" is dead. He wouldn't command us to do something we were too bad to do!

If looking to Jesus and getting our eyes off ourselves is the key to our transformation, then obsessing over our faults and failings is a dead-end street. The obsession over self-improvement is a road to nowhere. Transformation occurs through beholding Him, not our flesh! The Spirit changes us, not self-improvement techniques or discipline. Jesus never required the apostles to do anything but to follow Him and *imitate* Him. He was mentoring them as they beheld what He was and what He did. He modeled a new way of living, and He told them (and us), *"Greater things than this, you can do!"* It is possible for all of us to do these things if we keep our eyes on our primary purpose—to bring Jesus' Kingdom to the lost, the lame, the deaf, and the blind through a demonstration of His power and love! Surely we are to also extend kindness with provision for daily needs, and that will be obvious to us as we go along.

Do you believe what He said, and do you want to do the same? You can! And if you will only believe, you will!

ENDNOTES

1.   Charles Sheldon, *In His Steps* (Peabody, MA: Hendrickson Publishers, 2004).

2.   John Evan Smith, *Booth the Beloved* (Oxford: Oxford University Press, 1949), 123-124.

3.   StudyLight.org, *The New Testament Greek Lexicon Online,* s.v. "Metanoeo," http://www.studylight.org/lex/grk/view.cgi?number=3340.

CHAPTER 13

FROM BOTH SIDES NOW

To have a successful walk of faith, we need to be regularly aligning ourselves not only with the *words* of God but also with the *ways* of God.

> *Therefore I was angry with this generation, and said, "They always go astray in their heart, and* ***they did not know My ways"****; as I swore in My wrath, "They shall not enter My rest"* (Hebrews 3:10-11).

To be aligned with His Word and His ways gives us an understanding of the Kingdom. While God works in mysterious ways, we know God is mysteriously good, and if we grow in knowing the ways of God, we will have more and more confidence in Him and will be more capable of not just pleasing Him, but finishing well. Since we will never know *all* His ways (for they are unsearchable), we can still learn more and more of the ways of the Kingdom. The Scriptures are filled with them, and Jesus' lifestyle reflects it. We need to do what He says without rebellion, evasion, or delay. When Jesus said, *"Repent, for the kingdom of heaven is at hand,"* He meant for us to change our mind, the way we think. And when He says, "change your mind," *He already has something in mind for you to change into!* God is actually smarter than we think. We will have many opportunities God sets before us to make Kingdom choices, to "change our mind" and turn to something else. This is what abiding looks like. It is a lot like the French, German, and Japanese Maglev bullet trains.

166 LIFESTYLE

They go three times faster than a regular train. The reason they can go *so very fast* is:

1. They run on a separate track than the old rail lines— made of a continuous, seamless rail activated with a magnetic charge;

2. Their power comes from the rail and train itself;

3. They don't have wheels but magnets. They literally *fly* with *no* contact with the rail whatsoever.

By our alignment and agreement with Him, we get "on God's track" with Him! When we agree with Heaven, we get in on God's way of doing things, which is much faster, easier, and better than our old ways of doing things. If we follow His lead, He even says He will make us into someone and something we may not have felt comfortable being or doing before. He says if we follow, *He will make us fishers of men. Don't you think the Creator of all things can help you with your discomfort?*

> Then He said to them, **"Follow Me, and I will make you fishers of men."** They immediately left their nets and followed Him (Matthew 4:19-20 NKJV).

We have already surmised that His ways "go against the grain" of the way we might think, respond, or speak.

- We think, Exalt myself; He says, Humble yourself.

- We think, Be first; He says, Be last.

- We think, I need to understand, then I can believe; He says, Believe.

- We think, Let me reason this thing out; He says, Stop your reasoning.

- We think, God is like this or that; He's like me; He says, My ways aren't yours, neither are My thoughts.

- We think, If I can only do this or that first, **then** I can obey Him. He says, Do it.

> *For the wisdom of this world is foolishness before God. For it is written, "He is the one who catches the wise in their craftiness"; and again, "The Lord knows the reasonings of the wise, that they are useless"* (1 Corinthians 3:19-20).

The best our wisdom offers is foolishness to God. He laughs at all our wrangling about petty and irrelevant things. He sits in Heaven and laughs about His enemies even thinking they have the upper hand. While our culture portrays God as an archaic system of rules with sentimental value only acknowledged at weddings and funerals, we know better. The fool says in his heart, *"There is no God"* (see Ps. 14:1).

The problem with our nation today is that most people, including Christians, need to have an experience with God—a supernatural encounter with God that shakes them to the core. They need the kind of encounter that Saul, the angry persecutor of the Early Church had, one that *changed his mind.*

> *As he journeyed he came near Damascus, and suddenly a light shone around him from heaven. Then he fell to the ground, and heard a voice saying to him, "Saul, Saul, why are you persecuting Me?" And he said, "Who are You, Lord?" Then the Lord said, "I am Jesus, whom you are persecuting. It is hard for you to kick against the goads." So he, trembling and astonished, said, "Lord, what do*

You want me to do?" Then the Lord said to him, "Arise and go into the city, and you will be told what you must do." And the men who journeyed with him stood speechless, hearing a voice but seeing no one. Then Saul arose from the ground, and when his eyes were opened he saw no one. But they led him by the hand and brought him into Damascus. And he was three days without sight, and neither ate nor drank (Acts 9:3-9 NKJV).

A man with an experience is never at the mercy of a man with only an argument. Theory, opinions, and ideas are no match for solid experience in God. It is one thing to theorize about casting out demons. It is another to do it... and I have done it many, many times. This story of those posers, the sons of Sceva, attempting to do deliverance without any real faith and authority is one of my favorites in Acts.

Then some of the itinerant Jewish exorcists took it upon themselves to call the name of the Lord Jesus over those who had evil spirits, saying, "We exorcise you by the Jesus whom Paul preaches." Also there were seven sons of Sceva, a Jewish chief priest, who did so. And the evil spirit answered and said, "Jesus I know, and Paul I know; but who are you?" Then the man in whom the evil spirit was leaped on them, overpowered them, and prevailed against them, so that they fled out of that house naked and wounded (Acts 19:13-16 NKJV).

The enemy knows what you are truly living and walking in versus what you only know through others. These seven sons of Sceva were vicariously attempting to do something cool using the trick they had seen other Jewish exorcists use. There is a joke about the Royal "We." When someone says *we* need to do this or that, the truth is that one person somewhere has to take responsibility to get it done. When we say "we," what we really mean is "they" or "him" or "me."

> *My little children, let us not love in word or in tongue,* ***but in deed and in truth.*** *And by this we know that we are of the truth, and shall assure our hearts before Him. For if our heart condemns us, God is greater than our heart, and knows all things. Beloved, if our heart does not condemn us, we have confidence toward God. And whatever we ask we receive from Him, because we keep His commandments and do those things that are pleasing in His sight* (1 John 3:18-22 NKJV).

> *Now this is the confidence that we have in Him, that if we ask anything according to His will, He hears us. And if we know that He hears us, whatever we ask, we know that we have the petitions that we have asked of Him* (1 John 5:14-15 NKJV).

> *Consider it pure joy, my brothers, whenever you face trials of many kinds, because you know that the testing of your faith develops perseverance. Perseverance must finish its work so that you may be mature and complete, not lacking anything. If any of you lacks wisdom, he should ask God, who gives generously to all without finding fault, and it will be given to him. But when he asks, he must believe and not doubt, because he who doubts is like a wave of the sea, blown and tossed by the wind. That man should not think he will receive anything from the Lord;* ***he is a double-minded man, unstable in all he does*** (James 1:2-8 NIV).

*If any of you is deficient in wisdom, let him ask of the giving God [Who gives] to everyone liberally and ungrudgingly, without reproaching or faultfinding, and it will be given him. Only it must be in faith that he asks with no wavering (no hesitating, no doubting). For the one who wavers (hesitates, doubts) is like the billowing surge out at sea that is blown hither and thither and tossed by the wind. For truly, let not such a person imagine that he will receive anything [he asks for] from the Lord, **[For being as he is] a man of two minds (hesitating, dubious, irresolute), [he is] unstable and unreliable and uncertain about everything [he thinks, feels, decides]** (James 1:5-8 AMP).*

If our mind is not focused, single, and in agreement with God's mind in us, we will not have access to our heavenly accounts. Our check will not clear, and our (spiritual) funds will be put on hold. I am talking figuratively here. Scripture talks about "this mind" we are to have *in Him.*

Let nothing be done through selfish ambition or conceit, but in lowliness of mind let each esteem others better than himself. Let each of you look out not only for his own interests, but also for the interests of others. Let this mind be in you which was also in Christ Jesus, who, being in the form of God, did not consider it robbery to be equal with God, but made Himself of no reputation, taking the form of a bondservant, and coming in the likeness of men. And being found in appearance as a man, He humbled Himself and became obedient to the point of death, even the death of the cross (Philippians 2:3-8 NKJV).

What causes fights and quarrels among you? Don't they come from your desires that battle within you? You want something but don't get it. You kill and covet, but you cannot have what you want. You quarrel and fight. You do not have, because you do not ask God. When you ask, you do not receive, because you ask with wrong motives, that you may spend what you get on your pleasures. You adulterous people, don't you know that friendship with the world is hatred toward God? Anyone who chooses to be a friend of the world becomes an enemy of God. Or do you think Scripture says without reason that the Spirit He caused to live in us envies intensely? But He gives us **more grace**. *That is why Scripture says: "God opposes the proud but gives grace to the humble." Submit yourselves, then, to God. Resist the devil, and he will flee from you. Come near to God and He will come near to you. Wash your hands, you sinners, and* **purify your hearts, you double-minded** *(James 4:1-8 NIV).*

You [are like] unfaithful wives [having illicit love affairs with the world and breaking your marriage vow to God]! Do you not know that being the world's friend is being God's enemy? So whoever chooses to be a friend of the world takes his stand as an enemy of God. Or do you suppose that the Scripture is speaking to no purpose that says, The Spirit Whom He has caused to dwell in us yearns over us and He yearns for the Spirit [to be welcome] with a jealous love? But He gives us more and more grace (power of the Holy Spirit, to meet this evil tendency and all others fully). That is why He says, God sets Himself against the proud and haughty, but gives grace [continually] to the lowly (those who are humble enough to receive it). So be

191

subject to God. Resist the devil [stand firm against him], and he will flee from you. Come close to God and He will come close to you. [Recognize that you are] sinners, get your soiled hands clean; [realize that you have been disloyal] wavering individuals with divided interests, and purify your hearts [of your spiritual adultery] (James 4:4-8 AMP).

I love the Amplified Bible because it explodes the meanings of things, and you see them from nearly every angle. Basically the double-minded man is compared to an adulterer who has one wife but goes to another woman regularly. It describes this as like an affair with a mistress. Divided loyalties, allegiances, and disloyal affections have no place in the committed believer's lifestyle. We have become so used to certain things going on in our society that the politically correct posture is the one even the Church is taking. In the bid to be relevant and hip, the Church is lowering its standards, if that is possible. Several areas must be upheld as non-negotiable if we are ever to have the impact we want to in our society. The prime reason society is becoming more permissive and lawless is the Church is not preaching, healing, and delivering. We have bodies, buildings, and bucks, but why are we even doing these things if they don't work? Our message should either start a riot or a revival anywhere we take it. This message shouldn't be so watered-down that everyone likes it. We are not in a beauty contest but a war for souls and the future of our nation. Western culture is at stake.

The first area is the sanctity of marriage. Many have given up on the idea that a couple can get married and stay married. We need to applaud those who do and have grace and mercy for the divorced, and they shouldn't be ostracized from the Church. Then again, the divorced and remarried live complicated lives, and they shouldn't be the standard we look at. To look at a standard, however high, is better than to lower the standard to accommodate others and make them feel better.

The second area is homosexuality. Because the militant homosexual lobbies have worked for a generation to portray their cause as a civil rights and discrimination issue instead of an issue of lifestyle choice, we especially need to stand up for traditional marriage and hold the line that there is no redefinition to include homosexual marriage. We also must ramp up deliverance ministries to help those caught in this lifestyle get free.

The third area is abortion. Enough has been said about this by better people, but murder should never be allowed to be seen as normal. We have so compromised our message and our standards for so long; we need to realize watering down our message, ministries, and mandate only dilutes it and doesn't make it "go further."

> *Every good gift and every perfect (free, large, full) gift is from above; it comes down from the Father of all [that gives] light, in [the shining of] Whom there can be no variation [rising or setting] or shadow cast by His turning [as in an eclipse]. And it was of His own [free] will that He gave us birth [as sons] by [His] Word of Truth, so that we should be a kind of firstfruits of His creatures [a sample of what He created to be consecrated to Himself]. Understand [this], my beloved brethren. Let every man be quick to hear [a ready listener], slow to speak, slow to take offense and to get angry. For man's anger does not promote the righteousness God [wishes and requires]. So get rid of all uncleanness and the rampant outgrowth of wickedness, and in a humble (gentle, modest) spirit receive and welcome the Word which implanted and rooted [in your hearts] contains the power to save your souls. But be doers of the Word [obey the message], and not merely listeners to it, betraying yourselves [into deception by reasoning contrary to the Truth]. For if anyone only listens*

*to the Word without obeying it and being a doer of it,
he is like a man who looks carefully at his [own] natural
face in a mirror; for he thoughtfully observes himself, and
then goes off and promptly forgets what he was like. But
he who looks carefully into the faultless law, the [law]
of liberty, and is faithful to it and perseveres in looking
into it, being not a heedless listener who forgets but an
active doer [who obeys], he shall be blessed in his doing
(his life of obedience). If anyone thinks himself to be religious (piously observant of the external duties of his faith)
and does not bridle his tongue but deludes his own heart,
this person's religious service is worthless (futile, barren)*
(James 1:17-26 AMP).

Compromise means to let go of one thing and go halfway to another;
to modify so both sides can be in agreement. *Com-* means "with, together
or jointly"; *promise* means "a declaration that one will do or refrain from
doing something specified."[1]

Essentially, to compromise means to only go halfway on something.
In areas where there is ample give and take, like in a negotiation for
a business deal, to compromise on some things shows good will and
patience. However, when it comes to issues of integrity, ethics, or righteousness, compromise always leads to the loss of the purity and value of
things. When it involves those fine areas, there just can't be *any* cutting
corners or compromise. On most things, we have to be single-minded
and single-focused.

THE SINGLE EYE

The Greek word *haplous* means to be single or in union; to be braided
in union with God.[2] So we know that the eye represents our vision, our
ability to see and to clearly articulate our vision. Scripture says that if

we can have a clear vision, we will be filled with light. To be single in vision means to be in union with God, to be agreeing with Heaven and on God's track as we said earlier.

> *The eye is the lamp of your body; when your eye is clear, your whole body also is full of light; but when it is bad, your body also is full of darkness. Then watch out that the light in you is not darkness* (Luke 11:34-35).

> *The light of the body is the eye: therefore when thine eye is **single**, thy whole body also is full of light; but when thine eye is evil, thy body also is full of darkness. Take heed therefore that the light which is in thee be not darkness* (Luke 11:34-35 KJV).

> *Your eye is the lamp of your body. When your eyes are **good**, your whole body also is full of light. But when they are bad, your body also is full of darkness. See to it, then, that the light within you is not darkness* (Luke 11:34-35 NIV).

> *Your eye is the lamp of your body; when your eye (your conscience) is sound and fulfilling its office, your whole body is full of light; but when it is not sound and is not fulfilling its office, your body is full of darkness. Be careful, therefore, that the light that is in you is not darkness* (Luke 11:34-35 AMP).

EIGHT THINGS TO STAY SINGLE-MINDED ABOUT:

1. *Choose whom you are serving:*

And Elijah came to all the people, and said, "How long will you falter between two opinions? If the Lord is God, follow Him; but if Baal, follow him." But the people answered him not a word (1 Kings 18:21 NKJV).

2. *Cease all reasonings:* Don't think too hard! We must only operate out of hearing and obeying, not analyzing and wondering.

    But when Jesus perceived their thoughts, He answered and said to them, "Why are you reasoning in your hearts? Which is easier, to say, 'Your sins are forgiven you,' or to say, 'Rise up and walk'?" (Luke 5:22-23 NKJV).

3. *Simply obey:*

    For it is time for judgment to begin with the family of God; and if it begins with us, what will the outcome be for those who do not obey the gospel of God? (1 Peter 4:17 NIV).

4. *Watch what you say:* We need to have a victorious vocabulary, and we should drop all the "poor little old me" talk.

5. *Fix your eyes on Jesus:*

    Let us fix our eyes on Jesus, the author and perfecter of our faith, who for the joy set before Him endured the cross, scorning its shame, and sat down at the right hand of the throne of God. Consider Him who endured such opposition from sinful men, so that you will not grow weary and lose heart (Hebrews 12:2-3 NIV).

6. *Don't throw away your confidence:*

   Therefore, do not throw away your confidence, which has a great reward (Hebrews 10:35).

7. *Be a **victor**, not a **victim**:* You want to rule? Then act like you have dominion.

8. *Watch who you hang out with:*

   And if anyone does not obey our word in this epistle, note that person and do not keep company with him, that he may be ashamed. Yet do not count him as an enemy, but admonish him as a brother (2 Thessalonians 3:14-15 NKJV).

   He who walks with wise men will be wise, but the companion of fools will suffer harm (Proverbs 13:20).

ENDNOTES

1. *Merriam-Webster's Collegiate Dictionary*, 11th ed., s.v. Compromise.

2. StudyLight.org, *The New Testament Greek Lexicon Online*, s.v. "Haplous," see http://www.studylight.org/lex/grk/view.cgi?number=573.

CHAPTER 14

THE REAL OR THE IDEAL?

Blessed is the man who does not walk in the counsel of the wicked or stand in the way of sinners or sit in the seat of mockers. But his delight is in the law of the Lord, and on His law he meditates day and night. He is like a tree planted by streams of water, which yields its fruit in season and whose leaf does not wither. Whatever he does prospers.

—Psalm 1:1-3 (NIV)

At least there is hope for a tree: If it is cut down, it will sprout again, and its new shoots will not fail. Its roots may grow old in the ground and its stump die in the soil, yet at the scent of water it will bud and put forth shoots like a plant.

—Job 14:7-9 (NIV)

These two passages reveal that there is a supernatural thirst that we can have in God that can keep us going back for more of God. Thirst for God and His presence cannot be easily quantified, but it is readily visible and seen. Every day dozens of times a day we need water. We must have it. Most would say we need eight to ten glasses a day. In the same way, we need to be thirsting after God's Word and righteousness. Without water, we would die in three to four days; just so, we need to be drinking in the fresh water of God's Word, His presence, and His reality. But thirsting after righteousness brings us

166 LIFESTYLE

the blessing, and we need never thirst again after drinking one drink of His living water! One drink of His water creates a living fountain in us that has an unlimited supply. Every time we think of Him, we drink. Every time we read His Word, we drink. Every time we worship, we drink. That one drink when we came to Him has turned into a well that will never run dry!

> *Jesus answered and said to her, "Whoever drinks of this water* [natural water] *will thirst again, but whoever drinks of the water* [living water] *that I shall give him* **will never thirst**. *But the water that I shall give him will become in him a fountain of water springing up into everlasting life." The woman said to Him, "Sir, give me this water, that I may not thirst, nor come here to draw"* (John 4:13-15 NKJV).

NORMAL IS NOT NORMAL

As Christians, we have an idealism generated from our desire for Heaven and from our desire to worship and be like this wonderful, benevolent, omniscient Being we love and know as God. Because we have a hope in something better, we always are looking for something better. And when and if it doesn't happen, we tend to become surprised and even disappointed because we are experiencing less than what we think is "normal."

> *Beloved, do not be surprised at the fiery ordeal among you, which comes upon you for your testing, as though some strange thing were happening to you; but to the degree that you share the sufferings of Christ, keep on rejoicing, so that also at the revelation of His glory you may rejoice with exultation* (1 Peter 4:12-13).

We are always comparing ourselves to others or thinking we are missing some mark when we face these difficulties. It is as if we expect a life of "normal," with nothing to come to upset the apple cart. We expect to have plenty of money, never to have difficulties in our marriage, for our kids never to be sick, for all of our relationships to be smooth, and to always be loved, appreciated, blessed, and healthy. Not! While a lot of things happen because we are not believing God's Word or doing the works of Jesus, many times we are hindered because our faith is at such a low level.

1. Stuff happens to all of us. It may be a family curse (devil) or our own dumb fault (flesh) or something that comes upon us for our testing (world), but it still happens.

2. Don't compare yourself with others during this time. Comparison leads either to depression or discouragement because we may feel rejection. It also leads to pride and condescension when we are doing well.

3. Don't be looking for a way of escape first; be looking for what the Lord is saying or not saying in the situation. A lot of times the Lord is just showing you how to learn to fight and win!

   *Therefore let him who thinks he stands take heed lest he fall. No temptation has overtaken you except **such as is common to man;** but God is faithful, who will not allow you to be tempted beyond what you are able, but with the temptation will also make the way of escape, that you may be able to bear it* (1 Corinthians 10:12-13 NKJV).

4. Temptation is a test, but testing is not always about being tempted. You never have a testimony without a test. Testing is more about increasing your trust and hope in God and His Word!

5. Life is cyclical, like sound or light waves, and seasonal, like the weather. Life is really not supposed to be extremes—all pits or mountaintops; instead, it is more like life in the valley, a place of the mundane and everyday. Some of us so hate what is boring, we'd rather have a good trial than be bored.

6. If we are made to be warriors, we will be bored in peacetime, shining our weapons and always working at new war strategies. We should want to have fresh blood on our swords every day. Jesus spent His time "destroying the works of the devil" (see 1 John 3:8). I want to as well.

7. If we were more given to helping others, we might be more joyous. Nothing is more fulfilling than giving.

As we walk out this 166 lifestyle of operating in supernatural ministry, it becomes more "normal" to us. Many times we get questions as we train people in these things. Here are some of the most common:

ISSUE #1—DISQUALIFICATION

"How can I share the Gospel/move in power, etc., when I am full of sin, compromise, lukewarmness, etc.?"

That's agreeing with a qualifying spirit. Christ has qualified us. In addition, we have found that people who have an outlet where they preach regularly are those making the most progress, those who are growing in their relationship with the Lord. They are jettisoning their fleshliness and carnality.

> *For this reason also, since the day we heard of it, we have not ceased to pray for you and to ask that you may be filled with the knowledge of His will in all spiritual wisdom and*

*understanding, so that you will walk in a manner worthy
of the Lord, to please Him in all respects, bearing fruit in
every good work and increasing in the knowledge of God;
strengthened with all power, according to His glorious
might, for the attaining of all steadfastness and patience;
joyously giving thanks to the Father, who has qualified us
to share in the inheritance of the saints in Light. For He
rescued us from the domain of darkness, and transferred
us to the kingdom of His beloved Son, in whom we have
redemption, the forgiveness of sins* (Colossians 1:9-14).

We're not disqualified *from* the power of God based on the bad stuff
that we do or have done any more than we are qualified *for* the power of
God based on the good stuff that we do. We are qualified based on our
faith in what the blood of Jesus did on our behalf and on our faith in
His ability to use us with *His* power.

Do not be overcome by evil, but overcome evil with good
(Romans 12:21 NKJV).

The biggest reason believers are *not* overcomers is precisely this—*they
are not fulfilling their ministry, but instead are trying to avoid it.* They are
holding back because of this wrong teaching that only the perfect elite can
minister. They are using this false teaching as a validation for their own
weaknesses. None of us were designed merely to be pew-warmers. None
of us were designed to only barely get by. The average person is called to
do the ministry, and this means operating in the supernatural gifts. Just
because most Christians are ignorant about these things doesn't mean
they don't exist. It only means they don't exist *to them—in their current
frame of reference.* The ignorance or the lack of practice of something in
the local church doesn't mean it isn't available. It means leadership is not
offering it. The saints are the ones doing most of the ministry we see in
the New Testament. The apostles did the *extraordinary miracles.*

I pray that you may be active in sharing your faith, so that you will have a full understanding of every good thing we have in Christ (Philemon 1:6 NIV).

ISSUE #2—BURDEN

"How can I share the Gospel when I don't have a passion for the lost?"

Who says that we preach the Gospel because we have a passion for it or a passion for winning the lost? We preach the Gospel out of obedience, not burden, passion, gifting, or preference. The burden and love for lost people will come as we walk in obedience to the Word, which is the *revealed*, not the *veiled* will of God.

*I solemnly charge you in the presence of God and of Christ Jesus, who is to judge the living and the dead, and by His appearing and His kingdom: **preach the word; be ready in season and out of season; reprove, rebuke, exhort, with great patience and instruction.** For the time will come when they will not endure sound doctrine; but wanting to have their ears tickled, they will accumulate for themselves teachers in accordance to their own desires, and will turn away their ears from the truth and will turn aside to myths. **But you, be sober in all things, endure hardship, do the work of an evangelist, fulfill your ministry** (2 Timothy 4:1-5).*

ISSUE #3—GIFTING

"We don't really want to do what you're doing because we're not bold like you. I don't think that we are gifted to do what you are doing. We're more gifted in prayer and intercession for the unborn, etc. We feel led to tape our mouths shut and stand silently in front of abortion clinics. We are prayer missionaries."

P-L-E-A-S-E! This is yet another pathetic cop-out using gifting, burden, and feelings to define ministry. Sorry, but many of the "ministries" operating today in local churches and ministries don't even exist in the Bible! If you're not bold, then maybe you don't understand what it is to be righteous. Proverbs 28:1 says, *"...The righteous are bold as a lion."*

Boldness is the main request in the *only* prayer meeting about revival we see in the Book of Acts. Acts prayer meetings were a far cry from a lot of what goes on in many of our prayer meetings today. The believers in Acts got to the point, made their requests, and then acted! Preaching the Gospel is not a gift or suggestion, but a command. Sharing your faith is a command. Why does anyone act like it is an optional gift of the Spirit? All believers are called to be witnesses of His resurrection and walk in the power of God (see 1 John 2:6; John 14:12; Mark 16:15). Preaching has been falsely defined and is much more user-friendly in the Scriptures than in today's culture.

Nevertheless, there is *clearly no validation in Scripture for using prayer as an excuse for **not** preaching.* I'm sorry to tell some of you, but an intercessor is *not* a ministry gift in the Body. It was manufactured by people in a prayer room to validate and legitimize their being there. While we love and need praying people, please let's stay biblically authentic and get real.

ISSUE #4—WRONG UNDERSTANDING OF THE PURPOSE OF INTIMACY

"I feel called to worship at the feet of Jesus and get to know Him. Don't you think that knowing Jesus and truly being in love with Him is the most important thing? What about Mary? I think Martha is striving, and that your ministry is a striving ministry.

First of all, Jesus certainly loved Martha every bit as much as Mary. Remember, Lazarus was also Martha's brother, and Martha—not her sister Mary—talked and even pressed Jesus into going to raise him from the dead. While much has been made of the one time Jesus told Martha not to be overly concerned with natural things, without Martha Jesus wouldn't have been a guest in the house in the first place. She was a responsible, take-charge person. Of course, all duty and service must come out of relationship with Jesus. And, of course, loving and knowing Jesus *is* the most important thing! You can do acts of power without knowing the Lord (see Matt. 7:23), but you can't truly know the Lord and *not* do acts of power and preach the Gospel (see 1 John 2:6; John 14:12; Mark 16:15)! However, the second most important thing is fulfilling your purpose on the earth, not sitting around singing.... Oh, and by the way, the only reason that *you even know the story about Mary* is because someone got *off the floor* and preached the Gospel!

> *Truly I say to you, wherever this gospel is preached in the whole world, what this woman has done will also be spoken of in memory of her* (Matthew 26:13).

Prayer, fasting, and intercession are a regular part of a *believer's* life, and they allow us to have communion with God as well as fulfill our callings on the earth. Prayer is invaluable, but fits into our Christian life and faith as one key piece of our life and was *never meant to be the only priority* or exercise to the exclusion of all others. Prayer is like breathing. We all need to breathe to live. Breathing is a normal, irreplaceable part of our physical life and being. Yet, it is done primarily unconsciously and involuntarily, *without fanfare or hoopla*—indispensable to our existence, yet usually without us even recognizing it.

The perfect model for a believer's lifestyle, discipline, and doctrinal practice should be the model of the life and work of Jesus Christ. He is described as the *Firstborn* of a new race of beings that we are called to be part of! He is also called our elder Brother in this new family He allows us to be a part of. Most of Jesus' prayer meetings were private, and there is not one recorded stadium prayer meeting, corporate prayer meeting, or prayer fest in the New Testament. In fact, much to the chagrin and dismay of the army of "intercessors" in the Body of Christ today, most of Jesus' prayer times were private and usually occurred *after* His preaching and teaching ministry times. These encounters were a vital part of His communion with His Father. Yet He still remained very effective and fruitful in His ministry purpose on planet Earth. Never did Jesus become so closeted away with His Father that He became *unavailable* to finish His Gospel ministry to humans on earth.

If Jesus Christ, our great High Priest and the One who makes intercession for us (See Hebrews 7-8.) told us specifically how to pray, where to pray, and even in what spirit we are to pray, we ought to observe *His* example first of all.

> *And when you pray, **do not be like the hypocrites**, for they love to pray standing in the synagogues and on the street corners to be seen by men. I tell you the truth, they have received their reward in full. But when you pray, go into your room, close the door and pray to your Father, who is unseen. Then your Father, who sees what is done in secret, will reward you. And when you pray, do not keep on babbling like pagans, for they think they will be heard because of their many words. **Do not be like them**, for your Father knows what you need before you ask Him. This, then, is how you should pray: "Our Father in heaven, hallowed be Your name, Your kingdom come, Your will be done on earth as it is in heaven. Give us today our daily bread. Forgive us our debts, as we also have forgiven our debtors. And lead us not into temptation, but deliver us from the evil one." For if you forgive*

*men when they sin against you, your heavenly Father will
also forgive you. But if you do not forgive men their sins,
your Father will not forgive your sins* (Matthew 6:5-15
NIV).

He also told us something about fasting: how to fast, if we are to
fast—and He *even indicated His disciples didn't need to fast.* He speaks of
fasting as a desperate measure, done by those "looking to find God," *as
though He wasn't with them.* (He was.) He indicated when the Bridegroom
is present, there is no reason to fast. The truth is, He is with us today
through the Spirit. We have an open Heaven and have open access to
God's presence all the time. I fast, and we encourage people to fast, but
the "secret" of getting the results Jesus got isn't fasting. Our problem isn't
biblical ignorance of knowledge but a complete lack of application and
implementation.

*When you fast, do not look somber as the hypocrites do, for
they disfigure their faces to show men they are fasting. I
tell you the truth, they have received their reward in full.
But when you fast, put oil on your head and wash your
face, so that it will not be obvious to men that you are
fasting, but only to your Father, who is unseen; and your
Father, who sees what is done in secret, will reward you*
(Matthew 6:16-18 NIV).

*They said to Him, "John's disciples often fast and pray,
and so do the disciples of the Pharisees, but Yours go on
eating and drinking." Jesus answered, "Can you make the
guests of the Bridegroom fast while He is with them? But
the time will come when the Bridegroom will be taken
from them; in those days they will fast"* (Luke 5:33-35
NIV).

So how can thousands of believers then embrace a lifestyle of prayer that specifically violates everything Jesus says about prayer and fasting? And how then can thousands of believers substitute prayer, fasting, and intercession for the legitimate biblical "call" and "cause" of the believer to preach the Gospel of the Kingdom to the world? How? They are led by well-meaning people who have gone into erroneous emphases. The test is always the fruit.

> *Those who do wickedly against the covenant he shall corrupt with flattery; but the people who know their God shall be strong, and carry out great exploits* (Daniel 11:32 NKJV).

IDEALISM

One of the biggest dangers to walking in the truth is idealism. Spiritual or religious idealism isn't based in truth but in an imaginative view of how things should be and— doggone it—*ought* to be. While everything we think we hear from God we want to agree with, we must make sure every experience, every revelation, every angelic visitation or prophetic experience is grounded in the *Logos*, the Word of God. It is essential that we have a greater love for the truth than for what our feelings say.

> *And you shall know the truth, and the truth shall make you free* (John 8:32 NKJV).

> *Who desires all men to be saved and to come to the knowledge of the truth* (1 Timothy 2:4 NKJV).

It is not enough just to be saved from hell; we all need to come to *the knowledge* of the truth. This is not some personal, subjective knowledge of the truth. Lawlessness is a subjective knowledge of truth that we want to hold onto, but we then end up rejecting the rest. Lawlessness is really seen in our responses to people, especially those we love.

RUNNING TO THEIR DEFENSE

Many Christians are driven by overreactions or knee-jerk reactions, saying, "That's not right," or "That's not fair," when it comes to things like church discipline. False mercy or a faux "love" that really is a mushy tolerance for things God hates is a big problem. We have to be clear to separate the people from the problem. *Sometimes God was so stern with people He had them executed.* Apparently, both God and Texas still believe in capital punishment! If we don't get our allegiances straight, we may be in danger of getting on the other side of God. We have a big problem if we somehow suppose that we know how God ought to act or to think regarding a situation. As Bobby Conner teaches, many of us act familiar with a God we barely know. As we have already said, we must also know the severity of God if we are to ever fully know the goodness of God. It is unbalanced to only view God as a Santa Claus figure made in *our* likeness—you know, a really *nice* guy. When our view of God is wrong, we make judgment calls about ourselves and people in the Body and how they are treated. But with the results we see in Barna's poll mentioned in Chapter 11, how can we expect anything different? For all the talk about abuse and problems in churches, we can surmise by this survey that the majority of believers in America:

1. are puffed-up with pride;

2. idolize and elevate teaching over experience;

3. are ignorant of their gifts and what spiritual gifts even are;

4. are biblically illiterate on fundamentals;

5. go to church less and less;

6. think they are "not called" to preach; and finally,

7. feel they are "leaders."

Now this is *not* a good report card for American Christian leadership! With such dismal failure in the kind of Christians we produce and with our inability to fulfill our God-given mandate, the current crop of leaders deserve the same grade the leaders of many American financial institutions and businesses are getting today—an *F!* While this is disheartening, I am not discouraged, and because I have already invested 30 years in the Church, I want to be part of the solution! More and more pastors every day say to me, "Marc, I didn't think this stuff was possible, and I was so tired of doing *church as usual* with no fruit and little presence of God. This is the real deal I have been looking for!" To get these results, however, we have to actually confront sin and compromise and do things that bear fruit. This can be difficult for many pastors.

We may think, *Who are we to say, "That ain't right"?* However, the Bible is clear about what "ain't right." The Bible is clear about how to deal with sin in the Body and how to deal with restoring fallen people. If someone falls, it doesn't mean they are finished. It means they have lost their way and can't minister in integrity and have people trust them anymore. Our human nature wants to run to the defense of those with whom we can identify. But let me say, my biggest mistakes in 30 years of ministry have come when I supposed that I could help someone whom others couldn't. The truth is when someone shows up at your church door with all kinds of problems and needs, they may just be there to take you to the cleaners—to clean you out!

Two of the worst con artists I ever saw were women who broke my stereotype. One was a single mom with five kids. She ended up conning us and three other churches of $10,000 before we discovered that her cover story about her abusive husband, etc., was a story to elicit sympathy. It wasn't till I called her last three pastors that I got the right story. Another was a lady in a wheelchair. This woman used her disability to prey on people's sympathies. She scammed thousands of dollars out of several folks. But one family in particular felt we were treating her badly. I later discovered she had been thrown out of two other churches. She was a con artist who didn't want Jesus or His healing because losing her wheelchair would cut off her benefits and might cause her to lose the ear of gullible people. She was exposed for who she really was—a very divisive person. It wasn't pretty as she cussed me out every time I talked to her! I ended up putting her out of the church, and it was the smartest thing I could have done. But, boy, did she work up people's souls and their sympathies! We must not let ourselves listen more closely to people's souls than to their spirits. I should have done a better job training people's discernment. True discernment comes out of *love* anyway, not criticism.

> *And this is my prayer: that your love may abound more and more in knowledge and depth of insight, so that you may be able to discern what is best and may be pure and blameless until the day of Christ, filled with the fruit of righteousness that comes through Jesus Christ—to the glory and praise of God* (Philippians 1:9-11 NIV).

> *Do not be bound together with unbelievers; for what partnership have righteousness and lawlessness, or what fellowship has light with darkness?* (2 Corinthians 6:14)

Righteousness can't coexist with lawlessness. Lawlessness means every one doing what is right in their *own* eyes. It doesn't mean it doesn't look right; it just isn't right in God's eyes.

> *...Walk as children of Light (for the fruit of the Light consists in all goodness and righteousness and truth), trying to*

*learn what is pleasing to the Lord. Do not participate in
the unfruitful deeds of darkness, but instead even expose
them* (Ephesians 5:8-11).

Righteousness comes by faith, and lawlessness leads to dead works.
A lot of what we have had lately is a bit of anti-this and anti-that and
reacting to this and reacting to that. God is not reacting to *anything!*
While we regularly respond to injustice or mistakes with knee-jerk reactions and overreactions, God doesn't. He knows what is in the hearts of
people, and we could all use a big dose of discerning of spirits. It would
save a lot of headaches and problems with people. Unfortunately, we
regularly overreact. A funny example is the *Bill Cosby, Himself* comedy
video. It is rated PG or PG-13, and I highly recommend it for all parents.
You see in it the overreaction caused by a need for better, more attentive
parenting. When the kids were fighting, touching, and grabbing each
other, Cosby's response was, *"OK, that's it! From now on, no one is to
touch another child, ever again, ever!"* It is funny!

Most of our overreactions are caused by our passivity in dealing with
things in the first place. We don't need more overreaction but more truth.
Avoiding sin or living in idealism is not living in reality, and sometimes
we just need to learn to deal with things right away.

> *But let your "Yes" be "Yes," and your "No," "No." For
> whatever is more than these is from the evil one* (Matthew
> 5:37 NKJV).

> *But as God is faithful, our word to you was not Yes and
> No. For the Son of God, Jesus Christ, who was preached
> among you by us—by me, Silvanus, and Timothy—was
> not Yes and No, but in Him was Yes. For all the promises
> of God in Him are Yes, and in Him Amen, to the glory of
> God through us* (2 Corinthians 1:18-20 NKJV).

We also have to watch becoming anti-this or anti-that! That is that lawlessness again, a symptom of not confronting or dealing with things. When all we are is *anti*-everything, we are not *for* anything. The Gospel is about Jesus, and it is *good* news. We should not just be *anti* things and bad news! God is *for* things, not against things!

> *What, then, shall we say in response to this? If God is for us, who can be against us?* (Romans 8:31 NIV).

We must honestly embrace the reality of things and the way people *really* are, rather than what we just hope for or how we want people to be. At home we use the term *in real life*. If it doesn't work in real life, it probably won't work in church! As we see things as *they really are*, it may take more faith, but that's OK. Idealism is based on a wrong view of God, His Ways, and His Word and only leads to frustration and despair. We get expectations of things, and then we don't see them happen. We expect people to respond this or that way, and they don't, so we are disappointed. Hope doesn't disappoint: but put your hope in Jesus, His Ways, and His Word. Now that will work; that is reality. Jesus Christ is ultimate reality! He is *the* Truth, not simply *a* truth. Often we are trying to help people the "easy" way, and it never works! We get *dis-appointed* because we *appointed* something to happen that never should have.

President Obama won the 2008 presidential election mainly because he promised people hope for the future and a new way of doing things. People need to have hope! Hope is important because without hope people fade and quit. The Church needs hope, but putting hope in idealism *is* a false hope. And a little redecorating of the same old message won't work either. We need to see things as they really are. That is not cynical or idealistic, but it is realistic. On the other hand most of us only see what we got free *from*. We also need to teach people what they are *now free to do!* One of the Church's problems has been that we are always telling people, *"Don't do this,"* or *"Don't do that"; "You can't do this,"* or *"You can't do that."* We need to be telling the Church what they *can* do! They *can* heal the sick, they *can* preach the Gospel, they *can* raise the dead, and they *can* cast out demons! **Yes, we can!** Let's release them to a wide open door of opportunity outside the four walls of the Church the other 166 hours of the week! Once we stop limiting God's "work area" beyond our weekly service, any and all things might happen! We have got to remember:

1. We must not limit God or put Him in our little box!

Yes, again and again they tempted God, and limited the Holy One of Israel (Psalm 78:41).

2. We must never forget His *power!*

They did not remember His power: *The day when He redeemed them from the enemy, when He worked His signs in Egypt, and His wonders in the field of Zoan* (Psalm 78:42-43).

In October 2007, the Lord visited me one day—not literally, but He truly showed up in a way I didn't expect. He came to me and said that He was picking up the pace of everything and that I was going to need to run like Elijah did to keep up. Here are my impressions about this encounter:

- God is accelerating, and we don't have the time for debate and excuses anymore.

- God is accelerating His agenda for us and His Church and is using the supernatural to do it.

- Things that used to take years are being accomplished in months;

215

- Things that used to take months, weeks;

- Things that used to take weeks, days;

- Things that used to take days, hours;

- Things that used to take hours, minutes;

- Things that used to take minutes, seconds.

- Many things are instantly done when we agree with Heaven and God's will—that is, those things that are already decided.

- Whatever we agree with that is happening in Heaven we can possess here. We can have God's rule, His reign, His government, but we have to bring it.

- He is our King, but He is not only to be feared, but to be lavishly loved and worshiped!

- Salvation, healing, deliverance, and freedom have already been decided and determined in Heaven as God's will for people.

CHAPTER 15

THE MIGHTY WARRIOR LIFESTYLE

As we sat in a prophetic conference 14 years ago, my wife, Linda, and I were so excited about the things we were seeing there. We saw freedom in worship with new songs being written spontaneously by the Spirit. We heard apostolic teaching that rocked our very foundations and drew us closer to the Lord, and we saw awesome miracles, healings, and signs and wonders in His presence. I had this thought in my Spirit, *This is awesome, Lord; I want us to be a part of this!* But the quick, short response from the Lord came so clearly it was almost an audible voice: *"No, you're a Mighty Warrior."* I felt really humbled. God has a wonderful way of bursting our happy "balloons of our own expectations." He pulled out His pin and went *Boom!* I was crushed but excited. I was putting my future hope of where we would go next spiritually in this group, and then the Lord said, "No," just as a dad would do if his son asked to hang out with a friend on a Saturday but he had other stuff for the son to do. I trusted Him, but it took about seven years for me to even get a grasp on what that meant and the ramifications it had for us.

As I sought the Lord the next few years, things came up that directed me. I was asking about an association with a tribe, but He was speaking to me about my identity, "Mighty Warrior." So I looked up the Scriptures, and the term was used only in the NIV. There were five examples:

> *Cush was the father of Nimrod, who grew to be a* ***mighty warrior*** *on the earth* (Genesis 10:8 NIV).

*When the angel of the Lord appeared to Gideon, he said, "The Lord is with you, **mighty warrior**"* (Judges 6:12 NIV).

*Jephthah the Gileadite was a **mighty warrior*** (Judges 11:1 NIV).

*Cush was the father of Nimrod, who grew to be a **mighty warrior** on earth* (1 Chronicles 1:10 NIV).

*But the Lord is with me like a **mighty warrior**; so my persecutors will stumble and not prevail. They will fail and be thoroughly disgraced; their dishonor will never be forgotten* (Jeremiah 20:11 NIV).

I quickly eliminated the three verses that were genealogies. After that I found out that this term means: a dread champion, real fighter, and valiant soldier. A Mighty Warrior isn't the normal soldier; he is a real *bad* fellow (to the enemy, I mean). These guys were like a hybrid of all the *bad* tough action heroes ever imagined through the minds of the actors playing them: a *SchwarzenStalloneSeagalDammeDieselLiWillis* hybrid as it were… (Did I leave out someone you like?) Bottom line, these were real tough hombres. At a prayer event, I met a chief of the Creek Indians. He told me that there are three grades of fighters in their army. *First, the soldier,* who has training but no kills and little combat experience. *Second, the warrior,* who is experienced and has at least one kill. But then *third is the Mighty Warrior* who has many kills and trains others how to be great warriors. After hearing this, I then discovered that my literal name Marc or Marcus means the same thing: *Mighty Warrior.*

I really feel like it is time in our land for God to raise up the Mighty Warriors, the dread champions who will begin to take down the demonic giants in our land! The answer to bring change in our country isn't praying for the right political candidates or Supreme Court justices but to awaken the giant that is the American Church and get her to begin to preach the Gospel and win our nation back out of compromise and lawlessness! People who get authentically born again will not do drugs, destroy their marriages, or live licentious lifestyles. They will actually act like authentic believers. And this doesn't mean that every one has to have my personality or be a type-A choleric. The meek, the weak, the young, and the old all have a part to play. Just as we see in the Bible accounts of David, Gideon, Moses, Samson, Mary, Elizabeth, Naomi, Lydia, and many, many others, we see the *most unlikely heroes* come on the scene at a time when times are desperate! Gideon was a good example.

The story of unlikely Gideon taking a small band and defeating a vast army is compelling and gives anyone hope that God can use them. I went back to the passage about Gideon in Judges 6 where the angel of the Lord comes to him. It is interesting to note that Gideon was hiding in a winepress threshing wheat he didn't want stolen from the Midianites when his "call" came. He doesn't especially seem like a great candidate for this title, this designation—***Mighty Warrior.***

> *The angel of the Lord came and sat down under the oak in Ophrah that belonged to Joash the Abiezrite, where his son Gideon was threshing wheat in a winepress to keep it from the Midianites. When the angel of the Lord appeared to Gideon, he said,* **"The Lord is with you, mighty warrior."** *"But sir," Gideon replied, "if the Lord is with us, why has all this happened to us? Where are all His wonders that our fathers told us about when they said, 'Did not the Lord bring us up out of Egypt?' But now the Lord has abandoned us and put us into the hand of Midian." The Lord turned to him and said,* **"Go in the strength you have and save Israel out of Midian's hand.** *Am I not sending you?" "But Lord," Gideon asked, "how can*

I save Israel? My clan is the weakest in Manasseh, and I am the least in my family." The Lord answered, **"I will be with you, and you will strike down all the Midianites together"** (Judges 6:11-16 NIV).

Israel cried out to have the Lord rescue them from the Midianites, and God's answer was the unlikely Gideon who was hiding wheat in a winepress. Looking at Gideon's life, I see three things:

1. By all accounts, Gideon **was not** the most likely to free Israel. However, he was God's choice!

2. He wondered and questioned how God was going to pull it off, but he believed and agreed with Heaven about his designation! It is OK to ask questions as long as they aren't coming out of unbelief.

3. He was God's answer to the cries of God's people just as Moses was in his day. He was God's choice.

We need to be giant killers, destroyers of God's enemies, and Mighty Warriors! David's example of giant killing is an inspiration to all those who want to be Mighty Warriors. Gideon had to shift his thinking just a little to see himself differently. So did David with Goliath. All it takes is one giant shift in order for us to be able to view ourselves differently. David was 5 feet tall and change, yet Goliath was anywhere from 10 to 13 feet tall, with sandals as big as a large briefcase. But David didn't see his size; he saw God's size! God is *BIG!* When my daughter Amber was just a toddler, she saw an overweight man for the first time ever as we were eating lunch in McDonald's, and she yelled out to her mom, "Mommy, that man is B-B-B-I-I-I-G-G-G!!!" That is what the enemy needs to see—that we are B-I-G! When David faced Goliath, he saw God's reputation and credibility on the line. David didn't even "inquire of the Lord" about facing Goliath or killing him. He just knew inside it was wrong for this guy to intimidate and prophesy doom and accusation daily over God's people!

> But we all, with unveiled face, beholding as in a mirror the glory of the Lord, are being transformed into the same image from **glory to glory**, just as from the Lord, the Spirit (2 Corinthians 3:18).

BECOMING A GIANT KILLER!

The giants we see in Scripture are not a fairy tale; they were literally a race of physically large beings who stood in the way of Israel possessing her inheritance and the land God gave her. Standing between 9 and 10 feet tall, these giants had to be destroyed for Israel to enter the land. They are mentioned over 41 times in the Old Testament.

In the very beginning of the Bible, they are described:

> There were giants on the earth in those days, and also afterward, when **the sons of God came in to the daughters of men and they bore children to them**. Those were the mighty men who were of old, men of renown. Then the Lord saw that the wickedness of man was great in the earth, and that every intent of the thoughts of his heart was only evil continually. And the Lord was sorry that He had made man on the earth, and He was grieved in His heart (Genesis 6:4-6 NKJV).

My personal opinion: As these angels intermarried with human women, they brought into the gene pool the physical trait of gigantism along with great evil and lawlessness.

221

> *And **the angels who did not keep their proper domain**,*
> *but left their own abode, He has reserved in everlasting*
> *chains under darkness for the judgment of the great day*
> (Jude 6 NKJV).

I believe one of the main reasons God brought the flood was to completely eradicate this evil propensity out of the human DNA. God said that He wouldn't strive with man forever and that every inclination of man was evil continually. Could this be one of the causes of man's great capability for evil? Many theologians and historians have wondered if this angelic interbreeding with human women at the beginning of time caused many of man's ills, which precipitated God's decision to destroy mankind through the flood.

Moses ran into giants right after he sent spies to check out the land:

> *Now they departed and came back to Moses and Aaron*
> *and all the congregation of the children of Israel in the*
> *Wilderness of Paran, at Kadesh; they brought back word*
> *to them and to all the congregation, and showed them*
> *the fruit of the land. Then they told him, and said: "We*
> *went to the land where you sent us. It truly flows with*
> *milk and honey, and this is its fruit. Nevertheless the*
> *people who dwell in the land are strong; the cities are*
> *fortified and very large; moreover we saw the descendants*
> *of Anak there. The Amalekites dwell in the land of the*
> *South; the Hittites, the Jebusites, and the Amorites dwell*
> *in the mountains; and the Canaanites dwell by the sea*
> *and along the banks of the Jordan." Then Caleb quieted*
> *the people before Moses, and said, "Let us go up at once*
> *and take possession, for we are well able to overcome it."*

But the men who had gone up with him said, "We are not able to go up against the people, for they are stronger than we." And they gave the children of Israel a bad report of the land which they had spied out, saying, "The land through which we have gone as spies is a land that devours its inhabitants, and all the people whom we saw in it are men of great stature. There we saw the giants (the descendants of Anak came from the giants); and we were like grasshoppers in our own sight, and so we were in their sight" (Numbers 13:26-33 NKJV).

These "giants" were also mentioned in Deuteronomy:

For the Lord your God has blessed you in all the work of your hand. He knows your trudging through this great wilderness. These forty years the Lord your God has been with you; you have lacked nothing. And when we passed beyond our brethren, the descendants of Esau who dwell in Seir, away from the road of the plain, away from Elath and Ezion Geber, we turned and passed by way of the Wilderness of Moab. Then the Lord said to me, "Do not harass Moab, nor contend with them in battle, for I will not give you any of their land as a possession, because I have given Ar to the descendants of Lot as a possession." (The Emim had dwelt there in times past, a people as great and numerous and tall as the Anakim. They were also regarded as giants, like the Anakim, but the Moabites call them Emim. The Horites formerly dwelt in Seir, but the descendants of Esau dispossessed them and destroyed them from before them, and dwelt in their place, just as Israel did to the land of their possession which the Lord gave them.) (Deuteronomy 2:7-12 NKJV).

David faced and defeated one of them whose name was Goliath. The dimensions of his spear, coat of mail, shield, and height reveal his immense size. The Philistines stood on a mountain on one side, and Israel stood on a mountain on the other side, with a valley between them.

And a champion went out from the camp of the Philistines, named Goliath, from Gath, whose height was six cubits and a span. He had a bronze helmet on his head, and he was armed with a coat of mail, and the weight of the coat was five thousand shekels of bronze. And he had bronze armor on his legs and a bronze javelin between his shoulders. Now the staff of his spear was like a weaver's beam, and his iron spearhead weighed six hundred shekels; and a shield-bearer went before him (1 Samuel 17:4-7 NKJV).

A cubit was approximately 17½ inches, and a span is half a cubit, so Goliath was barely under 10 feet in height! His coat of armor weighed 5,000 shekels (a shekel is .4 oz), putting that between 125 to 130 pounds! Why did David take five smooth stones from the brook? Did he feel he needed all five to kill Goliath (see 1 Sam. 17:40) when only one was needed? No, it was because Goliath had four sons, and all five were necessary to take them all out! There was a real possibility that there would be a real giant killing that day.

When the Philistines were at war again with Israel, David and his servants with him went down and fought against the Philistines; and David grew faint. Then **Ishbi-Benob, who was one of the sons of the giant,** *the weight of whose bronze spear was three hundred shekels, who was bearing a new sword, thought he could kill David. But Abishai the son of Zeruiah came to his* *aid, and struck the Philistine and killed him. Then the men of David swore to him, saying, "You shall go out no more with us to battle, lest you quench the lamp of Israel." Now it happened afterward that there was again a battle with the Philistines at Gob. Then Sibbechai the Hushathite killed* **Saph, who was one of the sons of the giant**. *Again there was war at Gob with the Philistines, where Elhanan the son of Jaare-Oregim the Bethlehemite* **killed the brother of Goliath** *the Gittite, the shaft of whose spear was like a weaver's beam. Yet again there was war at Gath, where* **there was a man of great stature, who had six fingers on each hand and six toes on each foot, twenty-four in number; and he also was born to the giant.** *So when he defied Israel, Jonathan the son of Shimea, David's brother, killed him.* **These four were born to the giant in Gath,** *and fell by the hand of David and by the hand of his servants* (2 Samuel 21:15-22 NKJV).

The Bible uses these units of measure to describe the giants because *they really were giants,* even compared to the *huge* professional football and basketball players of today. These guys made the NBA and NFL's biggest look puny. We are talking a good two feet taller than the tallest men we see on earth today!

Look at what the Bible says of Og King of Bashan:

Then we turned and went up the road to Bashan; and Og king of Bashan came out against us, he and all his people, to battle at Edrei. And the Lord said to me, "Do not fear him, for I have delivered him and all his people and his land into your hand; you shall do to him as you did to Sihon king of the Amorites, who dwelt at Heshbon." So *the Lord our God also delivered into our hands Og king of Bashan, with all his people, and we attacked him until he had no survivors remaining. And we took all his cities at that time; there was not a city which we did not take from them: sixty cities, all the region of Argob, the kingdom of Og in Bashan. All these cities were fortified with high walls, gates, and bars, besides a great many rural towns. And we utterly destroyed them, as we did to Sihon king of Heshbon, utterly destroying the men, women, and children of every city. But all the livestock and the spoil of the cities we took as booty for ourselves. And at that time we took the land from the hand of the two kings of the Amorites who were on this side of the Jordan, from the River Arnon to Mount Hermon (the Sidonians call Hermon Sirion, and the Amorites call it Senir), all the cities of the plain, all Gilead, and all Bashan, as far as Salcah and Edrei, cities of the kingdom of Og in Bashan. **For only Og king of Bashan remained of the remnant of the giants.** Indeed his bedstead was an iron bedstead. (Is it not in Rabbah of the people of Ammon?) Nine cubits is its length and four cubits its width, according to the standard cubit* (Deuteronomy 3:1-11 NKJV).

Og's iron bed was 13 feet long by 5 feet wide! He was a big boy! Og was also described as one of the last giants:

*All the kingdom of Og in Bashan, who reigned in Ashtaroth and Edrei, **who remained of the remnant of the giants;** for Moses had defeated and cast out these* (Joshua 13:12 NKJV).

There was even a valley called *"the valley of the giants"*:

And the border went up by the Valley of the Son of Hinnom to the southern slope of the Jebusite city (which is Jerusalem). The border went up to the top of the mountain that lies before the valley of Hinnom westward, which is at the end of **the Valley of Rephaim** *northward* (Joshua 15:8 NKJV).

Then the border came down to the end of the mountain that lies before the Valley of the Son of Hinnom, which is in **the Valley of the Rephaim** *on the north, descended to the Valley of Hinnom, to the side of Jebusite city on the south, and descended to En Rogel* (Joshua 18:16 NKJV).

Why did God command Joshua to utterly destroy all these peoples? (see Deut. 7:2-3). It seems so cruel and even harsh for God to command Joshua to utterly destroy all the men, women, and children of these enemies of Israel. However, it's not because God isn't a loving God. It is because the remnants of these giants had to be utterly destroyed from their line. All possibility of any remnant of this race of giants had to be completely eliminated and destroyed.

And we utterly destroyed them, as we did to Sihon king of Heshbon, utterly destroying the men, women, and children of every city (Deuteronomy 3:6 NKJV).

The *bad news* is we are going to have to face some giants like these; the *good news* is that after awhile, they are no more. Even their remnants are gone.

There was not a city that made peace with the children of Israel, except the Hivites, the inhabitants of Gibeon. All the others they took in battle. For it was of the Lord to harden their hearts, that they should come against Israel in battle, that He might utterly destroy them, and that they might receive no mercy, but that He might destroy them, as the Lord had commanded Moses. And at that time Joshua came and **cut off the Anakim from the mountains: from Hebron, from Debir, from Anab, from all the mountains of Judah, and from all the mountains of Israel; Joshua utterly destroyed them with their cities. None of the Anakim were left in the land of the children of Israel; they remained only in Gaza, in Gath, and in Ashdod.** *So Joshua took the whole land, according to all that the Lord had said to Moses; and Joshua gave it as an inheritance to Israel according to their divisions by their tribes. Then the land rested from war* (Joshua 11:19-23 NKJV).

The names of these giants are significant as well:

- *Nephilim:* meaning "giants"[1]

- *Anak:* meaning "neck"; a Canaanite[2]

  Nevertheless they would not hear, but stiffened their **necks, like the necks of their fathers**, *who did not believe in the Lord their God* (2 Kings 17:14).

- *Emim:* meaning "terrors"; a Moabite[3]

- *Zamzummims:* meaning "scheme, purpose, plot"[4]

- *Goliath:* meaning "splendor"; also, "to strip or humiliate"[5]

Here are some things they all use against us: fear, bad reports, intimidation, and threats. They attempted to strike fear into the hearts of their enemies by spreading reports of their great size and intimidating posture and how terrible and awesome they were. They relied on their size and stature to intimidate and used this intimidation and threats to terrorize. They were the original "terrorists." Remember, *Emim* means "terrors." "Have you heard?" "Did you hear?" was the cry as word spread, and with each story, the threat grew bigger.

> *There were giants in the earth in those days, and also afterward, when the sons of God came in to the daughters of men and they bore children to them. Those were the mighty men who were of old,* **men of renown** (Genesis 6:4 NKJV).

They Set the Rules

> *Then he stood and cried out to the armies of Israel, and said to them, "Why have you come out to line up for battle? Am I not a Philistine, and you the servants of Saul? Choose a man for yourselves, and let him come down to me. If he is able to fight with me and kill me, then will we be your servants. But if I prevail against him and kill him, then you shall be our servants and serve us." And the Philistine said, "I defy the armies of Israel this day; give me a man, that we may fight together." When Saul and all Israel heard those words of the Philistine, they were dismayed and greatly afraid* (1 Samuel 17:8-11 NKJV).

Paralysis of Analysis

The key purpose of the intimidation and threats was to keep God's army so paralyzed that it would never engage the Philistines. Always mustering, but never engaging; always assembling, but never attacking.

There was a reluctance to commit for fear of loss. Isn't this what is happening with the American Church today?

> *Israel and the Philistines drew up in battle array, army against army* (1 Samuel 17:21).

Bogged Down in Politics

It wasn't politically correct to have David be chosen as king. He was too little, insignificant, and out of sight. But God chose him; only he had what it took. His time in the desert taking care of the sheep and flocks had uniquely prepared him to see beyond what everyone else saw.

> *Thus Jesse made seven of his sons pass before Samuel. But Samuel said to Jesse, "The Lord has not chosen these"* (1 Samuel 16:10).

WHAT DO WE DO?

So, how do we deal with these "giants"?

1. Realize that God always has a plan to defeat the giant: it may not be by using the politically correct or outwardly impressive.

2. Take action: God is looking for someone who cares about His interests first, who will take initiative to bring righteousness.

> *Then David spoke to the men who were standing by him, saying, "What will be done for the man who kills this Philistine, and takes away the reproach from Israel? For*

who is this uncircumcised Philistine, that he should taunt the armies of the living God?" (1 Samuel 17:26).

God never told David to go after Goliath, but he just had to! In contrast, Lot put up with the sins of Sodom and got absorbed into the atmosphere of the city. After awhile, he was compromised.

> *Now the two angels came to Sodom in the evening as **Lot was sitting in the gate of Sodom**...* (Genesis 19:1).

3. Declare and proclaim the destruction of your enemy: it is important to prophesy what is going to happen in advance to your enemy, to your giant!

> *Your servant has killed both the lion and the bear; and this uncircumcised Philistine will be like one of them, since he has taunted the armies of the living God* (1 Samuel 17:36).

> *Then David said to the Philistine, "You come to me with a sword, a spear, and a javelin, but I come to you in the name of the Lord of hosts, the God of the armies of Israel, whom you have taunted. This day the Lord will deliver you up into my hands, and I will strike you down and remove your head from you. And I will give the dead bodies of the army of the Philistines this day to the birds of the sky and the wild beasts of the earth, that all the earth may know that there is a God in Israel, and that all this assembly may know that the Lord does not deliver by sword or by spear; for the battle is the Lord's and He will give you into our hands"* (1 Samuel 17:45-47).

231

4. Expect to see victory over your giant: all God expects you to do is have the courage to get out there and face your giant! You need to declare his destruction and then face him, but if you do your part, the Lord will back up your little stone and make it have the impact of a Hummer in the head!

Then it happened...that David ran quickly toward the battle line to meet the Philistine (1 Samuel 17:48).

5. Utterly destroy him so that his army will flee: once you have killed him, it is important to cut off his head so his armies will flee! The symbol of holding his head over him is a frightening one to the enemy!

Then David ran and stood over the Philistine and took his sword and drew it out of its sheath and killed him, and cut off his head with it. When the Philistines saw that their champion was dead, they fled (1 Samuel 17:51).

ENDNOTES

1. StudyLight.org, *The Old Testament Hebrew Lexicon Online*, s.v. "Nephilim," http://www.studylight.org/lex/heb/view.cgi ?number=05303.

2. StudyLight.org, *The Old Testament Hebrew Lexicon Online*, s.v. "Anak," http://www.studylight.org/lex/heb/view.cgi ?number=06061.

3. StudyLight.org, *The Old Testament Hebrew Lexicon Online*, s.v. "Emim," http://www.studylight.org/lex/heb/view.cgi ?number=0368.

4. StudyLight.org, *The Old Testament Hebrew Lexicon Online*, s.v. "Zamzummims," http://www.studylight.org/lex/heb/view.cgi ?number=02157.

5.   StudyLight.org, *The Old Testament Hebrew Lexicon Online,* s.v. "Goliath," http://www.studylight.org/lex/heb/view.cgi?number=01555; http://www.studylight.org/lex/heb/view.cgi?number=01540.

CHAPTER 16

THE SHINING

O my love, you are as beautiful as Tirzah, lovely as Jerusalem, awesome as an army with banners!
—Song of Songs 6:4 (NKJV)

Arise, shine; for your light has come! And the glory of the Lord is risen upon you. For behold, the darkness shall cover the earth, and deep darkness the people; but the Lord will arise over you, and His glory will be seen upon you. The Gentiles shall come to your light, and kings to the brightness of your rising. Lift up your eyes all around, and see: They all gather together, they come to you; your sons shall come from afar, and your daughters shall be nursed at your side. Then you shall see and become radiant, and your heart shall swell with joy; because the abundance of the sea shall be turned to you, the wealth of the Gentiles shall come to you. The multitude of camels shall cover your land, the dromedaries of Midian and Ephah; all those from Sheba shall come; they shall bring gold and incense, and they shall proclaim the praises of the Lord. All the flocks of Kedar shall be gathered together to you, the rams of Nebaioth shall minister to you; they shall ascend with acceptance on My altar, and I will glorify the house of My glory. Who are these who fly like a cloud, and like doves to their roosts? Surely the coastlands shall wait for Me; and the ships of Tarshish will come first, to bring your sons from afar, their silver and their gold with them, to the name of the Lord your God, and to the Holy One of Israel, because He has glorified you. The sons of foreigners shall build up your walls, and their kings shall minister to you; for in My wrath I struck you, but in My favor I have had mercy on you. Therefore your gates shall be open continually; they shall not be shut day or night, that men may bring to you the wealth of the Gentiles, and their kings in procession. For the nation and kingdom which will not serve you shall perish, and those nations shall be utterly ruined. The glory of Lebanon shall come to you, the cypress, the pine, and the box tree together, to beautify the place of My sanctuary; and I will make the place of My feet glorious. Also the sons of those who afflicted you shall come bowing to you, and all those who despised you shall fall prostrate at the soles of your feet; and they shall call you The City of the Lord, Zion of the Holy One of Israel. Whereas you have been forsaken and hated, so that no one went through you, I will make you an eternal excellence, a joy of many generations. You shall drink the milk of the Gentiles, and milk the breast of kings; you shall know that I, the Lord, am your Savior and your Redeemer, the Mighty One of Jacob. Instead of bronze I will bring gold, instead of iron I will bring silver, instead of wood, bronze, and instead of stones, iron. I will also make your officers peace, and your magistrates righteousness. Violence shall no longer be heard in your land, neither wasting nor destruction within your borders; but you shall call your walls Salvation, and your gates Praise.

The sun shall no longer be your light by day, nor for brightness shall the moon give light to you; but the Lord will be to you an everlasting light, and your God your glory. Your sun shall no longer go down, nor shall your moon withdraw itself; for the Lord will be your everlasting light, and the days of your mourning shall be ended. **Also your people shall all be righteous; they shall inherit the land forever,** *the branch of My planting, the work of My hands, that I may be glorified.* **A little one shall become a thousand, and a small one a strong nation. I, the Lord, will hasten it in its time.**

The Spirit of the Lord God is upon Me, because the Lord has anointed Me to preach good tidings to the poor; He has sent Me to heal the brokenhearted, to proclaim liberty to the captives, and the opening of the prison to those who are bound; *to proclaim the acceptable year of the Lord, and the day of vengeance of our God; to comfort all who mourn, to console those who mourn in Zion, to give them beauty for ashes, the oil of joy for mourning, the garment of praise for the spirit of heaviness; that they may be called trees of righteousness, the planting of the Lord, that He may be glorified.* **And they shall rebuild the old ruins, they shall raise up the former desolations,** *and they shall repair the ruined cities, the desolations of many generations. Strangers shall stand and feed your flocks, and the sons of the foreigner shall be your plowmen and your vinedressers. But you shall be named the priests of the Lord, they shall call you the servants of our God. You shall eat the riches of the Gentiles, and in their glory you shall boast. Instead of your shame you shall have double honor, and instead of confusion they shall rejoice in their portion. Therefore in their land they shall possess double; everlasting joy shall be theirs. For I, the Lord, love justice; I hate robbery for burnt offering; I will direct their work in truth, and will make with them an everlasting covenant* (Isaiah 60:1-61:8 NKJV).

We have lived on the prophetic promises of these passages for 12 years now, and the promises are being fulfilled! It was a little over five years ago that we made a quality 166 lifestyle choice in our local church. For years, we had heard over and over from the prophets that God was going to show up on the streets, that we would see a move of God outside the four walls of our churches, and that it would be through a corporate anointing, where everyday believers, not Christian television superstars, would be regularly healing the sick, raising the dead, and doing the Gospel! We came to realize that for us to see the manifestation of this prophetic word we needed to respond to the invitation in it to step out and believe it was true. The fulfillment of the prophetic word depended on our response to it.

So we began to authentically challenge and equip believers to fulfill their personal callings—not just on Sunday mornings, but the entire rest of the week. We created intentional settings and situations where normal believers could rise and shine, doing their best to preach the Gospel. We began to base our schedules and existence not merely on a two-hour Sunday gathering attracting believers or seekers, but instead on practical, lifestyle-altering ways to intentionally equip believers. Instead of allowing them to remain in their day-to-day habits of being self-focused and absorbed, we challenged them to begin to think about a life of living for God and ministering to others. This 166 lifestyle is now progressively becoming a reality for all. Previously we had been duped into thinking that only an elite few are supposed to be doing this, the superstars. Unfortunately, this lie has been perpetrated mostly by the superstar-driven system and propped up by their unbiblical examples of excess and little fruit. It is kind of like the old adage of the "foxes guarding the henhouse." At home, as we put away those childish things that only catered to our needs and directed our attentions to the higher and nobler pursuits of doing the Gospel and living for the Kingdom, we started seeing the prophetic word come to pass.

But to do this, we needed to make concrete and intentional decisions to live by those certain principles. We started to make certain
daily, weekly, monthly, and yearly choices that allowed us to accommodate these things. Instead of making excuses for our lifestyles, we
started making prioritized choices that directed the course of our lives
and involved all the things that made up our day-to-day schedule. We
effectively raised the bar much, much higher, and we have had challenges. Some don't like a bar, let alone it being raised. However, people
who live for God usually want to do His will. If you and I are to live
for God today, we have to alter and remove out of our lives all thinking and things that hinder us, hold us back, or sap our faith. We must
live with a certain sense of purpose and know that destiny is a matter
of choice, not chance: *"For as he thinks in his heart, so is he..."* (Prov.
23:7 NKJV).

A lot of the "old guard" and the Christian establishment will say this
"won't work" (like they have ever really tried it), or will obligingly say,
*"Yeah, someone else somewhere else tried that a few years ago, and it didn't
work,"* or *"Stuff like that will not work in America."* But let me just say,
to quote Hicks from the movie *Aliens,* *"Maybe you haven't noticed, pal,
but we are getting our tails kicked out there."* The Gospel of the Kingdom
works in every nation, among every culture, tribe, and tongue—even
America. What the American Church is doing today by all objective
empirical data is a complete failure and waste of time. I am not saying
this because people don't have big hearts or because they have wrong
motives. But "more and better" of what we have already been doing, the
way we have been doing it, will still end up as dismal a failure. Biblical
changes modeled on Christ's lifestyle can be made; however, it will
require an end to failed programs and different kinds of endless teaching
services. *It will take the team "on the road" and out of the building.* Instead
of youth, women's, and singles' departments, this plan has one depart-
ment—the Saints. Our goal is to discover, develop, and deploy saints for
service. This can be done because we are doing it. It can be done!

YOU CAN IF YOU THINK YOU CAN!

If you think you are beaten, you are;
If you think you dare not, you don't.
If you'd like to win, but you think you can't
It's almost a cinch you won't.

If you think you'll lose, you're lost,
For out in the world we find
Success begins with a fellow's will;
It's all in the state of mind.

If you think you are outclassed, you are.
You've got to think high to rise.
You've got to be sure of yourself before
You can ever win a prize.

Life's battles don't always go
To the stronger or faster man;
But soon or late the man who wins,
Is the one who thinks he can.[1]

When Jesus said, *"Repent, for the Kingdom of Heaven is at hand,"* He was calling for people to change the way they think! (See Matthew 4:17.) The way we think about things is what affects every part of our life. Because of our religious stereotypes and mindsets, we have come to envision that when Jesus said this, it was in a great outdoor gathering of thousands, that somehow in the background a Hammond organ was playing, an altar call was being given, the apostles lined up down front (wherever that is), and then hundreds of crying, sobbing sinners and even saints ran down to give their lives to Jesus at some outdoor tree stump altar. But we would be *wrong!* It simply says in Matthew 4:17 that this was the *main message* Jesus preached *from that time on.*

The Church needs to do fewer altar calls, crusades, and church-as-usual activities and wake up to the fact that continuing to do what we have been doing—even bigger or faster—won't affect anything. It is time for a "regime change" in the mind. We have to completely alter the way we think. We have to throw out habits and lifestyles that have a form of godliness but don't work to produce Kingdom righteousness. We will *never* get to our destination, which is our destiny, if we don't change the way we think. And then we have to change everything else. What we think works probably doesn't, so why do we keep doing it? The reason? We don't know any better! So we keep repeating the same stuff that failed yesterday.

- What we think affects the course of our lives (destiny).

- Thinking affects what we feel (emotions).

- What we feel affects what we decide (decisions).

- What we decide affects what we do (actions).

- What we do we then begin to regularly do (habits).

- What we regularly do becomes our lifestyle.

- What our lifestyle is will determine our character.

- Our character allows us or prevents us from accomplishing our destiny and fulfilling our calling.

As you can see, the way you think can affect your life profoundly, either positively or negatively. The way we view things and ourselves is key if we are to be overcomers and adventurers in God, doing exploits for the Kingdom! If you haven't produced the results you wanted, chances are good that you've been thinking limited thoughts. You have taken God and His "impossible" vocabulary out of your thoughts, and you are only thinking things tied to your failures. Getting your thoughts off yourself is a good start. Are the thoughts you've been putting into your mind mostly positive and the truth of Scripture?

> *Finally, brethren, whatever is true, whatever is honorable, whatever is right, whatever is pure, whatever is lovely, whatever is of good repute, if there is any excellence and if anything worthy of praise, dwell on these things* (Philippians 4:8).

Do you expect to win more than you expect to lose, or the other way around? If you've been expecting to lose more than to win, don't worry. Today is a new day, and you can control and change what you put into your mind. While it may be hard for you to believe you can actually change your thinking habits this easily, you really can. It probably won't happen overnight, but if you start reconditioning your mind and expecting to achieve or win at whatever you do, your chance of succeeding will be greatly increased. Try it. You'll be surprised at the results. The next time a little voice comes in your mind and says, "You can't do it!" Just tell it to shut up and affirm yourself by saying, *"Yes! I can!"* After a short time, the little voice will become quieter and quieter, and eventually you won't be able to hear it anymore. It isn't always the devil; sometimes it's just your logical mind. The voice of reason is important to listen to at certain junctures, but you need to listen a lot more closely to your spirit! It actually agrees with and tells you what God is saying. Listening to your carnal thoughts will hold you back from being all you can be and keep you from accomplishing your aspirations.

One of the best ways to overcome limited thinking is to memorize Scripture and keep Scriptures in front of you—on the bathroom mirror, in the car, in the kitchen, wherever you go regularly. At work or school, put them around your work area. Another good thing to help your mind get in line is to read inspiring quotations from successful people—people who started with nothing but held to the belief that they had the potential to reach their dreams and overcame their fears so they triumphed. You do have the potential to achieve your desires, and the desires of your heart are those the Lord gives to you. So start believing in your ability to agree with Heaven as Gideon did! As you keep on working on your goals no matter what challenges you may face, very soon you'll see them turn into reality.

This principle in the Scripture is true: what you behold, you will become. If you behold depression, you will become it. If we behold Jesus and His lifestyle, we will become it! We can't separate His *life*style from His *life*. If you want the *life* of Jesus, pick up His *life*style! Your leaders have told you, "That won't work; you can't quit your job and walk around with a beard and a robe. That's not practical." No one is telling you to quit your job, but to change your life. People say, "But, Marc, I work at the power company" (or the school, etc.). I say, "Awesome. Has anyone ever been sick or depressed or experienced hardship at work? Then heal them, deliver them, preach to them! You are already in your harvest field; just don't forget to take Jesus with you. You have been leaving Him at home the last 10 years. Take Him in there with you!" Doing Matthew 10:6-9 isn't rocket science, only for the smartest; it is all about actually *doing*, not talking. American churches have actually been reproducing disciples, but these disciples just won't work.

> *For the time will come* [it's already here] *when they will not endure sound doctrine, but according to their own desires, because they have itching ears, they will heap up for themselves teachers* [the average seeker church]; *and they will turn their ears away from the truth* [the Gospel in its simplicity and ease] *and be turned aside to fables* [today's delusional Christianity]. *But **you be watchful in all things, endure afflictions, do the work of an evangelist, fulfill your ministry*** (2 Timothy 4:3-5 NKJV).

243

The Church right now needs to be doing these things:

1. Be watchful: *use discernment!*

2. Endure afflictions: today's Body needs to run toward persecution instead of running from it!

3. Do the work of an evangelist: the prophetic can evangelize, the pastoral can evangelize, even the teaching ministry can evangelize!

4. Fulfill your ministry: the leadership needs to train and release the Body. Most leaders are afraid they will be out of a job—they are wrong! They will be busier than ever!

We don't need more puffed-up teachers; we are already getting the fruit of that, and it doesn't work: lower church attendance, less evangelism, spiritual babies who have little Christian character and little change in their worldly lifestyle. That kind of disciple isn't going to change our nation! In a nation of teachers we have reproduced babies who think they are better than they are, but most don't even know their spiritual gifts or calling. Everyone can do the Gospel if they are trained. This must be modeled and can easily be replicated—and the cost? $0

There are times in each person's life where he or she can go down one clear path or another. It could be the person you marry; it could be the friends you hang around; it could be the church you are part of, or the job you take, or the neighborhood or house you move into. At these important crossroads, it is crucial that the right decisions are made. I look back at my life and see all the big decisions I made that were right and those that were wrong. Wrong choices can cause the ruin of many. God will hand us choices and give us opportunities, but we need to choose to accommodate those opportunities.

Many of us view our progress in the Christian life as a way of learning how not to lose so poorly. This is usually viewed as a battle where we go four steps forward, five steps back, six steps forward, five steps back. This may be the prevailing view in the Church, but it is defeatist and not valid for the Christian. We are called to be like Christ. In John 9, it is fascinating to see what became of the incredible opportunity Jesus had with this man who was blind from birth.

> *As He passed by, He saw a man blind from birth. And His disciples asked Him, "Rabbi, who sinned, this man or his parents, that he would be born blind?" Jesus answered, "It was neither that this man sinned, nor his parents; but it was so that the works of God might be displayed in him"* (John 9:1-3).

So this is another one of those opportunities where Jesus was "just passing by," and an opportunity for an extraordinary miracle came up. Do you know how many miracles happened "as Jesus passed by," or as He was "on the way"? Of course, because it was Jesus walking by, we all will say this was not a coincidence. But I don't believe anything happens by happenstance or coincidence, and since Christ is living within us that is all the more reason it is *not* an accident:

> *"We must work the works of Him who sent Me as long as it is day; night is coming when no one can work. While I am in the world, I am the Light of the world." When He had said this, He spat on the ground, and made clay of the spittle, and applied the clay to his eyes, and said to him, "Go, wash in the pool of Siloam" (which is translated, Sent). So he went away and washed, and came back seeing* (John 9:4-7).

Jesus expresses an urgency for us all to do God's will while we can because we won't always be able to. This is for us today! One Monday, which is my day off, I went with my wife, Linda, to a local Goodwill store because she was looking for some winter clothes. I remember it was in early December. As I was bored and ready to go I noticed a man walked in wearing a body brace from his neck down past his waist. He came in with two people whom I suspect were his parents. He seemed to be walking very slowly and deliberately as if in great anguish. Suddenly the Lord spoke to me, "You want to have some fun with Me?" I responded, "Yes!?" I knew what He meant—I was to go get the guy in the body brace healed! I looked around the store and a few people were in there. I remember thinking, "Come on Lord this is my day off." But I somehow knew He was insisting.

So I walked over to the man in the body brace and said, "Excuse me, my name is Marc, and I noticed you seem to be in some pain. If you don't mind me asking, why are you in such pain and what is the reason for that brace?" He said, "No, I don't mind telling you. I had a bad car accident seven months ago that crushed three of my back vertebrae. I have had many surgeries, am unable to work, and had to move in with my parents, over there. I am on four different pain medications." I asked him how bad the pain was on a scale of 1 to 10. He said right then it was a 9 and that was why he was shuffling across the floor. He said it hurt to move, let alone walk. I told the man, "I have good news for you! Jesus just sent me over here to pray for you so you can be healed. Would you let me pray for you?" He said, "Sure." So I said, *"In Jesus' name be healed of all the results of this accident. In Jesus' name, I command all pain to leave this man's body now, and may the Fire of God come on his body. Amen."*

I then turned and looked at him—his face was beet red and he looked flabbergasted! I said, "Sir, what is happening? What do you feel? Do you feel that pain?" He said, "No, but I feel HOT—like I'm on fire!" So I said, for some reason, "Let me pray again. *Fire of God, come on him NOW and completely heal this man of all pain and crippling disease in*

Jesus' name." Then I again asked, *"Now* what is happening?" He started grabbing his brace and the Velcro straps that held it across the front of his chest like a giant vest or long coat and began undoing them. He told me he felt like he was "on fire." I told him, "It's the fire of God that heals." He took the brace off his chest and neck, and his neck was bright red, as well as his arms, face, and all exposed areas. Other people in the store started turning to look and a small group of Hispanic ladies I had barely noticed before were by this time right there watching. I asked him to do something he couldn't do before. He said he couldn't walk around like he was doing, then he bobbed his head gently back and forth and sideways saying, "I couldn't do this either." Then he turned his head and circled it around it like he was stretching it. Then he started briskly walking around the store. He said he could not do that before! I asked, "Do you feel any pain?" He says, "No, but I am HOT!" The man was doing a victory lap in Goodwill on a random Monday morning in December because I agreed to go along with God's will for that man that day! Then he left the store with his parents, who were amazed and blessed. He was pain-free and thanking Jesus!

God is ready to do a miracle if you are! Jesus is ready, so the Father is too. Get it? He put spit on the blind man's eyes and told him to wash in the pool. Do you really think there was something magical or mystical about clay or the pool? *Nope.* The healing was in the command. If you will do this, God will do that. God wants to respond to us, but He likes to have something to work with. He always seems to like to use what we have.

Therefore the neighbors, and those who previously saw him as a beggar, were saying, "Is not this the one who used to sit and beg?" Others were saying, "This is he," still others were saying, "No, but he is like him." He kept saying, "I am the one." Therefore they were saying to him, "How then were your eyes opened?" He answered, "The man who is called Jesus made clay, and anointed my eyes, and said to me, 'Go to Siloam and wash'; so I went away and washed, and I received sight." They said to him, "Where is He?" He said, "I do not know." They brought to the Pharisees the man who was formerly blind. Now it was a Sabbath on the day when Jesus made the clay and opened his eyes. Then the Pharisees also were asking him again how he received his sight. And he said to them, "He applied clay to my eyes, and I washed, and I see." Therefore some of the Pharisees were saying, "This man is not from God, because He does not keep the Sabbath." But others were saying, "How can a man who is a sinner perform such signs?" And there was a division among them (John 9:8-16).

This is amazing, but we have seen the same kind of thing happen. We have seen teenagers in a Wal-Mart parking lot rise up when something supernatural happens. There was one instance where one of the gang leaders got belligerent with our guys because they preached the Kingdom to his friend, and he got healed. He got on the phone to ask his Baptist youth pastor, "How can this kind of thing be?" And his youth pastor told him it was the devil. When we show up and bring the Kingdom to people, there will be one of two responses—either revival or a riot. The religious spirit will always argue about *the way something happened*—how they prayed or what they said. The religious spirit is obvious because it deals in the how, when, and what, but it never cares about the *who*—the person.

So they said to the blind man again, "What do you say about Him, since He opened your eyes?" And he said, "He is a prophet." The Jews then did not believe it of him, that he had been blind and had received sight, until they called the parents of the very one who had received his *sight, and questioned them, saying, "Is this your son, who you say was born blind? Then how does he now see?" His parents answered them and said, "We know that this is our son, and that he was born blind; but how he now sees, we do not know; or who opened his eyes, we do not know. Ask him; he is of age, he shall speak for himself." His parents said this because they were afraid of the Jews; for the Jews had already agreed that if anyone confessed Him to be Christ, he was to be put out of the synagogue. For this reason his parents said, "He is of age; ask him." So a second time they called the man who had been blind, and said to him, "Give glory to God; we know that this man is a sinner." He therefore answered, **"Whether He is a sinner, I do not know; one thing I do know, that though I was blind, now I see."** So they said to him, "What did He do to you? How did He open your eyes?" He answered them, "I told you already, and you did not listen; why do you want to hear it again? You do not want to become His disciples too, do you?"* (John 9:17-27).

Here again, the Pharisees argue over what Jesus did or said—how it happened, rather than the glorious healing of a man born blind. This is a significant miracle, but the Pharisees were more interested in propriety and the proper protocol. You need to know that once you start stepping out in this you will be really persecuted and threatened and some may even die. At this same Wal-Mart parking lot, my son Jordan had someone put out cigarettes on his back as he was preaching. When you start healing and doing miracles, the questions come later: "What was that?" or "What did you just do to her?"

*They **reviled** him and said, "You are His disciple, but we are disciples of Moses. We know that God has spoken* *to Moses, but as for this man, we do not know where He is from." The man answered and said to them, "Well, here is an amazing thing, that you do not know where He is from, and **yet He opened my eyes.** We know that God does not hear sinners; but if anyone is God-fearing and does His will, He hears him. **Since the beginning of time it has never been heard that anyone opened the eyes of a person born blind. If this man were not from God, He could do nothing.**" They answered him, "You were born entirely in sins, and are you teaching us?" So they put him out* (John 9:28-34).

This is amazing! How can you revile a man with such a testimony? The priests had the testimony of a lifetime, but because it didn't *proceed from them* or *they didn't control how it occurred,* they put this guy out of the synagogue. He was just a young man and did nothing wrong, but because they couldn't control what was happening, they freaked out! One of the reasons the devil doesn't want God's power in the streets and "out in the open" is that he can't control it. The devil won't hang around empty buildings; he would much rather go to thriving churches and attempt to control things and keep God's Spirit out. He likes to work in and on the leadership, and he uses paranoia and fear to control.

*Jesus heard that they had put him out, and finding him, He said, "Do you believe in the Son of Man?" He answered, "Who is He, Lord, that I may believe in Him?" Jesus said to him, "You have both seen Him, and He is the one who is talking with you." And he said, "Lord, I believe." And he worshiped Him. **And Jesus said, "For judgment I came into this world, that those who do not see may see, and that those who see may become blind.**" Those of the Pharisees who were with Him heard* *these things and said to Him, "We are not blind too, are we?" Jesus said to them, "If you were blind, you would have no sin; but since you say, 'We see,' your sin remains"* (John 9:35-41).

The problem with these priests was that their preoccupation with doing things properly actually choked out the whole reason for their being there, which is to save sinners. It was Solomon who said, *"He who wins souls is wise"* (Prov. 11:30 NKJV).

For His Light to shine in us and come out of us, we have to be willing to go where the darkness is. Mind you, the darkness won't like you being there, and when miracles occur or the truth is declared, there is a conflict of light and darkness. But some of us need to learn how to get in the game, to fight and win against that religious devil. We will always win if we will only engage! The enemy has kept us on the sidelines for too long. This is not about talk but power, and His glory we carry in us will destroy the devil's works and will bring great joy as we go!

ENDNOTE

1.   Walter D. Wintle, "The Man Who Thinks He Can," *Poems That Live Forever*, comp. Hazel Felleman (New York, NY: Doubleday, 1965).

CHAPTER 17

ANIMAL FARM

We have met the enemy and he is us.

—Pogo (Walt Kelly)

He who walks with wise men will be wise, but the companion of fools will suffer harm.

—Proverbs 13:20

Who we associate with and allow to influence our lives is more than extremely important—it is a matter of life and death. Who we associate with defines *where we are going* more than *what we are doing.* Many times, we don't see the value or importance in who our friends are, but the wrong ones can make us bitter, and the right ones can make us better. The inheritance we have been destined by God to give to our children will never happen *if...*we hang around the wrong crowd. Alternatively, if we associate with like-minded people who want to go even further in God than we do, we will get a great blessing! In the NFL, the right team can take us to victory or to defeat in the Super Bowl, even before the playoffs. Jesus picked His disciples, and we need to do the same. He chose them, not the other way around. They can't just show up at our door and worm their way into our lives.

We have an ethic at home about the foolish and the wise. There are at least 30 characteristics of foolish people, and we try to train even our young people at an early age that there are a lot of foolish people who love God and show up at church, but that doesn't mean

166 LIFESTYLE

you make them your BFF (best friend forever). We need to pick our friends carefully and our disciples even more carefully. In ministry, they can either help you go to great heights in God or pull you into a religious spiral of bondage and failure. The devil will attempt to place in your path *(and bring into your ministry or church if you're a church leader)* stumbling blocks that come in the form of people.

A few years back, we were beginning to gather a number of young families and several young men who we were working with in ministry. Nearly all are still with us. It was a crucial time because we were forming then what has become much of our ministry team today. One day this man in his mid 50s showed up, a friend of someone in the church. It was obvious from the first handshake that he had rejection and a big wall around him. Over a matter of months, we saw his prophetic gifting and let him minister. As we did, we had to address some things he was doing wrong. He also had a number of problems with his money, marriage, and kids (which should have put up a red flag, but fixing stuff is what we do).

He told me that he had been in leadership *(nearly all Christians say that when they go to a new church)*, so I figured he could handle a little correction, but even a mild admonishing got to him, so he disappeared for weeks. He meekly made his way back with the excuse, *"There's been a lot going on,"* which meant, *"I was offended over nothing, but know I shouldn't be, so I'll try to forgive."* However, he then began talking to the young men. I had a check in my spirit, so I told him we needed to meet. When we did, I asked him what his call and areas of grace and fruitfulness in the past had been. *(He was a "leader," remember?)* He said he felt a call to "father" young men. I asked, "You say you have been doing this for 20 years now?" He said, "Yes." I said, "OK, then where are your sons? Can I meet one of them?" He said, "No, I don't have any; what I meant is that *fathering* is my calling." So I said, "If you have been doing this 20 years, and there's no fruit and no sons, why on earth should I let you work with mine? That's just not gonna happen." We talked some more, but I knew he wouldn't be back. It was good that I directed him to the door. He would have made a mess for so many just because he *needed* to minister and because he wouldn't let go of his rejection. We all need to minister, but he needed deliverance from rejection first so he could be fruitful, and he wouldn't receive it.

People can literally be a stumbling block to the growth and development of others. While this sounds harsh, that's exactly how Jesus referred to them. My biggest strength is to see potential in people and put them in their callings, but my biggest ministry failures have been my inability to see people who were stumbling blocks. Jesus says stumbling blocks come through people!

> *Woe to the world because of its stumbling blocks! For it is inevitable that stumbling blocks come; but **woe to that man through whom the stumbling block comes!*** (Matthew 18:7).

Relationships exist to serve and further God's purposes in the Kingdom, not the other way around. If you have been taught relationships are important, you are right, but it is essential you have the right ones. Certain relationships drain you and never challenge or confront you. We can't spend all our time attempting to prop up failed, draining, or "expired" relationships. It's also important that you know when a relationship is going nowhere fast. People who have the character trait of loyalty are the most prone to sticking with those who either are not going to change or have chaos in their personal life. There are also those who have a degree of stability in their lives but are not moving forward in God, and they can cost you, too. We need to know how we can best help people without becoming a casualty in the process.

UNHOLY COMPASSION

There is an unholy compassion that comes to the believer who has sinned that gives them a support system that can actually insulate them from godly leadership trying to bring them into repentance. It actually perpetuates lifestyles of sin and failure. This unholy compassion masquerades as love and care, but it really isn't. It is sympathy for the devil. It is sympathy for the sin that person is operating in because theirs (the sympathizers') is much worse, and they don't want to get theirs exposed either. God wants His Body to be real and transparent, which breaks unholy alliances that perpetuate sinful lifestyles. Because of this kind of compassion operating in some leaders their churches are Grand Central Stations for every manner of evil lifestyles. Some of the newer "emergent" churches are trying so hard to be relevant they allow everything imaginable to flourish in their congregations without it being confronted.

Friends who let you continue in a lifestyle of destructive living, bitterness, and slander without confronting you and holding your feet to the fire are not true friends. Jesus didn't say, "Go into all the world and make friends"; He commanded us to make disciples. Would you be willing to lose friends to do the will of God? You absolutely will be required to. Now He also said:

> But you will be betrayed even by parents and brothers
> and relatives and friends, and they will put some of you to
> death, and you will be hated by all because of My name
> (Luke 21:16-17).

We had a leader who was not fruitful and never seemed to do things we asked him to. When I told him there were things I needed him to handle, he said he would, but he wouldn't. He was just plain lazy, and he would never confront things, always having a really good excuse. It came out that he was squandering money, which forced him to go bankrupt, but he didn't tell me—or even his wife—till it was too late. I thought that his laid-back manner was cultural; I was wrong. Everyone thought he was "such a nice guy." But when I dealt with the problem, that unholy compassion was at work in people. I found out later he was undermining everything we were doing, and we later found out he squandered church money as well as time. I should have dealt with it sooner, but he was slippery, and I missed it till it was too late.

The enemy sends people into your life to ruin it and steal you away from God's destiny for your life. They come in smelling like roses, but leave smelling like sulfur. If you have seen the film *Lord of the Rings,* they are like the character Smeagol (Gollum), whose goal was to get the ring and to turn Frodo away or stop him from fulfilling his destiny—which was to destroy the ring. We must redefine fellowship. It is not just about having someone over. A fellowship that tolerates slander, gossip, and sinful lifestyles under the guise of "not being religious" is not real fellowship. Also, if people are sinning in their lifestyles, they are away from the Lord:

> *If we say that we have fellowship with Him and yet walk in the darkness, we lie and do not practice the truth; but if we walk in the Light as He Himself is in the Light, we have fellowship with one another, and the blood of Jesus His Son cleanses us from all sin* (1 John 1:6-7).

A few years back, I got a revelation about how some of these different kinds of people we should want to avoid are similar to the animals described in the Bible; this became a two-part message called "Animal Farm."

DOGS, PIGS, AND LEOPARDS

> *It has happened to them according to the true proverb, "A dog returns to its own vomit," and, "A sow, after washing, returns to wallowing in the mire"* (2 Peter 2:22).

These old sayings have merit today. Have you ever known anybody who just kept going back to his or her old ways? People like that keep making the same mistakes over and over and over and over. They keep going around the mountain. They seem to be snakebit, or even cursed. It seems like no matter what happens, they are programmed not to change. This reminds us of another animal the Bible speaks of—the leopard.

> *Can the Ethiopian change his skin or the leopard his spots?* (Jeremiah 13:23).

The leopard, of course, cannot change its spots. It is born with one coat of fur and one design of its spots, and that's it. These and other animals speak of kinds of people who never seem to learn, grow, or change. You probably know old school friends or fishing buddies or a guy at work or even family members who fit these categories. These kind of people are always around, and you need to avoid getting tangled up with them relationally. They can be a relational "black hole." Let's start with dogs. Dogs in Scripture are likened to religious spirits, those who spread trash, dig through garbage, and are unfit for the special things of God.

DOGS

Unholy

> *Do not give what is holy to dogs...* (Matthew 7:6).

The word *holy* means separated for a special purpose. This can be likened to a virgin preparing for his or her wedding or a special piece of china or dinnerware like a silver chalice.

Not Childlike

> *And He answered and said, "It is not good to take the children's bread and throw it to the dogs." But she said,*

*"Yes, Lord; but even the dogs feed on the crumbs which
fall from their masters' table"* (Matthew 15:26-27).

In this passage Jesus wasn't teaching so much about dogs as He was
giving a principle about the children's bread. While Jesus spoke about
the children's bread or necessary food, the woman understood that being
from Canaan, she was referred to as a little dog. At best this is a vivid
example of the lines He drew in ministering to people groups; at worse
it could be seen as insulting. Yet the woman gave a clever answer and
revealed the desperateness of her faith, which Jesus rewarded. She wasn't
childlike as much as she was desperate!

Strife

*And longing to be fed with the crumbs which were falling
from the rich man's table; besides, even the dogs were
coming and licking his sores* (Luke 16:21).

This is an interesting description, but there are people who aren't
content unless they are involved in gossip or slander, even going so far as
to massage people's unhealed areas and wounds, stirring up discontent.

Legalism

*Beware of the dogs, beware of the evil workers, beware of
the false circumcision* (Philippians 3:2).

Paul was referring here to those leaders or priests in the Early Church
who said that Christian believers, especially former Jews, should still be
circumcised as a sign of the rending of the heart. Paul called this the
false circumcision and insisted that true circumcision was of the heart.
This verse seems to link these leaders with legalism.

259

Separation

> *Outside are the dogs and the sorcerers and the immoral*
> *persons and the murderers and the idolaters, and everyone*
> *who loves and practices lying* (Revelation 22:15).

This implies a separation from the community of believers or those who have been expelled or removed or put out of the local church for discipline or those who choose to stay on the outside.

PIGS

Indiscretion

> *Do not give what is holy to dogs, and do not throw your*
> *pearls before swine, or they will trample them under their*
> *feet, and turn and tear you to pieces* (Matthew 7:6).

This is pretty straightforward: don't give your best things, your most precious revelations from God to these people because, like pigs, they will disregard how precious they are and might attack you for them. It is unwise to lay out our best to those people least respectful of it.

Keeping Bad Company

> *So he went and hired himself out to one of the citizens of*
> *that country, and he sent him into his fields to feed swine.*
> *And he would have gladly filled his stomach with the pods*
> *that the swine were eating, and no one was giving any-*
> *thing to him* (Luke 15:15-16).

The prodigal son, who threw away and burned through his inheritance, was a rebel against God, his father, and all common sense. He was a lazy fool by any account. I have heard many sermons on the prodigal son, usually involving evangelism. I have also heard some on the elder brother and how he had a wrong spirit toward his little brother. But the truth is that this passage is neither about evangelism or the wrong spirit toward the younger brother. The message is about those who have been given so great a salvation, have an incredible destiny, and abort it. Yes, when they come back to the "their Father's house," they eat of the Father's table, they have a feast, Dad is happy to have His son back home, and the prodigal gets his inheritance back, right? Wrong. Anyone who teaches that is wrongly adding their own sympathy for strays. Yes, "we all like sheep have gone astray" (see Isa. 53:6), but the prodigal consciously made a choice to burn through his inheritance, even early. *He never got it back.* I've even heard people teach that the father made the elder brother split his double portion with the younger. Nope. That didn't happen either. By custom, the older brother received double what the younger did anyway, so when his father died, he got *everything.*

> *And he said to him, "Son, you are always with me, and all that I have is yours. It was right that we should make merry and be glad, for your brother was dead and is alive again, and was lost and is found"* (Luke 15:31-32 NKJV).

The story is about the father telling his oldest, *"No, he won't get his inheritance, but he was dead and lost, and now he is alive and found, so we should be glad and have a party! We are not rewarding his foolishness; we are celebrating he is alive!"* As people hear this, they attempt to identify with the prodigal, and there is truth in that for all of us. But shouldn't we want to fulfill, not abort, our destiny? And shouldn't we want to wisely use our gifts and graces for the glory of God rather than squander them? Many of the greatest rock stars are running from the legitimate call they had in the Kingdom and they are like that prodigal, wasting their gifts for their own material gain. We should stop identifying with lazy fools. This only reveals how we have lowered the bar, lowered the standard.

The biggest reasons we keep identifying with the loser, the chronic failures, the unrepentant and willful sinner, and the rebel is we think that if we call them out for their behavior we may be held accountable for ours. This is one of the reasons churches don't come to a greater defense of righteousness. It's because they know they are lacking and weak in those areas, so they always say the same sappy thing: "Who am I to judge?" And the Bible is clear we aren't to judge what is happening. But those in leadership are called by God to have some semblance of holding the line on these great foundational boundaries. We can't say, "Who am I to judge?"

We **are** called to judge! We are called to police ourselves and admonish each other to conform to the Word of God. If we don't stand up about these ancient boundaries—like the definition of marriage being between a man and a woman—then we will lose this battle, and the next battles will be over crazy things like marriage between pedophiles and children or men and animals! While that may seem a stretch now, ancient cultures of great prominence like the Roman Empire allowed the erosion of their moral boundaries and consequentially, they no longer exist. We have also seen this with the ancient Aztec, Incan, and other empires. When any people forget the absolutes in the areas of ethics and morality and personal freedom and seek to do anything imagined in their hearts, it can lead to a complete breakdown of all boundaries.

> *Do not move the ancient boundary which your fathers have set* (Proverbs 22:28).

CHAPTER 18

ADVENTURING IN GOD

The Christian life is supposed to be more akin to an adventure or a pioneering journey than a nursing or retirement home. Our lives should more resemble what happens in an Indiana Jones movie, full of twists, surprise, and excitement than *The Office*. Instead, most *Christian churches today are like retirement homes:*

- They provide plush, clean, state-of-the-art facilities;

- You get fed just enough to keep you alive;

- All your needs are taken care of;

- The caregivers treat you really nicely;

- They take care of you till you die;

- They take all your money.

A lot of people now are withholding their time, energy, finances, and gifts because they are looking for the real deal!

OUR GUIDEBOOK—MATTHEW 10:5-14

These twelve Jesus sent out after instructing them: "Do not go in the way of the Gentiles, and do not enter any city of the Samaritans; but rather go to the lost sheep of the house of Israel. And as you go, preach, saying, 'The kingdom of heaven is at hand.' Heal the sick, raise the dead, cleanse the lepers, cast out demons. Freely you received, freely give. Do not acquire gold, or silver, or copper for your money belts, or a bag for your journey, or even two coats, or sandals, or a staff; for the worker is worthy of his support. And whatever city or village you enter, inquire who is worthy in it, and stay at his house until you leave that city. And as you enter the house, give it your greeting. If the house is worthy, give it your blessing of peace. But if it is not worthy, take back your blessing of peace. Whoever does not receive you, nor heed your words, as you go out of that house or that city, shake the dust off your feet."

These passages are our guidebook to another world, an open door to this Brave New World of adventures in God, a manifesto for the new millennium for the radical Church. This is our guidebook into a 166 lifestyle of miracles, signs and wonders, and advancement for the Kingdom. Just look how simple this is! We are told the following—and here is translation for today:

1. **What to do:** *go,* don't *stay;*

2. **Where to go**: to the lost sheep;

3. **Where not to go:** outside of the people group to which the Spirit is sending you;

4. **What to bring:** yourself and the Holy Spirit in you;

5. **What not to bring:** money—you'll be tempted to give people all your money, but they need the Gospel;

6. **What to say:** "God's here right now to bring Heaven into your life." A declaration of fact!

7. **How to act:** heal the sick, raise the dead, cast out demons, clean the unclean; give whatever God has freely given to you in whatever area;

8. **How to look for help:** ask if there is somebody who is a believer, then ask them to direct you to the worst cases;

9. **How long to stay:** as long as they receive you and listen to your words.

To enter into these adventures in God, we need to be clear about hearing from God. We need to listen to our new man so that we hear what the Lord is saying. God has given you a new man and a new way of living. From now on, we must stop listening to our old man, the flesh, and listen instead to our new man in Christ! The new man is filled with all righteousness and truth.

> ...*His purpose was to create in Himself one new man out of the two, thus making peace* (Ephesians 2:15 NIV).

You *aren't* only wrestling against your flesh, but the enemy wants you to think you are only wrestling with your flesh. The enemy doesn't even want you to think he exists, let alone is wrestling with you.

> ...*God is strong, and He wants you strong. So take everything the Master has set out for you, well-made weapons of the best materials. And put them to use so you will be able to stand up to everything the Devil throws your way. This is no afternoon athletic contest that we'll walk away from and forget about in a couple of hours. This is for keeps, a life-or-death fight to the finish against the Devil and all his angels. Be prepared. You're up against far more than you can handle on your own. Take all the help you can*

get, every weapon God has issued, so that when it's all over but the shouting you'll still be on your feet. Truth, righteousness, peace, faith, and salvation are more than words. Learn how to apply them. You'll need them throughout your life. God's Word is an indispensable weapon. In the same way, prayer is essential in this ongoing warfare. Pray hard and long. Pray for your brothers and sisters. Keep your eyes open. Keep each other's spirits up so that no one falls behind or drops out (Ephesians 6:10-18 TM).

Finally, be strong in the Lord, and in the strength of His might. Put on the full armor of God, so that you will be able to stand firm against the schemes of the devil. For our struggle is not against flesh and blood, but against the rulers (origins), against the powers (dunamis), against the world forces of this darkness, against the spiritual forces of wickedness in the heavenly places. Therefore, take up the full armor of God, so that you will be able to resist in the evil day, and having done everything, to stand firm. Stand firm therefore, having girded your loins with truth, and having put on the breastplate of righteousness, and having shod your feet with the preparation of the gospel of peace; in addition to all, taking up the shield of faith with which you will be able to extinguish all the flaming arrows of the evil one. And take the helmet of salvation, and the sword of the Spirit, which is the word of God. With all prayer and petition pray at all times in the Spirit, and with this in view, be on the alert with all perseverance and petition for all the saints (Ephesians 6:10-18).

Did you know another recent Barna poll (published March 2009) showed that the *majority* of born-again American *Christians* (60%) do not even believe the devil is real?[2] They believe the Scriptures about the Holy Spirit and satan are only words or types to represent good and bad. Do you know why? This is the fruit of the weak, inch-deep "teachings" coming from the majority of American churches every Sunday. Leaders are afraid that if they speak about the Holy Spirit or the devil, people will leave or will see them as "negative."

Our battleground is in the mind in thoughts and feelings. A spiritual war occurs when Jesus is beginning to be manifested in your life in a new way, when your "new man" is emerging in a new fashion. A 166 lifestyle of taking the Kingdom to others can really be an adventure if we see what we have to offer and are willing and bold enough to give it away. Nothing is more fulfilling or exciting than to hand His Kingdom to others. Bringing deliverance, healing, and glory to others is truly an adventure.

What is an adventure?

Adventure defined as a noun means "an undertaking usually involving danger and unknown risks; an exciting or remarkable experience." As a verb, it means, "to expose to danger or loss; to venture upon; to take a risk."[1]

God has called us to be the "bold and the reckless," doing adventures in God! Being careful, cautious, and safe is not our call or our lot in life. We are called to go where "no one has gone before" and do what few have been willing to do!

We can't even go in this direction if the main goal of our life is to be safe, careful, and cautious. I want to encourage all you parents to look at some of the things we say (often without thinking) and consider what that imparts to our kids. It would be better to tell our kids "be wise" than "be careful." When we say "be careful," we are really saying "be full of care, worries, and burdens." Even our vocabulary must be modified to accommodate the supernatural miracle faith release that we want to see! Are we men or mice? Are we chickens? No! We are not afraid!

WORDS CAN KILL OR BRING LIFE

...For out of the abundance of the heart the mouth speaks
(Matthew 12:34 NKJV).

Our vocabulary must equal our battle. If we are personally fighting
sickness, we do not possess or identify with it. It is not *my* headache,
my fibromyalgia, or *my* cancer. We teach people to *disassociate themselves
from the center of the battle. We won't let the enemy personalize anything.*
He is *out* there, not *in* here. The pharmaceutical companies spend billions to train you, even preach to you through television commercials,
to identify with your conditions—*my* allergies, *my* asthma, *my* diabetes,
my bipolar disorder, etc., etc. Drug company marketers know as long as
you personalize and *own* your condition, you will use *their* drugs forever!
If you don't believe this, just check the stock on all these companies and
also remember who does the preponderance of all daytime commercials!

We knew one man who had stage IV lung cancer in both lungs and
was given days to live. We went to this young man's house, commanded
the cancer to "shrink, shrivel up, and die," and the fire of God came on
his body! I declared he was healed, but told him how important it was
for *him* to own it, to *personalize* it. I told him he must open his mouth
and agree with what had happened to him. Scripture backs up this principle that it is a two-step process—believing in the heart, then confessing
or aligning with it by an action. When we say it, we "nail it down" here
on earth.

> *For it is with your heart that you believe and are justified,*
> *and it is with your mouth that you confess and are saved*
> (Romans 10:10 NIV).

Just as Elisha gave Naaman, the great commander of the Aramean
army, specific conditions to meet to receive his healing of leprosy (see

2 Kings 5), God gave me conditions for this man. I told him that he would instantly have a good report, and when the doctor could not find any more cancer, he was to come to my church and with his mouth testify what the Lord did for him. He swore up and down he would come and do it! And what I said happened; it came to pass! He had not been eating, he was losing about six pounds a week, his vital signs were plummeting, and he was not going to work or feeling like doing anything. We went to pray for him on a Saturday night. By Wednesday (four days), he felt so well that he went to work and played golf. By Friday (six days), he went for his weekly appointment, and he had gained eight pounds, and all vital signs were normal! Within two weeks, the doctors did a full battery of tests and *all the cancer in both lungs was completely gone—no elevated count, perfectly normal!* So when we heard this, we were ecstatic. I thought then that any upcoming Sunday would be a good time for him to come and share his testimony. So I called and invited him.

When we give a testimony, we are acknowledging what God has done with our tongue, which has the power of life and death! It also is humbling because we put our faith out there with our confession. *Anyway, he never came!* I called and asked, even begged him through his brother-in-law, for a couple months to no avail. Earlier I warned him this was part of the package. All the while his reports came back clean. His pride was such that he said to his brother-in-law, "I didn't want to say anything and then look bad if something bad happened to me later." When I heard that, I knew that he was creating his own future with his words. Many months later, he had a recurrence, and within seven months he was dead. I was very upset because the cancer was gone for at least three to four months. I truly believe he would still be here if he humbled himself before God and simply acknowledged God's work before men.

> *Whoever acknowledges Me before men, I will also acknowledge him before My Father in heaven. But*

whoever disowns Me before men, I will disown him before
My Father in heaven (Matthew 10:32-33 NIV).

The proud commander Naaman met God's conditions and was healed. But this young man's pride was too great to acknowledge the Lord's ability to heal *him*. Devils and sinners will both say God is able to heal and save others, but it means *nothing* until they make it personal and can say Jesus did it for *me!* This was a sad lesson, but a sobering one, revealing how little people know about God. Some people said, "If God really healed him, then he would have stayed healed." He was healed and cancer free for months, but he wouldn't meet God's conditions for *him*. Man has the problem submitting to God; God has no obligation to do things our way! Not in my Bible. Both Elisha and Jesus put conditions on miracles many times. Jesus told a blind man to wash in a pool and told the lepers to go tell the priests. I don't believe any of those men would have been healed if they hadn't met Jesus' conditions. Who are *we* to say, *"If it was God, they wouldn't have to do anything."* This just shows how much great pride but little fear of God people have.

Many things are instantly done when we agree with Heaven and God's will—that is, things that are already decided in Heaven. God is good and wants to do stuff all the time; however, He sometimes puts conditions on people. We have been taught, *"By grace through faith we are saved"* (see Eph. 2:8). But this was written by a proud man (Saul) who had to get the *you-know-what* knocked out of him and was struck blind for three days. How arrogant of us to presume we can dictate to God how He heals, saves, or does anything!

We must settle the issue of our access to an open Heaven once and for all so we are able to possess and keep what we possess. Once God's will on certain things is no longer obscure, we can then quickly figure out the reasons things break down and resolve them quickly through seeking, knocking, and asking. When we finally stop asking *if* it is God's will or not to do certain things, we then receive clarity quickly on the cloudy things, and we can ask *how?* Light will shine on our ways. I think this also means that when we find ourselves doing His will, we will also find ourselves using His ways, which will keep us balanced.

> *Then your light shall break forth like the morning, your healing shall spring forth speedily, and your righteousness shall go before you; the glory of the Lord shall be your rear guard. Then you shall call, and the Lord will answer; you shall cry, and He will say, "Here I am." If you take away the yoke from your midst, the pointing of the finger, and speaking wickedness, if you extend your soul to the hungry and satisfy the afflicted soul, then your light shall dawn in the darkness, and your darkness shall be as the noonday. The Lord will guide you continually, and satisfy your soul in drought, and strengthen your bones; you shall be like a watered garden, and like a spring of water, whose waters do not fail* (Isaiah 58:8-11 NKJV).

When our ways are His, the lights go on and stay on! We will have a great confidence when we are clear about what we know are the basics of God's will. I am not saying we will ever fathom all His ways, but we can know some basics of His will toward us.

> *For there is hope for a tree, if it is cut down, that it will sprout again, and that its tender shoots will not cease. Though its root may grow old in the earth, and its stump may die in the ground, yet **at the scent of water it will bud and bring forth branches like a plant*** (Job 14:7-9 NKJV).

People have lost hope, but Jesus wants to restore it. There are a lot of people who just know there must be a whole lot more, and after we see it, we need to help them see it!

GOD'S BASIC WILL 101

1. God is good—even better than we could ever imagine—and has a loving Father's heart toward us.

> *How great is the love the Father has lavished on us, that we should be called children of God! And that is what we are!* (1 John 3:1 NIV)

If I know God is good but unfathomable by human efforts and only can be searched by His Spirit, I will be OK.

> *Therefore consider the goodness and severity of God: on those who fell, severity; but toward you, goodness, if you continue in His goodness. Otherwise you also will be cut off. And they also, if they do not continue in unbelief, will be grafted in, for God is able to graft them in again* (Romans 11:22-23 NKJV).

2. He is also severe.

If we are to understand His amazing goodness, we also must see it contrasted with His severity.

How is it that we do not fully understand either the grace and mercy of God or His severity? When we communicate something that has two sides and omit one part, we tend to give permission to one side and communicate that the other side is unimportant. But the Word of God is a *two*-edged sword! We can't only focus on the parts we like and feel good about. There are mysteries of God that scare me.

> *For the word of God is living and powerful, and sharper than any two-edged sword, piercing even to the division of soul and spirit, and of joints and marrow, and is a discerner of the thoughts and intents of the heart. And there*

*is no creature hidden from His sight, but all things are
naked and open to the eyes of Him to whom we must give
account* (Hebrews 4:12-13 NKJV).

3. In Christ, we live under an open Heaven.

*He then added, "I tell you the truth, you shall see heaven
open, and the angels of God ascending and descending on
the Son of Man"* (John 1:51 NIV).

*Jesus opened the heavens, and we can do nothing to open them less or
more.* It is faith that is the key, and when we preach the Kingdom, the
windows of Heaven are open. Obedience to God's will is a Kingdom
key-turner!

4. We have been given our commission.

*Zaccheus stopped and said to the Lord, "Behold, Lord,
half of my possessions I will give to the poor, and if I have
defrauded anyone of anything, I will give back four times
as much." And Jesus said to him, "Today salvation has
come to this house, because he, too, is a son of Abraham.
**For the Son of Man has come to seek and to save that
which was lost"*** (Luke 19:8-10).

But a big question is, what was lost? Without God's dominion,
there is injustice and inequality. God's dominion over the earth is to be
enforced through Jesus operating and manifesting His love and life out
of His people. The devil's work is to take God's rule and reign away from
the earth. We are called to bring it back in—or, rather, to enforce what
man gave away!

*...The reason the Son of God appeared was to destroy the
devil's work* (1 John 3:8 NIV).

God's will is for all men to be saved, healed, delivered, raised, and preached to, and it is revealed in our Gospel commission, Matthew 10:7-8:

> *As you go, preach this message: "The kingdom of heaven is near." Heal the sick, raise the dead, cleanse those who have leprosy, drive out demons. Freely you have received, freely give* (NIV).

But you might say, "I'm a plumber; how can God use me?" That's fine; so were Smith Wigglesworth and Bob Jones. God has used them. "But I have a business, Marc." "That's great! Run it for the glory of God and make sure the business serves the Kingdom, not you, and let it serve God's purposes on the earth!" "But I'm a mom with three little kids, so how can you expect me to preach and use my gifts?" "Awesome, while you are at home you can train in and exercise all your spiritual gifts on the kids, especially healing, deliverance, and discerning of spirits!"

One time when our youngest two children (we have five) were 4 and 7 years old, Linda had an especially busy time running around to birthday parties, either for ours or taking ours to their friends. She was in the car crying out, "Lord, I'm sorry I have been so busy going to parties I haven't had time for You." He abruptly answered out of the blue and said, "That's OK, I *love* birthday parties!" It totally blessed her to know He was right there all along! The Lord is always accompanying you young moms, even when you are wiping noses and cleaning bottoms!

5. It is the Lord's will for us to have what is in Heaven here on earth.

> *This, then, is how you should pray: "Our Father in heaven, hallowed be Your name, Your kingdom come, Your will be done on earth as it is in heaven"* (Matthew 6:9-10 NIV).

6. *Our inheritance is reserved in Heaven for us. In other words, there are already things in Heaven decided on for us to do here on earth.*

> *Peter, an apostle of Jesus Christ, to those who reside as aliens, scattered throughout Pontus, Galatia, Cappadocia, Asia, and Bithynia, who are chosen according to the foreknowledge of God the Father, by the sanctifying work of the Spirit, to obey Jesus Christ and be sprinkled with His blood: May grace and peace be yours in fullest measure. Blessed be the God and Father of our Lord Jesus Christ, who according to His great mercy has caused us to be born again to a living hope through the resurrection of Jesus Christ from the dead, to obtain **an inheritance which is imperishable and undefiled and will not fade away, reserved in heaven for you,** who are protected by the power of God through faith for a salvation ready to be revealed in the last time* (1 Peter 1:1-5).

7. *We can pull from Heaven to the earth.*

> *"Have faith in God," Jesus answered. "I tell you the truth, if anyone says to this mountain, 'Go, throw yourself into the sea,' and does not doubt in his heart but believes that what he says will happen, it will be done for him. Therefore I tell you, **whatever you ask for** in prayer, believe that you have received it, and it will be yours"* (Mark 11:22-24 NIV).

You can decree things into being that are God's will (see Job 22:28).

275

8. Blessings, blessings, and more blessings are our lot in life on earth.

> *From the fullness of His grace we have all received one blessing after another* (John 1:16 NIV).

> *For I am not ashamed of the gospel, for it is the power of God for salvation to everyone who believes, to the Jew first and also to the Greek. For in it the righteousness of God is revealed from **faith to faith**; as it is written, "But the righteous man shall live by faith"* (Romans 1:16-17).

> *They go from **strength to strength**, every one of them appears before God in Zion* (Psalm 84:7).

Grace is agreement with God's predetermined things for us—His revealed will, not His mysterious will. God is mysteriously good, not mysteriously bad, anyway. This is where the grace is.

9. Whatever is happening in Heaven we can agree with and possess here: God's rule, His reign, His government.

It is God's revealed will to bring His dominion here on earth. Salvation, healing, deliverance, and freedom have already been decided and determined in Heaven as God's will for people.

10. Whatever God does in us has to be done from the inside out.

Remember the car assembly illustration? A car is built in stages, and from the inside out.

Furthermore, there are many things already settled in Heaven that are awaiting other things to be fulfilled so as to allow them to happen. And there are awesome things we have already received that we haven't yet signed for or allowed into our house. We can order from Heaven and even have marvelous things delivered from the Lord, but if we don't receive them in our lives, they will just sit outside, on our porch. For example, if you receive a FedEx Package, *you must sign for it to acknowledge you have received it!* That could be similar to God asking people sometimes to do this or that in order to get things from Heaven. Another time you might not have to sign for it, but if it is delivered to you and is sitting on the front porch and you don't go out and look for it, open it up, and use it, what good is it to you? Some of us don't sign for things, some of us don't even see if it has been delivered, some of us have it *in the house,* but we don't take the time to open it up!

11. This is a Body thing.

As Joshua led the Israelites into the Promised Land, they could not start working their own land without helping their brothers to get theirs. When we rejoice at another's blessings, then the *earth will yield up her strength,* and none will lack. We will be blessed because we *choose* to rejoice at others' blessings and to think of others more highly than ourselves. It is more blessed to give than receive! What we're called to do will require *more patience as we wait for others to come into their portion.* If people only see what we do and they don't have understanding why we're doing it, then they end up doing the same thing just because everyone else is.

We must offer some degree of understanding and clarity to these random acts of Christianity.

> When you come together, it is not the Lord's Supper you eat, for as you eat, each of you goes ahead without waiting for anybody else. One remains hungry, another gets drunk. Don't you have homes to eat and drink in? Or do you despise the church of God and humiliate those who have nothing? What shall I say to you? Shall I praise you for this? Certainly not! For I received from the Lord what I

also passed on to you: The Lord Jesus, on the night He was betrayed, took bread, and when He had given thanks, He broke it and said, "This is My body, which is for you; do this in remembrance of Me." In the same way, after supper He took the cup, saying, "This cup is the new covenant in My blood; do this, whenever you drink it, in remembrance of Me." For whenever you eat this bread and drink this cup, you proclaim the Lord's death until He comes. Therefore, whoever eats the bread or drinks the cup of the Lord in an unworthy manner will be guilty of sinning against the body and blood of the Lord. A man ought to examine himself before he eats of the bread and drinks of the cup (1 Corinthians 11:20-28 NIV).

One of the sad things about the condition of the Body presently is there is such a lack of acceptance of something that doesn't proceed from "us"—it is so often perceived as "not being God." Everyone is desirous of having more of God, but we get bogged down in the "package" it comes in, as we just talked about. We must realize that weakness, sickness, and even death are frequently a result of this great pride in the Body that rejects other parts of the Body as unimportant.

> **For anyone who eats and drinks without recognizing the body of the Lord eats and drinks judgment on himself. That is why many among you are weak and sick, and a number of you have fallen asleep.** *But if we judged ourselves, we would not come under judgment* (1 Corinthians 11:29-31 NIV).

We ought to pray for God to send judgment in the Body! If we starting judging each other *properly,* we would start getting these answers because we wouldn't be saying to another part, "I don't need you!" Peter told the man at the gate Beautiful, *"Silver and gold I do not have, but what I do have I give you…"* (Acts 3:6 NKJV). *What I do have* implies we have all the things He has. Peter went on to tell the people that the miracle occurred not *"by our own power or godliness"* (see Acts 3:12). We have *nothing,* but we have full access to *everything…*

We have the opportunity to reach into Heaven's treasury and release strategic miracles, just as the disciples did: *"And they were casting out many demons and were anointing with oil many sick people and healing them"* (Mark 6:13).

Wrong and traditional views of Jesus must be demolished, and so we must bring a recovery of faith. He taught us a brand-new set of operating principles, which we have to model, teach, and train. We have to think long-term and have a multi-generational vision as well. As we truly have our hearts set on getting the true riches, He is also going to give us the least—monetary wealth. We need to know how to handle wealth, but it is both deceitful and temporary. Don't get jealous of others when they get blessed.

> *The worries of this life, the deceitfulness of wealth and the desires for other things come in and choke the word, making it unfruitful* (Mark 4:19 NIV).

We are going to have a systematic vision of increase from the natural to spiritual; God wants to break the spirit of poverty when we have poverty of spirit because supernatural power brings material blessing. God is going to abundantly compensate those who are going after the true riches. We must change the view in the American and Western Church from the Laodicean mindset and instead, model a needy, desperate, hungry Body!

> *You say, "I am rich, have become wealthy, and have need of nothing…"* (Revelation 3:17).

We are the ones to take this new "166 lifestyle" and turn America and the Church upside down! When God told Abraham He was going to bless him and make him a great nation, he said *"in you..."*:

> *I will make you a great nation, and I will bless you, and make your name great; and so you shall be a blessing; and I will bless those who bless you, and the one who curses you I will curse and **in you** all the families of the earth will be blessed* (Genesis 12:2-3).

With faith and *patience* you will get the promises (see Heb. 6:12). We have to keep pressing in, and soon we will possess the land.

ENDNOTE

1. *Merriam-Webster's Collegiate Dictionary*, 11th ed., s.v. "Adventure."

2. "Barna Survey Examines Changes in Worldview Among Christians Over the Past 13 Years," March 6, 2009, http://www.barna .org. Used by permission.

OSTEOARTHRITIS HEALED!

Recently, one of our church members was returning home after work and saw a lady standing on the side of the road, looking very confused. When he inquired what she needed, she burst into tears and told her story of physical infirmity and poverty. Giving her a ride back to her home, he found out that she had colon cancer and crippling osteoarthritis, being in horrible pain. She had just walked in that condition to pawn her valuables to buy groceries and was in terrible shape. Not wanting to be insensitive, but also knowing what was about to happen, he exclaimed, "Honey, today is a good day for you!" After explaining the Kingdom of God to her and its nearness to her problems, he interviewed her, and she rated her pain from the osteoarthritis at a "10" on a 10-level pain scale. "Watch this," he said, and he began to pray that the Kingdom would come into her body. The power of God gave her a jolt, and she exclaimed, "What did you do!?" After checking, *all the pain was gone!* When asked what had happened, she said, "All the pain left when the goose bumps came!" ***All things are possible!***

SHOPPING WITH THE HOLY SPIRIT!

One of our church members gives this testimony:

281

I was up at Wal-Mart waiting on a friend and had time to spare, so I decided to go and pray for whomever I could find. I found a Spanish woman in a motorized buggy back in the electronics section. I asked her what sickness she had that required the buggy. She told me she had a pain in her leg caused by a blood clot.

Long story short, I prayed for her—wrongly even as I stated "in Heaven as it is on earth," but then I fixed my mistake afterward (I just let people know this so that they don't think there is a specific formula/recipe). Anyway, after praying, I asked her how she felt, and she replied "Good." Well, I was looking for a little more, so I asked her, "Did you feel anything?" She replied that she felt something inside of her. I was screaming, praising God on the inside but calm, cool, collected on the outside (except for my mixed up prayer that is, lol). I asked her if she could do something that she couldn't have done before without difficulty. She said that it hurt when she walked, so I walked with her down the Wal-Mart aisle as people looked on, and I continued to pray for her. After around 25 feet, she turned to me and said the pain was gone. Praise God! I told her she needed to make that into a testimony and went on my way, trying to find other candidates for a hit-and-run. ***Come on, Jesus!***

TUMOR *GONE!*

From an outreach team in Jonesboro, Georgia:

A few months ago we had the chance to minister to a lady in Jonesboro, Georgia. At first she didn't seem interested in hearing what we had to say, but after some specific words of knowledge we led her and her son to the Lord. For a while now, we have been discipling this single mother of four. We noticed during one of our visits that she was losing weight. She told us she had a tumor and needed surgery. We prayed for her many times, and her health improved, but the tumor remained.

She works two jobs to keep food on the table, so one afternoon we brought dinner to give her a rest. After pizza, we prayed again. The fire of God came on her, and she said that she felt hot all over. From that day, all her symptoms disappeared, and the tumor is nowhere to be found!

TEN YEARS OF PAIN *VANISH*!

After a recent ministry trip to Fort Worth, Texas, we received a phone call from one of the gentlemen who received ministry during the conference. For ten years, he had lived with debilitating pain and lack of mobility in his right ankle due to an accident. Immediately after prayer all pain left him. He called to let us know that the pain has never returned and never will.

A 4-YEAR-OLD'S HEARING HEALED!

A family attended meetings recently and brought with them their little 4-year-old boy who had severe hearing and speech problems. When he spoke, he spoke unintelligibly, and only his parents could really understand him. He came in with these huge hearing aids on both ears, which had what appeared to be a drainage tube attached to them. Definitely not something that a little 4-year-old needs!

Several folks in our church gathered around him, asking mom and dad if they could pray. Little kids, mommies, grandparents, and businessmen all pressed in to "take care of this." Someone asked his parents if they could remove the hearing aids, and they did. They kept praying, and then began to test the little boy's hearing, asking him if he could hear them. After a few minutes, they got the mom and dad to speak to him from behind, and the little boy swung his head around, responding to their calls! You should have seen the face on his dad!

His dad had come in acting calm, cool, and collected, but after hearing his little boy call his name clearly and respond quickly to the slightest whisper, again and again, he was floored! Dad was *so* blown away that he simply couldn't believe it. For more than an hour after his child started hearing and speaking, he kept testing his little boy's hearing, in total disbelief; each time his child responded. Tears streamed down his face, and he worshiped God. I asked him what this did for him, and he said, "This stuff is real!"

DIABETES DESTROYED

While our outreach team was recently in Jonesboro, Georgia, they knocked on a door. A gentleman came to the door, and after hearing that the Kingdom of God was on the earth, he told the team that he was a diabetic. The team called forth healing and cleansing of the blood. Several weeks later, the man explained that after the team left, he believed that he was healed. In response, he stopped injecting himself with insulin, after injecting himself twice a day for almost two years.

He explained further that he had been diagnosed with diabetes after going into a coma for 14 days in the summer of 2006. If he did not inject himself, he would risk going back into a coma. After two full weeks of no medication, he gave the team his empty bottles of medicine, leftover syringes, and blood sugar tester. He has called his doctor and told him that he was healed, and the doctor wants him to come in for a number of tests so that the diabetes can be erased off his record. When his records are cleared, he will be allowed to get his big rig license back and go back to truck driving again.

Thank You, Jesus!

Additional copies of this book and other
book titles from DESTINY IMAGE are
available at your local bookstore.

Call toll-free: 1-800-722-6774.

Send a request for a catalog to:

Destiny Image® Publishers, Inc.

P.O. Box 310
Shippensburg, PA 17257-0310

*"Speaking to the Purposes of God for This
Generation and for the Generations to Come."*

For a complete list of our titles,
visit us at www.destinyimage.com.